Hanoak
Traditional Korean Homes

Hollym
Elizabeth, NJ·Seoul

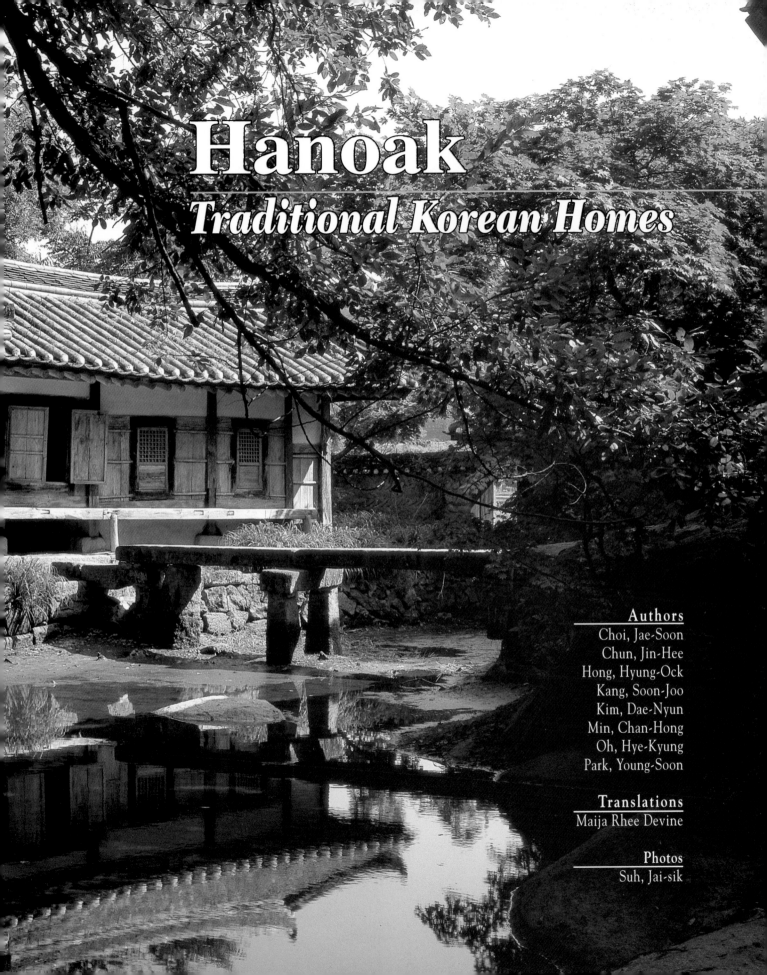

Hanoak
Traditional Korean Homes

Authors
Choi, Jae-Soon
Chun, Jin-Hee
Hong, Hyung-Ock
Kang, Soon-Joo
Kim, Dae-Nyun
Min, Chan-Hong
Oh, Hye-Kyung
Park, Young-Soon

Translations
Maija Rhee Devine

Photos
Suh, Jai-sik

Hanoak: Traditional Korean Homes

Copyright © 1999
by Hong, Hyung-Ock et al.

First published in 1999
Fifth printing, 2010
by Hollym International Corp.
18 Donald Place, Elizabeth, New Jersey 07208, USA
Phone 908 353 1655   **Fax** 908 353 0255
http://www.hollym.com

ʃ] Hollym

Published simultaneously in Korea
by Hollym Corp., Publishers
13-13 Gwancheol-dong, Jongno-gu, Seoul 110-111 Korea
Phone +82 2 734 5087   **Fax** +82 2 730 8192
http://www.hollym.co.kr   **e-Mail** info@hollym.co.kr

ISBN: 978-1-56591-298-4
Library of Congress Control Number: 99-65246

Printed in Korea

P·r·e·f·a·c·e

This book has been written by the faculty members who teach housing and interior design in several Korean universities to inform the world on the Korean traditional house and interiors. The main chapters are on the Korean traditional way of space planning and furniture arrangement. Also, the chapters focus on the fact that nature and socio-cultural background have been the major factors in forming the Korean traditional house plan and furniture design.

The chapters in this book mostly cover the style of the typical upper class houses in the Chosun Dynasty. The upper class houses represent the best form of Korean traditional housing including the interior space planning and furniture, the colors and patterns, and the house style, since they had been built without any financial limitations.

Chapter 1 covers Korean geographical and socio-cultural background and how they affected the form of the Korean traditional house.

Chapter 2 covers the relationship of family life and space planning since family life and social norm in the Chosun Dynasty were the major factors in forming the house form and style. In this chapter, upper class houses and lower class houses are compared.

Chapter 3 covers basic space planning and major characteristics of the floor, wall, ceiling, window, door and other interior elements.

Chapter 4 covers major furniture pieces, their functions and characteristics, and also lighting fixtures, accessories, and other household items.

Chapter 5 covers traditional furniture layout in the master bedroom(*An bang*), living room (*Sarang bang*), and kitchen.

Chapter 6 covers typical colors in the traditional house and its interiors, and typical patterns used in the traditional house and interiors, and the meanings and symbols the patterns represent.

Chapter 7 covers how Korean traditional form has been established through Korean geographical and cultural influences, considering all of the aforementioned elements in previous chapters. The general Korean perception that there should be a harmonious relationship among nature, people, and house, is reflected in the traditional houses of tile roofed or rice straw roofed houses in the Chosun Dynasty. The upper class, although possessing wealth and power, preferred to show their power and status in a simple and restrained life style rather than a luxurious and wasteful one. This was due to their philosophy in life to be in harmony with nature, avoiding complexity and greed.

Thus, the Korean traditional house, that is derived from Korean philosophy of life, exhibits unique and apparently paradoxical characteristics that seem very "full", yet "empty" at the same time, and seem "weak" on the outside space shows a dynamic energy and balances, which is very unique, and which can not be found in any other county. This unique traditional house that has been formed through a long period of time possesses practicality and artistic beauty, and we hope that those who visit Korea can see the merits of the Korean traditional house. This book will guide those who search for Korean tradition, practicality, and beauty of the traditional houses that were formed in its long history.

The authors

C·o·n·t·e·n·t·s

CHAPTER 1
The Development of Traditional Korean Houses

T hroughout the world, the first forms of human habitats were crude structures without significant distinguishing characteristics. In time, as people's lifestyles diversified and the functions of shelters expanded to accommodate individual, social, and religious needs and activities, houses began to assume national, regional and individual characteristics. Natural surroundings along with such cultural elements as people's values, life styles, and customs also played an important role in the evolution of architectural styles. Korean houses, as those in other cultures, showcased people's everyday activities as well as their history and traditions.

Since natural and geographical as well as social and cultural factors influenced the development of Korean homes, a study of the natural environment and culture of Korea yields insights into the rationale and evolution of traditional Korean homes. A discussion on these topics follows.

1. Natural environment

1 Geographical characteristics

Korea is a peninsula that juts from the southeastern corner of Asia. Her land borders China on the north with the Amnok and Tuman Rivers. To the south and across the sea lies Japan. The easy access to China both by land and sea resulted in the spread of Chinese culture throughout Korea, and in turn Korea participated in the dissemination to Japan of its imported culture.

A society situated on a peninsula reflects dual characteristics: continental as well as insular. Thus, one finds a dualism in Korean culture and temperament: easy-going laxity and emotional intensity, carefree optimism and sentimentalism, and adaptability to change and rigid conservatism. Exemplifying this duality, traditional Korean homes exhibited an interesting mix of both Chinese and Japanese qualities, showing the similarities to and contrasts with both cultures.

The beauty of *kumsugangsan*, "the shining rivers and high mountains", of Korea is well known. Four distinct seasons and generally clear weather characterize the climate of this peninsula. Prompted by nature's harmonious beauty, Koreans developed a passion to live in tune with nature, and this conviction laid the foundation of architectural concepts.

Approximately 75% of the surface area of Korea is covered by mountains and mountain ranges. However, there are few extremely high mountains, most of them being relatively low as typically seen in aged terrains. Hillocks, peneplains, and pockets of plains scattered among mountains and small streams flowing into rivers compose typical vistas. Taking advantage of these geographical characteristics and also in keeping with the ideas of feng shui, communities formed their

1. Photo: The view of a traditional village. The village of Nagganupsong shows the typical layout of a cluster of thatched roof houses whose roof lines harmonize with the shapes of the surrounding hills.

villages with mountains to the back and rivers to the front. This practice of feng shui often influenced the choice of locale for both communities and individual dwellings.

The ubiquitous presence of hills and their gentle slopes provided powerful design motifs for the arts, crafts, and architecture. The roof lines of houses and the shapes and designs of ceramic pottery bear witness to the correlation. The contours of thatched roofs and the low ceiling of these structures reveal Koreans' choice to live in unison with nature rather than in opposition to it (photo 1).

High quality stones such as granite, gneiss, andesite, limestone, and sandstone were used as building materials. People used granite especially for cornerstones, foundations, and walls. As for wood, because of a low level of rain fall and a dry climate, Korea did not produce an ample supply; so, to make more efficient use of an available supply of good quality wood, builders devised various techniques of using it more effectively.

2 Climate

Because the principle function of a home was protection against the cold and heat of the weather, climate had a direct impact on architecture. The climate of the Korean peninsula is relatively mild as the result of the mingling of both the inland and oceanic climates.

Korea has four distinct seasons, and the average temperatures are typically lower than those of other regions on the same latitude; the northern region of the Korean peninsular averages 10°C or lower, mid region 10-20°C, and the south 12-14°C. Winters are long; from November to March the average temperature drops below 0°C. But while the winter season is long, warm and cold days alternate on a seven-day cycle in patterns of 3-warms-to-4-colds, 2-colds-to-5-warms, or 5-colds-to-2-warms. This phenomenon tempers the harshness. Summer lasts for four months, from June to September, with temperatures of 18°C or higher. August may see many continuous days with temperatures as high as 30°C. The month with the longest daylight hours is July; the shortest is December. The average annual precipitation is 600-1500 mm. The summer being the rainy season, the rain fall of June through August accounts for 50-60% of the annual total.

Throughout centuries, Koreans viewed a setting with "a mountain to the back; river to the front" as the most ideal for a village. The mountain not only acted as a wind-deflector, but also supplied villagers with fire wood. The river provided drinking water and agricultural irrigation.

The duality found in the climate of Korea—the characteristics found in continental and oceanic regions—produced a similar duality in the architectural designs of Korean homes. Namely, two contrasting floor structures of *ondol* (heated floor) and *maru* (wood-floored hall with an empty space beneath for ventilation) appeared; and despite the fact that Korea is a small land, each region developed different types of homes showing various combinations of these two floor patterns.

It is an established fact that traditional Korean homes utilized the opposing architectural elements of both *ondol* and *maru*, showing excellent adaptation to the climate and natural setting. The *ondol* was first developed in long winters of the northern climate among the lower classes, but gradually spread to the south and the upper class. The *maru*, on the other hand, originated from the upper class in the south

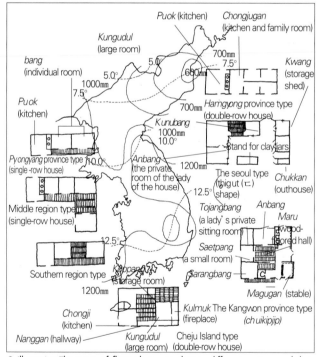

2. Illustration: The types of floor plans prevalent in different regions and their climatic patterns. The floor plans of houses varied from region to region, reflecting the amounts of annual precipitation and other climatic variables. Cold regions, such as the Hamgyong Provinces, had double-row houses while middle regions favored a *kiyok* (L- or bent-shape) layout. Warmer climates preferred *ilja* (—) single straight line houses equipped with large central *marus* (wood-floored halls). The Samch'ok area in Kangwon Province and Cheju Island featured double-row floor plans.

with its long, hot, and humid summers. This structural characteristic made its way to the north and was adopted by the lower class as well.

The typical house of the common people evolved to a structure with three major elements: *pang*s (individual enclosed rooms), *taech'ong* (wood-floored main hall with one open side), and *puok* (kitchen). A study of the layout of these three living spaces in different regions reveals a correlation between the layout and the regions' median temperatures (illustration 2). The northern region of Korea has extreme weather conditions, with severe winters and short summers, characteristics typically found in the interior of continents.

Therefore, houses in the north were designed for heat conservation and protection from extreme cold. Individual enclosed rooms were arranged in double rows for this purpose, as seen in the houses in Hamgyong Province. On the other hand, the south, with its wide plains, has long summers. To withstand these hot days, the people in those regions built *maru*s (wood-floored halls) and designed homes composed of several scattered structures. As a result, each structure tended to be relatively smaller than their northern counterparts and featured a single-row room-arrangement pattern, which maximized ventilation.

The Kangwon Province and Wullung Island regions receive the heaviest snow falls. The annual average snow accumulation in the north measures 40-70mm and the middle region gets 40-100mm. Meanwhile, the south, except for the Ch'up'ung Range and Mokp'o regions, receives a mere 20mm. The most typical example of the way climates influenced the shapes of houses can be seen in the *kwit'ul* (log houses) and *wudegi* (outer walls) found in Wullung Island.

These islanders erected *wudegi* walls, made of eulalia or bush clover branches, in order to keep path-

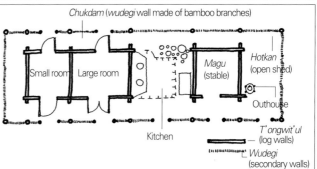

3. Photo and illustration: The exterior view (photo) and layout (illustration) of a *t'ubangjip* (log house) typical of Ullung Island. The sturdy log walls withstood heavy snow falls. Secondary *wudegi* walls were constructed all around the house to prevent blockage of passageways between buildings by snow accumulation.

ways between buildings from becoming impassable with snow accumulation. These walls extended from the eaves and along the outside of the interior walls. People used logs for the interior walls to withstand the weight of snow (photo 3).

While coniferous trees proliferate in the north and mid regions, and broad-leaved trees grow in the south, pines cover the entire peninsula. Because of this abundance, pine was the most commonly used material and figured prominently in the designing and building of homes.

2. Social and cultural environment

1 Philosophies

Korean people are believed to belong to the Tongi Tribe, sometimes known, according to ancient classics, as Puyo or Yemek. They migrated into the Korean peninsula during China's Ch'unch'u Warrior State Period. Anthropologically, Koreans are Mongolian while their language falls into the category of the Ural-Altaic language group. Culturally, Koreans trace their origins to the civilization of the Northeast Asia, which reigned the Asian continent as a predominant force. Spreading southward throughout Korea from this region, Buddhism flourished and, after acquiring a unique Korean flavor over time, became the basis of Korean culture.

Other popular religious practices existed from ancient times in the forms of shamanism or regional beliefs. The roots of these spiritual practices can be traced to the attitudes held by the agricultural population toward nature: reverence and fear. *Hanul* ("the sky" in literal translation) or "the heavens" represented an absolute spiritual presence. Throughout history, Koreans attempted to avert natural disasters by worshipping this deity. This folk belief led to the acceptance of and submission to nature as a providential force.

Numerous stone monuments stand as testimony to such a form of worship. In architecture, as with culture in general, Koreans adopted Chinese models, but imbued these with their own distinct character. Chinese theories of Yin-Yang-and-Five-Elements School, feng shui, astrology, Buddhism, Confucianism, Taoism, and other philosophies also left a lasting imprint on the process of architectural evolution. When exactly the theories of feng shui and Yin-Yang-and-Five-Ele-

ments were introduced to Korea is unclear. However, according to a record on Panwol Fort in The History of Three Kingdoms, the Koguryo and Pakchae Kingdom tomb wall paintings depicting feng-shui-related Four Animal Gods, and books on the theory of Yin-Yang-and-Five-Elements, one can deduce that the practices of feng shui and the Yin-Yang-and-Five-Elements came into Korea around the onset of the ancient kingdoms.

Once the philosophy of feng shui took root throughout the land, people sought to optimize their fortunes through a careful choice of home as well as burial sites. The discerning of portentous locations was believed to be of utmost importance in determining the fortunes of descendants, and professionals providing needed services emerged.

Because Buddhism led to much corruption during the Silla and Koryo Periods, under the Chosun Dynasty the religion met with official oppression and the building of Buddhist temples came to a temporary halt while construction of Confucian shrines, local Confucian schools, and larger Confucian halls accelerated. The Confucian ancestor worship entered into the population's moral consciousness. With this development, the family, not the individual, emerged as the basic unit of the society. This paternalistic, extended family system left a lasting stamp on the architectural designs of houses.

(I) Buddhism

Buddhism reached Korea through China during the Three-Kingdom Period (57 B.C.- 688 A.D.). However, Koreans did not absorb it in the form it was introduced; rather, they imbued it with a distinct Korean flavor by grafting it onto existing traditions and customs. Because of this localization of the religion, the acceptance of the alien religion by the general public became more palatable, and the way for the religion to become the principle system of belief and cultural foundation was paved.

Buddhism views man's journey through the life stages of birth, old age, illness, and death as the basic reality and sees suffering as an inevitable human condition. Pain derives from man's desires and obsessive drives. The elimination of these desires and drives can liberate a person from suffering and makes it possible for him/ her to experience freedom and peace. Buddhism also teaches that the reality we face is uncertain and because actuality continually changes, all beings are non-beings.

Since life is devoid of meaning and value, desiring and pursuing wealth and fame or being obsessed with the birth/old age/illness/death cycle is all in vain. Only accepting everything as is, resigning oneself to the meaninglessness of it all and living in harmony with nature is the only desirable way of life. These ideas opened a radically new world view and philosophy to Koreans, who had been accustomed to less refined systems of beliefs. The Buddhist view left little tolerance for such efforts as striving to leave one's individual mark on history, let alone lavishly decorating luxurious houses. In addition, exploiting nature to procure building materials went directly against the grain of Buddhist respect for nature.

(2) Confucianism

Confucianism, a philosophical system based on the ideas of Confucius of China and expounded in Four Books and Five Classics, teaches the ways of establishing social and political order through moral codes of behavior. Obeying Heaven's decrees, one must labor to cultivate the virtues of benevolence, righteousness,

propriety, and knowledge. During the Chosun Period (1392-1910 A.D.), this philosophy of individual moral development and proper governmental practices became a state policy approaching the status of a cult.

Confucianism not only became the basis for all governmental policy-making, but also the principle by which people ordered their family and social lives. Members of the governing stratum (gentry) relied on Confucianism as their sole guide and for the *yangbans* (nobility); and studying Confucian classics, passing the government exams, and procuring official positions became their supreme goal in life. If not granted office, even after passing the examinations, because of the limited number of positions, the non-titled continued to practice Confucian ideals in their daily lives through cultivating a virtuous and noble character. Ancestor worshipping ceremonies and other rituals derived from this culture.

Grounded on metaphysics, the Confucian philosophy viewed the universe as operating under one eternal order of the cosmos and concluded that everything in the universe, including man and nature, were intricately interrelated in carrying out the course of the order of the cosmos. Actualizing this world view in the daily lives of men translated into striving for the cultivation of three fundamental principles and five moral disciplines. The three principles describe the proper behaviors to be developed between the ruler and his subject, parents and children, and wife and husband. The five moral disciplines were applied to the building of five basic relationships: affection between father and son; righteousness between ruler and minister; attention to the separate functions between husband and wife; order between elder and younger brothers, and good faith between friends. These Confucian theories spawned a strong patriarchal family system in Korea.

Soon throughout the land there appeared *tongjokch'on*s (tribal villages) formed of patriarchal blood relations—a type of an expanded form of the extended family system. Mutually dependent, the tribal members looked after one another. According to the census of 1933, there were about 7,800 villages with 30 or more families; 3,000 with 50 or more, 1,200 with 70 or more, 400 with 100 or more. These tribal villages were more prevalent in the south.

Because *tongjokch'on*s necessitated the acquisition of large pieces of land, such communities proliferated first among the upper class. The villagers provided one another with social and economic support. Marriages were generally arranged among members of similar social standing, and this custom led to the establishment of *t'onghonkkwon*, a system of giving permission for marriage only between certain classes. But because these landowners needed laborers to work on the farms, people with different surnames often

lived among the blood-related members. The Hahoe Village in Andong, Yangdong Village in Kyongju, and Myodong Village in the North Kyongsang Province are well-known examples and still show the typical layouts and life styles of such villages (photo 4).

The families within a tribal village branched out like a tree. The heir and his dependents were called the "head family". Subsequent offsprings and their dependents were "little families". The root or head family of the whole village was called *taejongga*, and the head of this served not only as the man of his own family, but of the entire village.

People had the home of the head family built either at the center or apex of the village. The "little families" claimed sites nearest to the head family. The hired farmers occupied locations farthest from the center or occupied the lower area of the village (illustration 5).

Confucianism also left its mark on the system of

4. Photo: The Yangdong Village in North Kyongsang Province. The Sohns from Wolsong and the Yis from Yogang formed this tribal village. Well preserved, it reveals much about ancient tribal villages.

5 Illustration(right) : The layout of Myodong Village in North Kyongsang Province. The head family homestead occupied the top (northernmost) plot, while the houses of hired farmers were concentrated in the lower (southern) or outlying section.

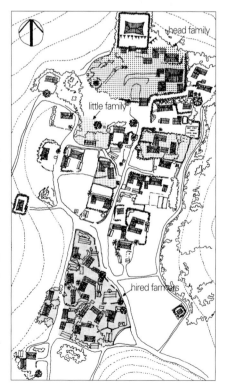

6.Photo:A *sarang-ch'ae* (men's quarters) equipped with a young son's *sarang* (study and living quarters). The ancient estate of Chong Yo-ch'ang, pen-named Il-du, boasted men's quarters featuring a large study (for the man of the house) and a small study (for his son). The large study (left) consisted of two *kans*, while a young man (seen behind the veranda on the right), was of one-*kan*.

respecting the birth order of male offsprings and leaving the inheritance to the first-born male. In the early stages of the Chosun Period, the difference in treatment of the eldest and younger sons was not pronounced. For example, the word *"jungson"* ("offspring") was used for all the sons including step sons. But later, as seen in *Saraep'yollam*, a volume on propriety and case histories, the heir was called "primary" while the others were termed "secondary" offspring. The Confucian teaching of conducting business by birth order firmly established the rights of the first-born son as the heir. This practice led to the placement of the first son's study near the master study used by the head of the family (photo 6).

The nobility of the Chosun Period practiced Confucianism in the strictest fashion, believing that doing so was an inalienable duty of man. Ancestor worship formed the core of this sacred obligation. People erected separate *kamyos* (family shrines) in their homes. Chong Mong-ju of the last period of Koryo established the *hyangkyo*, a country school annexed to a Confucian shrine, and encouraged the populace to build family shrines. Min Yu-ui was the first to do so. In the sixth year of King T'aejong, a eunuch in government service drafted an imperial recommendation that instituted the establishment of family shrines among the upper class as official policy. That year Ho-ung of the Ministry of Justice exhorted that the establishment of fam-

7. Photo:The shrine of a head (heir) family. Featuring a *matpae* (tiled) roof, the family shrine of a literati household occupied a secluded spot farthest away from the front gate. Three *kans* and surrounded by walls, this site of ancestor worship functioned as separate quarters.

ily shrines be complied with from members of literati to the lower classes. In the thirteenth year of King T'aejong, the Ministry of the Capital City decreed that those not establishing family shrines would be punished. As the family shrine law became a national policy, each upper class household constructed a family shrine (photo 7).

In order to keep traffic away from the shrine, where ancestral tablets were housed, the structure was built farthest from the front gate. However, the lower class population could not afford a separate shrine. In such cases, people set aside a room in the house to hold ancestral worship ceremonies. The ancestor worship took on religious fervor, and in the *yangban* (gentry) households, the male members paid respect at the family shrine twice daily--morning and evening--and bowed to the shrine before leaving the house and when important events took place at home. This practice was based on the belief that the living

and the dead resided together under the same roof and family fortunes could not be made without the intercession of ancestral spirits. The populace kept a spirit jar on a ledge in the *anbang*. This spirit was a type of a folk house god watching over the wellbeing and fortune of the family members. The upper class in particular viewed the home as a site where Confucian ideals and proper behavior could be put to practice and where the family's social standing could be showcased. Upholding the class status, however, amounted to distancing themselves from the common classes while maintaining privacy. Therefore, generally, high walls surrounded the buildings, yard and other inner spaces, and the servants' quarters occupied wings built into the front gate unit. This layout served as a means of distancing and protection of both property and persons. Walls and gates separated the servants' activity areas from the owner's quarters.

Because many generations lived communally under the Chosun Period's patriarchal, extended family system, large living spaces were required. Therefore, numerous buildings composed one family compound. The *k'unsarang* (study and living quarters of the man of the house), *chagunsarang* (son's study and living quarters), *haengnang-ch'ae* (servants' quarters), *an-ch'ae* (women's quarters), and *pyoldang* (annex) all provided separate living areas, used by designated members of the household.

The Confucian teachings of the three fundamental principles and five moral disciplines permitted a double standard to be applied to men and women in terms of the lines of authority, the types of daily activities, educational opportunities, inheritance rights, and overall social standing. From the mid Chosun Period on, discriminatory treatment of women developed into a full-blown, socially accepted pattern; and the requirement that opposite sexes keep their distance from each other became a primary design and layout concern. After the age of seven, males and females were forbidden to occupy the same space. Eating at the same table was taboo. Thus, the Confucian "attention to" men and women's "separate functions" dictated that the living spaces of men and women be isolated from each other. Therefore, by way of walls, the women's quarters were detached from the men's. Living in such seclusion, only after bearing male offspring did women receive credit for having contributed to the wellbeing of her husband's family. Women proved themselves able persons only to the extent that their worth served the pleasures and purposes of her husband's family (photo 8).

(3) The philosophies of yin and yang and feng shui, and beliefs in astrology

Three systems of thoughts, namely, the Yin-and-Yang-and-Five-Elements theory, feng shui, and astrology, also permeated the political, social, and private lives of

8.Photo: An *ilgak* (one-*kan* width) gate. This small gate served as a passageway between men and women's quarters, which were separated by walls.

Koreans during the Chosun era. The Yin-and-Yang-and-Five-Elements School taught that everything in the universe was formed of yin and yang, which, when combined, manifested as five elements of metal, wood, water, fire, and earth. An offshoot of this philosophy was feng shui, which spells out the principles governing the spiritual forces that operate on land as well as underground. Astrology, a body of ideas used to predict good and bad omens, then joined forces with feng shui, and exerted powerful influence on the Chosun people.

The Yin-and-Yang-and-Five-Elements philosophy

According to the beliefs of ancient Asian societies, among which China served as the cultural center, the origin of the universe owes its existence to a primal, chaotic state. The universe as we know it, with the heaven and earth, the sun and moon, and plant and animal life, was created by a force; and this force continues to move and transform the world. Named *ki*, this force expresses itself as yin and yang.

The yin (-) and yang (+) are opposites of each other, webbed in an interdependent relationship. Everything in the universe contains opposites of strong and weak, hard and soft, spiritual and material, large and small, long and short, and quality and quantity. It was believed that these opposites, through their circular movements and harmonizing acts, propelled the course of the universe and human lives. The idea that the yin and yang manifest themselves into five elements developed into a philosophy of Five-Elements-School. According to this theory, everything in the universe moves through the creative activities of the five elements--wood, fire, earth, metal, and water--combining and separating and operating in circles. Wood refers to a state of being ready to spring forth; fire sig-

nifies the bursting of energy; earth serves as the medium through which the yin and yang interact; metal denotes a state of containment of energy within; and water is identified as the state of readiness of the contained and condensed energy to give birth to a life force.

An important concept of *sangsaeng* in the Five-Elements theory refers to the order by which the reciprocal conversion process occurs to the five elements as they move through stages of transformation-- namely, the order of wood-fire-earth-metal-water. This means that yang begins its ascension through the stages of wood and fire. Then, utilizing the service of the medium—the earth—the yang reaches the metal and water phases, where the yang becomes condensed and yields to yin, which in turn works to prepare for the next cycle. Applied to the way seasons change, the same process begins with the yang bursting into action through spring and summer, condensing during autumn and winter, and yin taking over and preparing for the coming of spring. Fire functions as a catalyst of the transition of the yang to yin and expedites their harmonization.

Another important concept of the Five-Elements theory is *sangguk*--the order or hierarchy of ascendancy or of overpowering among the elements. Namely, metal has power over wood, fire over metal, water over fire, earth over water, and wood returns to overpower earth. Interlocked with one another in this fashion, the five elements move together in eternal cycles.

The theorists of the Yin-and-Yang-and-Five-Elements School believed that the principles applied to nature held true for human beings as well. From this standpoint, the practitioners of the philosophy established the profession of predicting the future of men. According to the philosophy, as man, as well as nature, is under the influence of *ki*, the primal force, men and nature must live in unison with each other. In addition, since the force responsible for giving forth life, causing changes, and wielding power over humans living above ground moves underground, it is critical to identify the spots in the land where *ki* is concentrated. Two philosophies, based on the Yin-and-Yang-and-Five-Elements theory, which affected the architectural designs are feng shui and astrology.

Feng shui

Feng shui, which came to the scene in China in 4000 B.C., but did not formulate into a systematic thought until 3 B.C., is a body of knowledge which attempts to explain the principles of nature by finding corresponding principles directing the courses of nature and human lives. The feng (*p'ung* in Korean) means wind; shui (*su* in Korean) refers to everything that is associated with water. Reinforced by astrology, the basic principles of feng shui took deep roots. According to feng shui philosophy, a current of life force takes certain courses, just as blood flows through determined routes in the human body. Thus, when a person is born with a certain life force, he will realize riches and fame. If a house is built upon the spot where the life force is concentrated, the family will prosper for generations. If the capital is established on such a site, the nation will flourish; and if a tomb rests at an auspicious plot, the descendants will achieve greatness. Namely, the location of the house, village, town, or grave is directly connected to good and ill fortunes.

Feng shui is divided into two types: yin feng sui, an effort to procure fortunes and good government jobs through proper burying of ancestors remains; and yang feng shui, a way of achieving the same goals but through the proper selection of the house site. The ways (*-bop*) of selecting the location and direction of sites for houses include *kanyongbop* (dragon), *changp'ugbop* (geography), *tuksubop* (water), *chonghyolbop* (grave or "blood"), *chwahyangnon* (direction), and *hyonggungnon* (geographical formation) methods.

The dragon method is a way of divining the good and bad omens by studying the configurations of mountain ranges. When building or buying a house, finding a mountain range that flows in a dragon shape near the site is essential. The geography method makes use of the layout of the surrounding area and served to determine the sites for graves, houses, and villages. The water method involves discerning through the waters in the area, water being the critical factor in the harmonizing of the yin and yang.

As for the grave or "blood" method, in the feng shui vocabulary, the *hyol* (blood) refers to the part of the grave that comes in contact with a body. If such a contact point is chosen correctly, the life force will flow. Within a house, the *hyol* signifies the living space, and the sites of both the grave and house must be right on the course of the *hyol*. The direction method is used to determine the optimal direction of a structure. Identifying an auspicious direction is the most critical task of feng shui. Considered constant factors are such things such as the amount of sunshine, the effects of the sunlight, and the region's seasonal winds. Relative factors or instruments include the clock, centripetal point, and directions. All these go into the detecting of the proper direction.

Using the geographical formation method, one takes an overview of the entire area in question and makes impressions. The images taken from these impressions, which correspond to the five elements, fall roughly into several contoured shapes of animals,

10. Photo: A geographical configuration in the shape of a lotus floating in water, an example of which can be found in Hahoe Village in Andong.

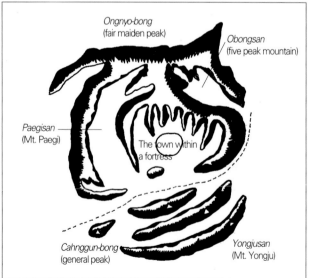

9. Illustration: The geographical contour of Nagganupsong Village resembled the figure of a beautiful-woman's flowing-hair, combing her hair and putting on make-up in preparation for the ritual of handing a helmet and rice cake to her warrior.

objects, human figures, plants, or letters. However, in reality animal shapes were most commonly sighted. These configurations "tell" about the life force and spirit that move in each location. The lower class population simplified their understanding of these impressions by looking only for plant, animal, and human figures. Considered most propitious were the figures of a hen-hatching-an-egg, a lotus-floating-in-a-pond, a boat-sailing-away, or a beautiful-woman's-flowing- hair (illustration 9 and photo 10).

An area with mountains surrounding it and protecting it from the winds while being cradled by a turtle-shaped mountain to the back, a bird shape to the

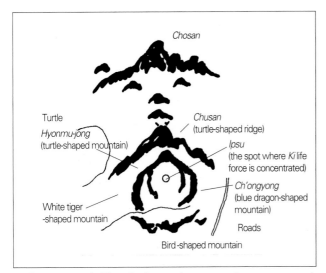

11 Illustration:An ideal feng shui location for a town. A large mountain to the back, a small mountain to the front with a stream flowing before it, and several surrounding low ridges all marked this as an ideal site for a village.

front, a dragon to the left, and a tiger to the right was considered the ideal location, having four godly animal protectors on guard in all directions. The turtle shaped mountain was the most important element and was called *chusan*, the head mountain. The bird-shaped mountains were divided into two types of *chosan* and *ansan*. The *chosan* was deep and large; the low-ridged *ansan*'s height was about midway between those of the head mountain and *chosan*.

The dragon and tiger figures were believed to provide protection to the whole site. To discern the course of the life force, one studied the flow and contour of an area. The spot where the flow stopped was called *kuk*. The central point where the life force gathered was named *hyol*, the most desirable spot for a house or grave (illustration 11).

Even aside from feng shui considerations, the ideal site discussed above, with its mountain ridges swooping downward and rivers coursing in an easy manner, would have provided interesting vistas and

inspired a sense of security and comfort — a desirable location. Building a house feng shui way meant beginning the whole process with the selection of the site. However, unlike grave sites, homes needed to be situated in locations equipped with certain essential services. Therefore, beginning the latter part of the Chosun Period, realists moved away from strict observance of feng shui, opting for more practical considerations, including economical, social, and educational needs.

After a site for a house was selected, decisions were made on the exact location of the foundations and the direction of the house, namely, the direction seen from the back of the house toward the front. This task was by no means a trifling manner, as the direction the house faced was believed to determine the destiny of the head of the household. Deciding on the directions of the *anbang* (room of the lady of the house), kitchen, and the front gate was likewise of critical importance and a feng shui expert's professional service was sought. The rest of the living spaces were chosen according to their functions and to the principles governing the five elements.

The structural design of the house also reflected the feng shui philosophy. The layout needed to resemble the shape of a letter that had propitious meaning. The characters meaning the sun (日) and moon (月) were considered excellent. The character meaning a mouth (口) was also favored, believing that such a layout would provide bountiful subsistence. Most other architectural elements, including the shapes of spaces, the forms of the front gate and walls, the placement of doors and windows, and the size of the entire site, were all required to follow the principles of feng shui and the five elements.

The timing and process of the construction were

also determined according to feng shui. The job of discerning which year a man must build his home was called *songju unbogi*, a type of fortune-telling. If a house was built in a year without a lucky streak, misfortunes would plague the owner. The dates for laying the foundation, placing the corner stones, erecting the support columns, installing the ridge beam and moving into the structure all called for feng shui consultation. While there were specialists performing only *taek-il* (selection of dates), general feng shui practitioners frequently carried out this task. The feng shui ideas also applied to the builder, his construction methods and the materials to be chosen. There were certain practices and materials he was required to avoid. For example, he was never to construct the outer walls or the exterior gate first. The pillar timber was never to be marred with cracks or used upside down. Other lumber also needed to be perfect: not bent, not eaten by worms, no wood that had been dead a while, never dried mulberry wood, and neither maple nor bamboo wood struck by lightening. Timber left over from building shrines, temples, government offices or ships was avoided. Also disliked were *sinsu* ("spirit" trees), trees from around shrines, or trees once inhabited by animals.

In this thorough fashion, feng shui controlled all aspects of building, from the selection of the site, the placement and direction, the structural design, the timing and sequence of construction phases, and materials and methods employed.

Toch'am philosophy (astrology)

The Five-Elements philosophy spawned *toch'am*, a supernatural and superstitious set of beliefs in which good and bad omens are predicted and promises to

12.photo:The *Changsung*, which are village guardian poles

help avert bad luck are made. Throughout the Chosun Period, all major areas of political, social, and private life fell under the sway of *toch'am* and Five-Elements philosophies. However, today, only *changsung* (village guardian poles), *songhwang-dang* (guardian deity alters), *tangsan* (prayer mountains), mountain spirits and various family guardian spirits remain in folk beliefs (photo 12).

The faith in family guardian gods became most visible in such practices as *kut* or *ant'aekkosa*, religious rituals held in the home or those held while a house was being built. There are regional variations on the names of these spirits, but generally the *songjusin* (the head spirit) was believed to be the chief god of the *taech'ong* (wood-floored main hall), *samsin* was the god of birth in the women's quarters, *chowangsin* guarded the kitchen, *madaejisin* the stable, *ch'uksin* the outhouse, *kutuljisin* the gate, *nojukchisin* the yard, *changdoksin* the cellar or earthenware jar stand, and *yongwangsin* (dragon god) protected the well.

Of all these gods, the *songjusin* was revered as the main deity, ensuring the overwall fortunes of the household and protecting the man of the house in particular. Artifacts that symbolize the *songju* god included bundles of money and rice paper threaded together, layers of rice-paper folded many times, jars filled with rice, pieces of hemp or other cloth or paper, and the ceremonial garb worn by the sorceress who performed a *songju kut* (photo 13).

The *songju* god artifacts were placed on the main ceiling beam, a post supporting *chungdori* (middle cross beam), in a corner of the main wood-floored hall, or on a shelf or ledge in the women's quarters (photo 14). These artifacts were symbols of or ritual offerings to the *songju* god. His "body" was believed to be the house itself, or more specifically the main building.

Because these domestic deities were believed to protect their respective areas and be in charge of directing the fortunes of the household, worship rituals were performed on a regular basis. They were held at home because homes were considered places of worship just as much as official temples.

2 Life styles

A look at the arrangement of living spaces yields insights into the people's life styles, and vice versa. Therefore, a discussion of various aspects of Chosun People's daily lives is included below. The study includes patterns in clothing, food, and shelter shown in everyday routines, as well as special ceremonies which included rituals of coming-of-age, marriage, funeral, and ancestral worship.

13. Photo: The *songjusin* (family guardian spirit) enshrined in rice jars. In keeping with religious folk practice, Koreans kept such rice-filled jars in storage rooms and worshipped their guardian spirits.

14. Photo: Symbolic artifacts that represented the *songjusin* (family guardian spirit) placed in *taech'ong maru* (wood-floored hall). Rice paper, folded in many layers, together with a skein of thread, symbolized the presence of the household guardian spirit. The paper and thread were kept in one corner of the *taech'ong maru*.

(1) Daily life

Because Confucian philosophy taught strict observation of segregating ("attention to separateness of functions") of men and women, the arrangement and functions of living spaces were determined according to this cardinal principle. For example, girls lived in the *anch'ae* (women's quarters) learning housekeeping and feminine decorum. Meanwhile, once beyond nursing age—Korean children nursed much longer than in Western civilization—boys slept in the *sarangchae* (men's quarters) and under the direction of their grandfather or father. There, the boys participated in male pursuits of studying classics, building competency in performing correct rites and rituals, and mastering Confucianism in general. The *anbang*, the central room in *anch'ae* (sleeping as well as daytime activity area of the lady of the house) was located in the innermost spot of the household and away from outside traffic. According to the Confucian rule of segregating the sexes, males, other than members of the immediate family, were strictly forbidden from entering the *anch'ae*. The position and responsibility of the lady of the house to oversee the operation of the household was symbolized by her ring of keys, particularly those to the storeroom and *twiju*s (grain bins). These keys passed from her hands to the wife of her eldest son, but only after the younger woman proved herself worthy of such a recognition by fully assimilating the character and heritage of her husband's family. This consisted of mastering the intricacies of the administration of the household, and, most important, giving birth to children, especially males, and raising them properly.

The formal clothing of government officials from the royalty down to the literati and military personnel were closely modeled after those of the Chinese throughout the Three-Kingdom and Chosun Periods. However, typical Korean women's clothes, consisting basically of blouses and skirts, originated in China, but in their typical way, Koreans transformed the designs to fit their own aesthetic sense and customs. The types of women's clothing included *changsams* (ceremonial robe of royal ladies), *wonsams* (ceremonial robles of green, yellow, and red colors), *hwalot* (bridal gown of the princesses and other women of noble lineage), *tanguis* (overblouses without side seams), *surans* (floor-length skirts with hems decorated with gold border designs), *tansokkots* (trouser-like underwear worn under skirts), *chokturis* (women's formal crown-like headpieces), *hwakans* (women's ceremonial coronets), and *posons* (white cotton socks with upturned, pointed toes). Off-season family clothing was stored in various cabinets and chests in the women's quarters.

Another characteristic of Korean clothing was its predominant color: white. This color was used partially because common class people were deficient in the knowledge of dying agents and because of the cost involved in obtaining them. Therefore, the majority of common people made use of natural colors of fabrics.

Another Korean outstanding characteristic lay in the design of clothes. Literally observing the Confucian view of sensuality as undignified and an element to be drastically reduced or covered up, Koreans constructed women's clothes to hide traces of physical feminine beauty shown in the lines and fullness of breasts, waist, hips, and legs.

Accommodating house guests was considered to be one of the most important activities for males of the *yangban* (nobility) class for their social, political, and networking purposes. Such activities occurred mainly at the open great hall of the *sarangch'ae* (men's quarters) or in the *sarang* (study/private room of the man of the house). In the summer, men used a *numaru* (wood-floored verandah). When relatives or close friends visited, however, they were entertained in the women's quarters or the *pyol-dang* (annex). The guests' periods of stay sometimes lasted up to many months or even longer. In households guests frequented, hosts were always prepared to provide food and lodging.

Confined by their natural environment, Koreans developed their own unique taste and style in food and food preparation. Surrounded on three sides by bodies of water, Koreans became skilled producers of sea foods. Agricultural harvests also yielded foods of great varieties. Influenced by the heritage of hunting tribes from earlier eras, Koreans relished grilling. They also discovered fermentation techniques and made their own wines. In readiness for long winters, Koreans pickled foods, *kimch'i* being a prime example. Naturally, a variety of utensils and containers needed for pickling was developed. Particularly during the Chosun Period, people made great advances in the art of food preparation and many of the favored recipes similar to those used today originate from this era.

The main part of a meal was rice, which was placed in individual rice bowls. Side dishes, each in a separate bowl or platter, complemented the rice well and rounded out the table. A soup, *tchigae* (stew), and *kimch'i*, in addition to rice, formed the basics of a meal. Optional dishes included fresh salads, cooked vegetable salads, roasted meats, hard-boiled items, pickled seafood, dried vegetables seasoned with soy sauce, other dried meat or fish, pan fried, pan-cake-shaped meats or vegetables, or raw fish. Depending on seasonal availability, the individual family's taste, and the finances of the household, any combinations of the fol-

lowing graced the meal table, *kimch'i*, pickled seafoods, and dry vegetables seasoned with soy sauce were staples that were prepared in large quantities and kept ready to be served at a moment's notice. Storing these foods required space and a great number of jars and other containers. Therefore, some households built a kitchen annex.

The kitchen was dirt-floored. The fireplace cook-top counter was equipped with slots for small, medium, and large pots; these were used mainly for cooking rice and soups. In the summer, when maintaining fire in the hypocaust fireplace was not needed, women set a portable stove outside the kitchen. A large clay water jug stood just inside the kitchen door. Women used a large basin for washing dishes. Waste water flowed into a drain set in the inner courtyard. Numerous large clay jars stood in rows on the roof tops of specially constructed, elevated cellars. Light and air kept the foods in the jars well ventilated and preserved. In addition, other storage spaces including a *kwang* (storeroom), *kokkan* (warehouse) *kobang* (closet) and *ch'angan* (pantry) were utilized. In Honam, a southwestern district, people set aside a space called a *chotkoggan* (pickled seafood storage room).

In strict observance of the Confucian rule of respecting the elders, the eldest members of the family took meals first. Men and women ate at separate tables, and the father-in-law of the house ate alone at a table set exclusively for him. Because of this custom of eating separately, a variety of small, portable tables was used. Human waste was recycled as fertilizer. An outhouse was built close to the courtyard gate in order to facilitate the transporting of the waste to the fields. At night, chamber pots were kept handy to save the waste. As for bathing, because of a certain wariness taken toward the activity during the Chosun Period,

15.Photo: The back side of the domestic work area. A mortar and water basin are often placed here. In the summer, women used this secluded area for bathing.

little bathing space and few toilet items were developed. In the summer, people bathed in nearby streams or washed themselves in a corner of their back yard. In winter, warm baths were taken in a room or in a dark corner of a kitchen, quietly and secretively (photo 15).

In small-sized lower class families, the couple and their children occupied the *anbang*. In large families, the husband's parents took the *anbang*. When the father-in-law died, the mother-in-law generally continued to occupy the *anbang*, sharing it with her grandchildren. If the father-in-law was widowed, he usually gave up the *anbang* to his son and son's wife and moved to *aratpang* (outer wing room). The *sarang* (study/private room of the man of the house) was then used either by the widowed father-in-law or the couple's grown sons.

Feng shui principles also determined which direc-

In homes equipped with *sarang*, men entertained there. In the absence of such a room, the *konnobang* (room across the hall from *anbang*) was used. The host always offered guests the *aranmok* (area on the floor closest to the fireplace—the warmest spot). Even in households that had a *sarang* (man's study and living quarters), guests visiting the lady of the house were received in her room. In the summer, for informal visitors, the *maru* (wood-floored hall) was used.

(2) Ritual life

The major rituals in Korean life fell into four types of ceremony: *kwalle* (a rite of passage), *holye* (marriage), *sangnye* (funeral), and *cherye* (ancestor worship) ceremonies. *Kwalle* symbolized and marked a male's passage into adulthood. At the ceremony, almost always held among upper class households, the youth's hair was combed into a top knot, and thereafter he donned a black hat. The entire process of this ritual began with the selection of the young man's wedding date. This was followed by the dispatching to the bride's home of a letter which contained the groom's *saju*, the "Four Pillars"—the year, month, day, and hour of his birth. Once the date for *kwalle* was chosen, the father of the groom-to-be "announced" the event to the ancestral spirits at the family shrine. An outside master of ceremonies was invited, and after the groom-to-be donned his official garb, he was called to make his appearance at the ceremony. The father again "announced" the proceeding to the ancestral spirits. Upon completion of the *kwalle*, the young man made his formal bows to the elders. A party followed with all the guests attending.

The *holye* (the marriage ritual) was deemed extremely important, and its complex procedure proved its gravity. In traditional Korean society, mar-

tion to place one's head while sleeping: east for riches, west for poverty, south for long life, and north for short life. Needless to say, people slept with their heads toward east or south. In the common class homes, windows were installed on east and south sides, and people slept with their heads toward the courtyard. The fireplace, used for cooking as well as for heating floors of bedrooms, was set on the opposite side of the windows.

16.photo: A traditional wedding ceremony. The groom took a seat on the east side of the table, the bride on the west side.

ried men were allowed to have more than one wife. But women were bound to the marriage vow of loyalty and sexual purity to one husband only, dead or alive. Naturally, to women, marriage was for life.

A marriage ceremony was performed according to the intricate, ritualistic propriety detailed in the Confucian Book of Rituals. Traditionally, the ceremony was held at the bride's home, and the groom's trip to the bride's homestead was called *ch'ohang* (the first visit). Before his departure, the groom "informed" his ancestral spirits at the family shrine of his upcoming marriage. Wearing his formal

17 Photo: A table set in a courtyard for a wedding ceremony. The table setting consisted of two candles, a vase filled with evergreens, bowls of chestnuts, jujubes, rice, a hen and rooster tied in cloth wraps and skeins of red and blue threads.

groom's outfit, including a tall, black hat with wings, he headed for the bride's house on horseback. A man called *sanggaek*, with the special duty of carrying a wooden wild goose, walked ahead of the groom. Known for an affectionate relationship between the male and female, a wild goose symbolized the groom's intention to maintain conjugal happiness for "one hundred years".

The ceremony was conducted in the main hall of the bride's home. At the center and to the back of the hall, a folding screen embroidered with peonies was arranged and in front of it the ceremonial table. On the table were placed two candles; a vase displaying either pine, bamboo, or evergreen branches; plates of chestnuts, Chinese dates, and rice; a hen and a rooster tied and wrapped in cloth wraps; skeins of blue and red threads; and small dried halved gourds. Some regional variations of the table setting existed, but in general similar functional as well as symbolic items filled out the table. The pine and bamboo symbolized women's *cholgae* (conjugal faithfulness); the hens represented the force that ushered in each day's beginning and fought off sundry evil spirits; and the skeins of blue and red threads signified the providential union of the couple. The groom took a seat on the east side of the table, the bride on the west side. Bowing to each other several times and the groom's drinking of the three glasses of wine offered by the bride completed the ceremony (photo 16, 17).

A party followed in the inner courtyard. After the ceremony, the newly weds spent their first night together in the nuptial room prepared at the bride's home. They remained with the bride's family several days, weeks, or even months. The bride then moved to her husband's house where she made formal bows to her parents-in-law, other elders of the family, and various relatives. This event, termed *p'aebak* today, marked the beginning of the rest of the bride's life to be spent with her in-laws. Viewed as an outsider by her own family once she was married off, she was allowed by her in-laws to visit her home only sparingly--perhaps only a dozen times in the remainder of her life.

Funerals and ancestor worship ceremonies were also considered extremely important in a Confucian society. *Sangnye* referred to the proper rituals to be performed when someone died. The procedures were complex, and because of the importance of the occasion, every effort was made to spare no expense. Holding a grand funeral was a supreme duty of the surviving family members and a way of showing the most revered of all virtues: filial piety. Following feng shui, the descendants made painstaking efforts to choose the most auspicious burial plot: one flanked by a dragon shaped hill to the left and a tiger-shaped mountain to the right. By doing so, survivors sought to increase their chances for better fortunes.

People with elderly parents used the professional services of feng shui practitioners to select the burial sites ahead of time. Generally a dry spot facing the south was chosen. Once such a location was identified, sometimes holes for the coffins were dug in advance in order to avoid having to conduct affairs in a chaotic and hurried matter after the elderly died. Also, it was customary to prepare the garments for the dead ahead of time in a leap month. Such practice was considered a show of the younger generation's wish for their parents' long life.

The many steps of the funeral ritual began even before the hour of death. When a parent was gravely ill, he/she was moved to the *anbang*. Sons stayed outside the room. Failing to perform this duty was consid-

18.Photo: Male mourners. Mourners donned roughly sewn hemp garbs. Male mourners wore head gear called a *dugon* and *kulgon*, which were fastened by a straw rope intertwined with dried hemp peels.

19. Photo: A table set for an ancestral worship ceremony commemorating the deaths of a couple. The table setting varied slightly from region to region. However, fruits of red coloring, fish, and sweetened rice beverage were generally set to the east, while fruits of pale coloring and various meats including strips of dried, seasoned meats were placed to the west.

ered an act of *pulhyo*, a breach of filial piety. Once the parent took the last breath, sons plugged the mouth and nose of the deceased with pieces of fresh cotton. Then someone in attendance took a piece of clothing of the deceased, climbed to the roof top, and called out to the departing spirit. This part of the ritual was called *kobok*. All the furniture was removed from the room where a person died, and people stopped heating that room by plugging the opening of the fireplace. After *kobok* was completed, a board was set over pieces of wood or straw pillows, and the body was placed on the board. This phase was called *susi*. Next came the setting of a table for the messenger of *yomradaewang*, the lord of the dead or lower world. This was done to ease the way to be taken by the messenger who would lead the dead to the lord of the lower world. The table was usually set on a mat either in the courtyard or outside the front gate. Three bowls of rice, three glasses of wine, three dried whiting fish, some coins, and three pairs of straw shoes filled the messenger's table.

The chief mourner knelt in front of the body and accepted condolences from guests. At this time, all the mourners let out loud ritualistic cries (photo 18). After bathing the body and putting clothes on it, the body was bound, which was called *yomsup*. Next came the placing of the body in the coffin. A special ceremony was held before the coffin was carried out and taken to a mountain. The chief mourner carried a temporary spirit tablet to the grave site. There, at the feng-shui-designated time, the coffin was lowered into the hole with the head of the body facing north and the feet to the south. People placed a twin knot on the top of the coffin and covered the coffin with a red pennant bearing the name, official position and rank, and family origin of the deceased written in white. Dirt was poured and pressed down over the coffin. When the grave was filled to the level of the ground, a leveling ceremony ensued. The chief mourner returned home (now his home inherited from the deceased, if the deceased was his father) taking the same roads he had taken while carrying the ancestral tablet or temporary spirit tablet on the way to the grave. This completed the funeral ritual (photo 18).

For three years after the death of a parent, the family maintained an area where the ancestral tablet was kept. Twice daily, in the morning and evening, sacrificial meals were offered to the deceased. After three years, the ancestral tablet was moved to the family shrine located in a corner of the courtyard. The family maintained ancestral tablets of four generations of ancestors, and conducted solemn and well-prepared worship ceremonies on the anniversary dates of each deceased ancestor.

Thus, families observed filial piety throughout their parents' lives and years and generations after their deaths. Families performed the *ch'arye* (memorial service), *kije* (anniversary memorial service), and *myoje* (grave-site) rites. The preparer of these services never bargained on the prices of foods and other materials. Before preparing the food, the cook bathed and took care not to allow any flawed materials into the food. The food offerings were similar for all the memorial services. Placements of various foods followed certain rules: fruits of red coloring on the east side; fruits of pale coloring on the west; fishes on the east; and meats on the west; and slices of dried meat seasoned with spices to the left; and *sikke* (sweetened rice dessert beverage) to the right (photo 19). Of course, following these rules was believed to precipitate good fortunes and blessings.

A *ch'arye* (memorial service) was generally held during special festivals such as the lunar New Year's Day, *hansik* (the 105th day after the winter solstice), *ch'usok* (a harvest festival held on August 15 on the lunar calendar), and the *tano* (a festival observed on the fifth day of the fifth month of the year on the lunar calendar). The *kije* memorial service was held at midnight of the anniversary date of each of the four generations of deceased ancestors. The ancestral tablets of ancestors beyond four generations were buried in front of their respective graves and, following the instructions of the Four Rituals Manual, men held grave-site memorial services at mid-day in early March each year. Services for the older ancestors came first. But before these could be carried out, a ritual of worshipping the mountain spirits occurred.

In homes with family shrines, where ancestral tablets were properly housed, people made bows to the spirits before "inviting" the spirits, which was done by lighting incense or pouring wine into a bowl filled with sand. In homes without shrines, ceremonies were held in the *anbang* or the main hall, and the procedure of bowing and "inviting" was reversed.

As discussed in this chapter, natural elements influenced Korean architectural designs as did social, cultural, religious, and philosophical ideologies and practices. A discussion follows on the various aspects of living spaces in homes and how these reflected Korean culture.

T he layout of the living spaces in Korean houses underwent significant changes, riding the tides of various philosophical and social currents that flowed each era in Korean history. These currents included power struggles waged between the central government and rural leadership and the challenges Confucianism had to overcome along its long road to increased influence and final establishment as the unshakable, ultimate moral yardstick of public and private lives.

The traditional homes remaining today and examined in this volume are from the latter part of the Chosun Dynasty. Therefore, rather than systematically showing the process of the entire architectural evolution, they point to the layouts found at the end of the long history of transformation. This chapter examines several historic residences in relation to the social and cultural mores in vogue during the Chosun period, particularly its class system and the differing Confucian life styles of the upper and lower classes.

1. Upper class residences

The population of Chosun was divided into five classes: *yangban* (gentry); *chungin* ("middle"—low ranking government worker) class; *igyo* (semi-official employees); *yangin* ("good," common people); and *ch'onin* (the lowest class). *Yangban* referred to the upper or government official class, both military and literati. More specifically, the designation signified the members of the nine classified offices of the military and literati branches of the government. They included those who qualified for government jobs by passing examinations, but were not granted offices because of the limited number of government positions. The "middle" class lay between *yangban* and common classes. The members of this class could not hold high government offices, but worked for institutions such as the *naeui-won* (royal medical center) or *sayok-won* (office of translation/interpretation). The class of *igyo* fell between the government official class and the common people. The *igyo* class could hold only certain positions. The *yangin* meant average citizens. The *ch'onin*s worked in positions of the lowest classification, and their privileges were severely limited.

The Chosun dynasty imposed regulations on the size of private residences of the upper class, as well as lower classes, and depending on the ranking of the position held by the master of the house, certain rules applied on the types of decorations and accessories as well.

1 The size and decoration of the house

The upper class men held government offices. The extra high front gates of the homes of this class signified the superior ranking of the master of the house. The middle class homes were large houses of non-*yangban*s, including low-ranking government workers, or rich farmers, but the distinction between them and the members of the upper class sometimes blurred because the middle class homes included the residences of *yangban*s without government positions. The *minga* meant the houses of non-government-officed or civilian population. Reflecting climatic influences more directly than those of the upper class, the designs of these structures showed a greater regional variety. The thatched *karabjip*s were very humble shelters of *ch'onin*s (the lowest class people, including retired servants with homes of their own), usually not larger than three *kan*s (one *kan* is a space made by 2×2 columns) scattered in the vicinity of a master's home. Sometimes, these people lived in the *haeng-nang-ch'ae* (the servants' quarters) of the upper class homes.

(1) Size of residences

The Chosun citizens, even those of the upper class, did not have the freedom to build their homes in any sizes they wished. The government regulated the sizes of the land as well as the house itself according to the ranking of royalty or government positions.

A debate on whether such regulations needed to be formalized into government policies began during the 12th year of Chosun King Sejong (1430 A.D.), thirty years after the moving of the seat of government to Seoul. By that time, the initial phase of the building of the capital was completed, and the majority of government structures, as well as private residences, had already been built. As citizens settled in the capital city, they began exhibiting extravagance in the size and decoration of their homes. King Sejong addressed this issue by enforcing Rules of Domiciles. In following years, these regulations underwent several amendments.

The Rules of Domiciles were observed fairly well during King Sejong's time, but during the subsequent reigns of Kings Yejong and Songjong, the rules, according to records, met increasingly lax enforcement. During the Songjong period, people observed the regulation concerning the sizes of homes, but not the sizes of materials. Therefore, the government amended the rules to regulate both areas. But, the sizes of residential structures remained constant: 60 *kan*s for the *tae-gun* (rank of princes by the king's first wife); 50 *kan*s for the ranks of *kun* (princes by the king's secondary wives), and *ongju* (princesses by the king's secondary wives); 40 *kan*s for the *chongch'in* (king's relatives) of Class Level Two or above, 30 *kan*s for Class Three and lower, and 10 *kan*s for *sohin*s (non-titled citizens).

Even though the sizes of residences remained unchanged following the 13th year of King Sejong, *chongch'im* (the ancestral worship space in the *an-ch'ae*--the inner/women's quarters) and the length of the servants' wings extending off both sides of the front gate continued to expand. Faced with such frenzy for larger residences, the government reluctantly allowed grander homes to be built. According to the *Kyongguktaejon*, a book of the principles of government, published in 1419 A.D., the section on the requirements of the sizes of homes specified only the square footage. People complied with this requirement, but by using larger and taller building materials, they exceeded the limits in other areas. The *Kyongguktae-jon* shows that the members of nobility were the first failing to comply with regulations. In fact, the king himself did not adhere to them strictly.

For example, in the 21st year of King Songjong, a princess by one of the king's secondary wives had a house built which exceeded the regulation of 40 *kan*s. When she came under criticism, the king ruled that she was not in non-compliance with the law. Again, in the 23rd year of Songjong, records show that the king came to the defense of his own sons and daughters of his secondary wives by ruling that their residences became larger than government requirements only as the result of utilizing materials left over from building the palace. As Songjong did not require compliance from the sons and daughters by his queen, he set a pattern whereby subsequent generations constructed even grander palaces. This trend continued through the reign of Yonsan-gun; and Song Hi-an built a palatial residence far exceeding 40 *kan*s. According to a survey taken of the capital city during King Chungjong period, the number of people who breached the Rules of Domiciles reached 280. In the spring of the 18th year of King Chungjong *Ongju* (Princess) Hyejong was allowed to have her palace built the same size as that of *Kun* (Prince) Kumwon, and each residence was well over 70 *kan*s.

By this time, not complying with regulations became the norm, and even King Chungjong himself declared that since such a building pattern was unavoidable, no corrective action needed to be taken. In addition, unlike the practices followed under King Sejong, the servants wings began to be excluded from the total count of the size of residences, further demonstrating how completely government regulations had been ignored.

Similar laxity occurred with the rich people in the country side. For example, the grand home Wunjo-ru, built in Kurae in the 52nd year of King Yongjo and expanded gradually in the next 18 years, measured 78 *kan*s by the time its founder passed away and left it to his descendants. The government regulations were already in place when infractions such as this occurred; however, many local wealthy men erected residences exceeding 60 *kan*s. According to oral history, the Wunjo-ru estate was known to have measured 99 or 100 *kan*s, but the structures still remaining measure only about 73 *kan*s. The parts of the Wunjo-ru that no longer exist totalled to about 26 *kan*s. Therefore, the whole estate, at its peak expansion period, must have occupied about 99 *kan*s, and if the second-story storage spaces were included, the mansion well exceeded 100 *kan*s.

Yun Hyon-jo, a well-known official who served all three Kings Sukchong, Kyongjong, and Yongjo, drew criticism when he built a 101-*kan* home in Yangju. A private residence exceeding 100 *kan*s was unheard of. The Yongyong-dang within the Ch'angdok Palace in Seoul, built in the 28th year of King Sunjo (1828 A.D.) upon the request of the king's second son to have a home similar to that of a literati, stands on a 1500-*pyong* piece of land and has the living space of 99 *kan*s. Because of the increasing demand for constructing residences exceeding regulation sizes, oral history maintains that eventually even private citizens were granted permits to build 99-*kan* homes. But evidence of this cannot be found in any written records.

Amidst the widespread breaking of regulations, some individuals like Yi Won-ik, who served as the prime minister for forty years during King Sonjo period, lived in a small, humble house of only a few *kan*s. His example demonstrates that depending on the financial standing and philosophy of life, some people view the maximum limits set by the government as obstacles to wrestle with while others voluntarily lived in humble environment far below official guidelines.

The census of 1897 and a survey taken in the same year on domestic artifacts in Uiryong-gun in the South Kyongsang Province yielded interesting discoveries. The records revealed that in the reported sizes of

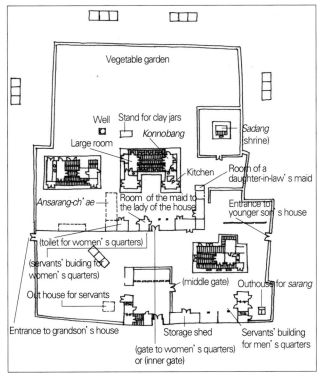

Vegetable garden

Well
Stand for clay jars
Konnobang
Large room
Kitchen
Sadang (shrine)
Room of a daughter-in-law's maid
Ansarang-ch'ae
Room of the maid to the lady of the house
Entrance to younger son's house
(toilet for women's quarters)
(servants' buiding for women's quarters)
Out house for servants
(middle gate)
Outhouse for *sarang*
Entrance to grandson's house
Storage shed
(gate to women's quarters) or (inner gate)
Servants' building for men's quarters

20. Illustration: The layout of the Kim's house in Chongup. At 87 *kan*s, this house seemed to have exceeded the government regulation; however, if only the rooms and *maru*s in the *sarang-ch'ae* and *an-ch'ae* were counted, the size of this house totaled 39.5 *kan*s, well within regulation.

houses, the kitchen and adjunct structures were excluded. For instance, a building with an actual size of four *kan*s was reported as a three-*kan* home, having excluded the kitchen from the total count. The fact that the government documents restricting the sizes of houses did not make specific mention of support structures was believed to have been the cause for such a practice. However, the validity of such assumption has not been proven. What seems certain is that, as seen in the example of the Kim residence in Chongup, which was a house of 87 *kan*s exceeding the government limits, but was reported as 40 *kan*s, a number reached by counting only the individual rooms and *maru*, people reported the sizes of their houses without counting certain spaces when responding to census or investigations on the compliance of regulations (illustration 20).

(2) Residential decorations

Decorations included the painting of surfaces, the sculpting of stones, the heights of pillars and shapes of decorative pillar tops, and the shapes of pillars themselves. These were all regulated by the government according to the official status of the man of the house. The first indication of the imposition of government restrictions on decoration was found in a public proclamation made in the 11th year of King Sejong. This document forbade the painting of buildings in red, with the exception of royal palaces. But as in the case of the rules on residence sizes, this decree was also frequently ignored.

In the 14th year of King Sejong, when *Chinsa* (an office awarded to a person who passed only the basic examination for office) Sin Hyo-ch'ang used sculpted stones for the corner stones and walls of his house, he was, records show, admonished and punished by the Ministry of Justice. In the first year of King Munjong, when a petition was presented to the king to have a *tanch'ong* (bright multi colors) Chinkwan-sa Temple, he granted it. This set into motion the trend of painting government buildings and temples in such a fashion.

According to the *Kyongguktaejon*, a volume on governance, the punishment for those decorating private homes with *tanch'ong* was 80 floggings. The *Taejonhoet'ong*, another book on government administration, published during King Kojong's reign, concurred with the punishment for such criminal act. Pak Sung-jong aroused much ire with the *tanch'ong* done on his residence during King Songjong period. By mid-Chosun Period, namely during the King Chungjong period, according to records, the restriction on *tanch'ong* was largely ignored. In the 8th year of King Chungjong, when one of his top ministers, Song Chil, was denounced for indulging in luxury by having

21. Photo: Chong head family residence in Hamyang. Though forbidden in private residences by the government, round pillars, considered more stately than square ones, often graced the *taech'ong*s of grand upper class houses, as seen in this example.

his residence painted in *tanch'ong*, and his resignation from office was demanded, the king ruled that "A house can be rebuilt, but a minister cannot be replaced."

These occurrences seem to indicate that there were other private homes being decorated in *tanch'ong*. During the King Myongjong period, when the mistress of Sim Yon-won, the Minister of Interior, not only had pillars with an arch built but also had them painted in *tanch'ong*, she aroused much excited criticism; reportedly, she was forced to have the *tanch'ong* washed off. It seems then that the govern-

ment regulations were strictly enforced in some cases, but in other instances mostly involving rich individuals, were able to get away with *tanch'ong*, and thus contributed to the perpetuation of the inconsistent enforcement. In the 7th year of King Chungjong, a petition to forbid *hwagong* (a special technique of carving--an epitome of luxury) of the beams that traversed across pillars was presented, and the king granted the petition.

This seems to indicate that such a practice was already in existence, but the government intended to prohibit it as a general rule. Beginning the 13th year of

King Sejong, *hwagong* was forbidden, but using *suksok*s (sculpted stones) was permitted only for corner stones. However, Song Hi-an of King Chungjong's era attracted criticism because he used *suksok*s for other areas as well.

A study of the artifacts from Chosun residences reveal that despite the government prohibition against the use of round pillars except within palaces, such materials were found to have been used widely in the *sarang-ch'ae* and *an-ch'ae*, and by the main wood-floored hall and *apt'oe* (front side hall) of even private houses in various locations. In the Injo period, when a princess had round pillars erected in her palatial residence, she was ordered by the Ministry of Justice to eliminate them, citing the rule that no private residency should feature such pillars. But they were frequently used in homesteads of powerful and rich individuals, as seen in photo 21. Still, it was clear that the government made attempts to curb excessive decorating of houses.

2 Space arrangement in relation to daily life

Even before Confucianism was introduced, Koreans were already advancing toward a patriarchal extended family system. But before the system became a universally accepted social norm, certain customs foreshadowed the eventual acceptance of patriarchy. One such example is the marriage arrangement in which the groom lived at the bride' home until their children grew up and then moved his family to his parents' home. According to records from Koguryo period, the men's length of stay at their wives' homestead was from three to 24 years and the women's ages when they joined the in-laws were between 18 and 39.

Another custom that existed before patriarchy became the norm was the tradition of equally dividing the parents' estates among the children. However, during the 18th century, the moral and social mores that had supported such practice changed.

With the advancement of Confucianism as the state religion and policy, ancestral worship and preferential treatment for the eldest son became the core life principles, especially among the leadership class. As tribal villages and patriarchal communities formed of blood relations became established as institutions, exclusion toward non-blood relations emerged. This emphasis on blood as the crucial tie brought about the demise of the marriage system whereby the males lived long periods at their wives' homesteads. Also, the new custom of leaving one's inheritance to the eldest son solidified and led to discriminatory treatment of daughters. All these new practices of maintaining a patriarchal, extended family system, men returning to their own home after staying only three days at their bride's house, preferential treatment of the eldest son, and inequitable inheritance laws received unequivocal official endorsement until the end of Chosun Dynasty.

One of the institutions that cinched an unshakable foothold for Confucianism was its family shrine system. This practice, which was the nucleus of ancestor worship, was not truly and firmly established even during the early Chosun period. Until shrines later acquired a symbolic significance, the system languished from lack of support, and in some cases shrines to ancestors were even torn down. However, by mid Chosun period, the shrine emerged as the symbol of the status and lineage of a household and became a medium of even stronger amalgamation among blood relations, with the shrine of the eldest son's house serving as a crucial symbol. Once this shrine system was

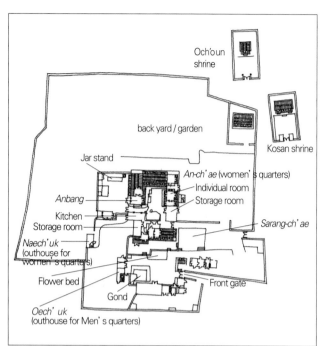

Och'oun shrine

back yard / garden

Kosan shrine

Jar stand

An-ch'ae (women's quarters)

Individual room

Anbang

Storage room

Kitchen

Storage room

Sarang-ch'ae

Naech'uk
(outhouse for
women's quarters)

Flower bed

Front gate

Gond

Oech'uk
(outhouse for Men's quarters)

22. Illustration: The layout of the ancient estate of Yun Ko-san in Haenam. This residence featured three family shrines: the Ko-san Shrine established at the order of the king, the Och'oun Shrine established in honor of Yun Ko-sans deceased father, and a family shrine where four generations of ancestors were worshipped.

(1) Space arrangement in a patriarchal system

As discussed above, the Chosun families' position of power resided with the male, and the father-son relationship formed the basis of the family unit. Because more than three generations lived together within one compound, and because other close relatives also lived with them, relationships could become quite complicat-

firmly set, the Confucian way of life blossomed.

As the shrine's importance increased, the rate of movement among the upper class dropped virtually to zero, and the male head of the household placed himself in the inalienable position as the individual with the responsibility of performing ancestral rites and as the person of absolute power of the patriarchal family. Four generations of ancestors became objects of worship ceremonies held at the family shrine. In addition, some households had ancestral tablets bestowed upon them by the king himself, so that the outstanding service to the king by the late ancestors could be honored through eternity by the descendants. The Yun family in Haenam had two such tablets; therefore, the Yun residence require three separate family shrines (illustration 22).

ed. Therefore, maintaining order in the family and the family's place in the community required strong male leadership.

The *sarang* (men's quarters) reflects the position of power of the eldest male. During the first half of Chosun, *sarang* meant a small room annexed to the inner/women's quarters and was used to accommodate guests. But in the latter half of Chosun, *sarang-ch'ae* (with a different Chinese character than the former *sarang*) emerged as a separate quarters to serve as a symbol of the male position and power. This change occurred partly because of the Confucian rule of *nae'oe*, (attention to the separate functions of male and female) which required separate living spaces for the sexes.

23. Photo: The Hwallae-jong pavilion at Songyo-jang estate in Kangnung. A series of doors formed the sides of this pavilion, which included a tea room. Built partially on stilts, this structure commanded a beautiful view of the pond and its lotus blossoms.

Sarang-ch'ae, the status symbol of the household, served as the living space of his eldest son, and an arena of training for the young man. In upper class residences, the master *sarang*, being the first structure one encountered inside the front gate, made its presence felt as the command post of the household. People lowered their heads as they passed the *sarang*, and the master, seated high in the center of the six-*kan* great hall, would look down at the tops of the bowed heads. In some cases, the foundation of the *sarang-ch'ae* was built 100 cm high, and even round pillars, forbidden in private residences, appeared. Some *sarang-ch'ae*s featured side *maru*s framed by regal round pillars, which added to their majesty a decorative yet dignified element.

A master *sarang* room for the father, a junior one for the eldest son, a *taech'ong* (a great *maru* hall), bedroom, study, library or reading room, and *numaru*s (verandahs) composed the *sarang-ch'ae*. Sometimes, the *sarang-ch'ae* included pavilions for men's enjoyment of nature and music (photo 23). When the status and responsibilities of the master passed onto his eldest son while the father was alive, a separate "hidden" *ansarang-ch'ae* (*sarang-ch'ae* in the inner quarters) was made available to the retired master.

As discussed earlier, as the patriarchal family system settled as nationally accepted institution, living space arrangements responded to this change. Preferential treatment, including additional space allocation, was given to the eldest son of the family for a variety of reasons. Among them were his duty to support his parents during their life time, perform ancestral ceremonies, entertain dignitaries, and oversee the operation of the "house"—the main portion of estate he would inherit. Various artifacts prove the existence of the practice whereby generations of direct-line eldest sons lived in the same house. Moving into the large *sarang* room in the *sarang-ch'ae* and the *anbang* in the *an-ch'ae* signified that the position of power transferred from the master of the house to his eldest son and from the lady of the house to her daughter-in-law, respectively.

The design and size of the master and junior *sarang*s (studies) set the two structures apart. The relatively humble structure and furnishings of the latter were to instill humility in the young man in training. The Wunjo-ru estate in Kurae is typical of the space arrangement used in upper class households which strictly observed the Confucian family hierarchy (illustration 24). The master *sarang* and a veranda/pavilion, called Wunjo-ru, belonged to the master; the junior

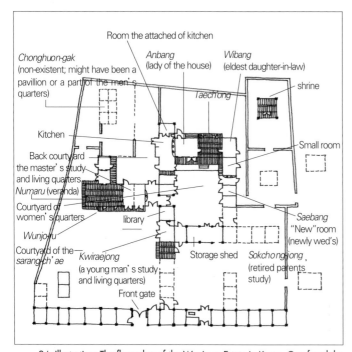

24. Illustration: The floor plan of the Wunjo-ru Estate in Kurae. One faced the men's quarters upon stepping inside the front gate. A plaque bearing the name Wunjo-ru ran across the top of the *taech'ong* of the *sarang-ch'ae*, the living space of the master of the household. To the right was a study called the Kwirae-jong, used by the master's son. Once occupied by the master's retired parents, the structures inside the women's quarters (indicated by dotted lines) were destroyed.

sarang room and its veranda, Kwirae-jong, to the eldest son; and the *ansarang* (the study in the inner quarters) and its veranda, Sokjong-jong, to the retired grandparents. Various separate servants' routes existed for the transportation of food and other items out of the *an-ch'ae* (the women's quarters) to these diverse areas. This floor plan fulfilled two purposes: it allowed each area to serve as a familial position symbol and permitted a degree of privacy and independence among members of different generations. In the *an-ch'ae*, the lady of the house (mother-in-law), her eldest son's wife and younger son's wife occupied respective spaces. The *sarang-ch'ae* included a *kulpang* (study) for married sons. Unmarried daughters used a *ch'odang* (annex) and unmarried sons studied in *sodang*. It took ingenious arrangements to accommodate the needs of numerous family members according to their places in the family hierarchy while at the same time maintaining the cardinal Confucian rule of keeping males and females distanced.

An equitable inheritance system existed even until 1600's, namely the mid-Chosun period. But, particularly with the publication of the *Kyonggukt'aejon*, the institution gradually gave way to unequal treatment of the sexes and favoritism for the eldest son. The ideas stressed in that document, particularly those dealing with ancestor worship, patriarchal privileges to perform ancestral ceremonies, emphasis on blood ties and the impracticality of dividing farm lands into smaller pieces, all contributed to the formation of the new inheritance system which left the entire estate to the eldest son, passing all rights to him and providing a discriminatory treatment to the females. Another factor that tipped the scale toward the inequitable inheritance system might have been political in nature. As a defense against the power struggles

waged among political factions that plagued the latter half of Chosun, the blood-related members of clans felt the need to unite as male-centered units. For these reasons, the non-discriminatory attitude toward sexes that existed in early Chosun period gave way to the practice of ensuring the perpetuation of the blood lineage. Childless couples adopted the sons of close male relatives and eventually, during the later Chosun period, even the sons of distant male relatives rather than considering the adoption of non-blood relations. Because once married, a daughter was considered an outsider, couples without sons made the sons of their close or distant male relatives their heirs rather than considering the sons of their daughters. Records concerning the change from the type of marriage which the groom living with the bride's family for three-24 years before moving back to his home to *ch'inyong* (the bride resided with her in-laws) or *panch'inyong* (the married couple lived with the bride's family for a short time—several months to a few years—before moving to groom's home) during the mid-Chosun period correlates with the above-mentioned preferential treatment of the eldest son and the blood-line adoption practice. According to records, the *panch'inyong* continued among the general population, but it was forbidden among the royal families.

The traditional inheritance practices generally fell into four types: the at-retirement type prevalent in the North and South Kyongsang Province areas; the at-death type seen in the South Cholla and Ch'ungch'ong regions, independence type in Cheju Island, and recurrence type in the Hamgyong Province. Two examples representing the at-retirement and at-death types follow. The at-retirement type denotes passing all rights of the patriarch to his eldest son all at once at the time of the elder's retirement. In this system, even though the privileges and duties changed hands, as long as the father was alive, he still retained the right to make the first offering at ancestral ceremonies. The time of passage of leadership to younger generation varied from region to region and from family to family. In terms of space arrangement, in the at-retirement system, the retiring couple continued to live in the same house, but gave up the *sarang* and *anbang* to their eldest son and his wife. The older couple moved to a smaller or less important room or annex.

A look at the head house of the Chongs at Hadong in Hamyang shows that the *sarang-ch'ae* consisted of a large study for the master, a junior study for the eldest son, and the *ch'imbang* (bedroom of the master). The *an-ch'ae* included the *anbang* of the mother-in-law, her personal servant's room next to it, and *konnobang* of the wife of the eldest son across the *anbang* on the other side of the *taech'ong*. This space arrangement changed with the retirement of the master. The eldest son occupied the master study and the *ch'imbang*, his eldest son moved into the junior study in *sarang-ch'ae*, and the wife of the new head of the household took the *anbang* in the *an-ch'ae*. The retired couple moved to the *sarang-ch'ae* in the *an-ch'ae* used as a *kulpang* (small study and living quarters for unmarried sons) until then.

In the at-death system, the position of power transferred after the death of the master of the house. Even when the parents were aged and feeble, and their eldest son managed the household and performed ceremonies, he was only an acting head of the family. In this custom, various rights transferred in increments. The first to be handed over to the son was the right to represent the father. Next came the power to deal with financial matters. The third to transfer was the operation of the household. The last to be

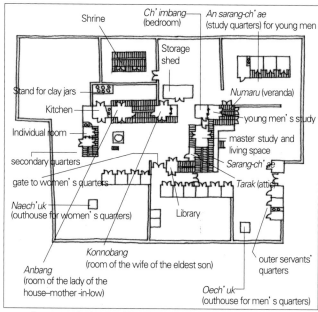

25. Illustration: The layout of the Chong head (heir) family from Hadong. This estate of Chong Yo-ch'ang, pen named Il-du, was built during the latter part of the Chosun Dynasty and showed traces of the at-retirement type of inheritance system practiced by the family. The back (north) right corner of the estate housed an *ansarang-ch'ae* used as young grandsons' study/library. This area was later converted to a space for the elderly grandparents after their retirement.

passed on was the right to perform ancestral rites. But the changing of living spaces occurred only after the death of the father.

As mentioned, in this at-death inheritance custom, the father continued occupying the *sarang* and the mother-in-law did not pass the use of *anbang* to the daughter-in-law; therefore, when the parents lived well into old age, and the age difference between the mother-in-law and daughter-in-law was not great, the younger woman never got her chance to move into the *anbang*. The same held true for the son. The two types of inheritance customs directly affected the floor plans, the sizes of rooms and furnishings. A good example demonstrating such a correlation were the homes of the Chongs' house at Hadong in Hamyang (illustration 25) and the Kims' house in Chongup (illustration

20). The Chongs observed the at-retirement inheritance system while the Kims followed at-death system. A look at the *an-ch'ae*s of the two households follows.

While the house of the Chongs featured an *anbang* with an adjacent personal servant's room, the daughter-in-law's room across the hall was smaller and decorated sparsely. Also, in the *sarang-ch'ae*, the master study for the head of the family occupied two *kan*s with an attached bedroom while the junior study for the eldest son was mere one *kan*. These inequities occurred because the Chongs observed the at-retirement inheritance custom and the eldest son and his wife were expected to eventually move out of their humble, temporary quarters into the larger rooms. On the other hand, in households that followed at-death inheritance custom, in order to allay the desire to occupy larger living spaces on the part of the younger couple, the older couple generally built rooms of similar sizes for the young people, used similar decorations and equipped them with comparable accessories as well. The Kims' residence at Chongup showed an almost perfect symmetry between the *anbang* and the daughter-in-law's room, with similar decorations and accessories, an identical type of ceiling finish, a built-in storage space and an attic. The two women's rooms resembled each other, each complete with its own adjacent room, side wooden ledge, same number of windows of similar sizes and shapes, and a personal servant's room located at similar distance in the inner servants' quarter.

However, such symmetry did not apply to the *sarang-ch'ae*. The *sarang* used by the head of the family featured two rooms of one *kan* each. In addition, his large *sarang* had an attic, and the ceilings were finished in a *panja* (drop ceiling covered with paper—a fancy ceiling finish). Also, a set of sliding doors

installed between the two rooms could be lifted out in the summer, allowing the combined spaces to be used as one large room. An errand boy's room was located nearby and to the back. A beautifully fashioned *pulbalgi* window separated the *sarangbang* from the *taech'ong* (main hall).

But the ceiling of the small *sarang* occupied by the eldest son had a rough finish: a paper surface covering a sheeting woven with arrowroot vines. The room was smaller than his father's and was decorated sparsely. Facing the west, it had only a small side ledge. It seems that such disparity existed because the parties involved believed that the strength of the blood bond between the father and son was powerful enough to overshadow any competition that might exist between them and any resentment the son might harbor, even if the trade in living spaces never materialized.

The inheritance pattern of Cheju Island was termed "an independence" type, which allowed a measure of independence to both the older and younger generations. With his marriage, the eldest son achieved his own independent head position of his own household. If the son lived in the same house as his father, in some cases the father held the power of family representation; otherwise, the son did. The ancestor worship duty always belonged to the father and passed onto the son only upon the older man's death. Even when the father and son lived in the same residence, the two men led lives independently of each other. The daughter-in-law maintained her own kitchen and cooked for her family only, and the mother-in-law and daughter-in-law cultivated separate vegetables gardens. They often even kept separate wells and outhouses. When the mother-in-law died, the daughter-in-law prepared meals for her father-in-law;

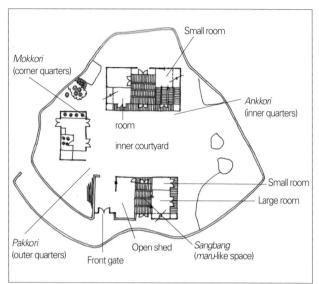

26. Illustration: The floor plan of a typical Cheju Island house. This exemplified the layout of the Cheju Island inhabitants, who practiced an independence type of inheritance system. Houses following this arrangement maintained separately functioning family units within the same walled compound. Called inner, outer, and corner quarters, these units were complete by themselves with their own food preparation facilities.

however, in the event of the father-in-law's death, the daughter-in-law did not cook for her mother-in-law. In this fashion, in Cheju Island each married woman acted as her own independent agent and lady of her own household. Therefore, even within the same living compound, different family units carried out their own lives, using separate spaces named the *angori* (inner quarters), *pakkori* (outer quarters), and *mokori* (corner quarters); they also kept separate outhouses and entrances (illustration 26).

(2) Space arrangement in relation to life cycles

As discussed earlier, the ideal traditional Korean family system was a patriarchy formed of immediate blood relations. The father, the household head, and his son, the family heir, created a vertical line. The son was an absolutely essential figure in a family line; therefore, the eldest son received a more special education and

treatment than the second or third son.

A household progressed through changes following life-cycle patterns of expansion and compression through marriages, births, establishment of separate households, and deaths. The family needed to accommodate such changes and went through many fluctuations in space arrangements until it stabilized with the firm positioning of the head couple and the eldest's son and his wife.

For example, the eldest son occupied various living spaces during his lifetime. He started out sleeping next to his mother during his nursing period, but once a sibling was born, he was weaned and sent off to his grandmother's room. When more than two children began to share the grandmother's room, the children moved to their grandfather's quarters—roughly around the ages of five or six, but sometimes ten. Upon marriage, the eldest son moved into a small *sarang* only to move again into the larger *sarang* when he became the head of the household.

In the case of the eldest son's wife, while she was a nursing infant, she lived in her mother's room and remained there until a sibling was born. Then she moved to her grandmother's room. At the age of about seven, she took one of the smaller rooms or a room in the annex; however, in some cases, she remained in the grandmother's room until her marriage. Sometimes, she slept in grandmother's or mother's room.

After marriage, she lived in the *konnobang* (room across from *anbang*--the mother-in-law's room) in the *an-ch'ae* of the husband's house. Sometimes, she stayed in a corner room for a year and moved to a *wuitpang* (room next to the mother-in-law's), after yielding the corner room to the second son's wife of the family upon his marriage. Upon the deaths of her parents-in-law or at a designated time, she moved to the

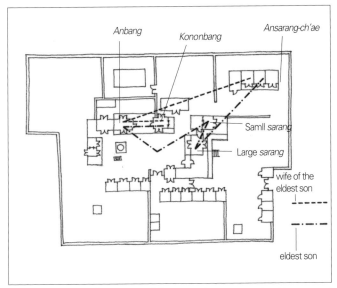

Anbang Kononbang Ansarang-ch'ae

Samll *sarang*

Large *sarang*

wife of the
eldest son

eldest son

27. Illustration: The locations of the various living spaces the eldest son and his wife occupied throughout their lives. The eldest son of a family, practicing the at-retirement inheritance system, began his life in the *konnobang*, moved to *anbang* after the birth of a sibling, migrated to his grandfather's room when two or more siblings joined the *anbang* population, occupied the young man's study after his marriage, moved to the master's study after he inherited the estate, and finally retired into the *ansarang-ch'ae* after passing his position on to his son.

Such increases affected the structure of homes. For one, they necessitated a great number of rooms in order to accommodate multi-generations. Therefore, instead of classifying rooms by their functions, they were divided and named according to the size, location, and materials used. Also, because Koreans sat directly on the floor, rooms remained free of furniture, such as chairs, and lent themselves to serve as multi-activity rooms.

The *anbang* and *sarangbang* were generally one *kan* (space made by 2×2 columns) each. The *anbang* and *sarangbang* were built as expandable rooms, consisting of two one-*kan* rooms with sliding doors between them. If the *anbang* or *sarangbang* was only a one-*kan* room, a half *kan* addition was made to the room and used as storage. However, most rooms were of one *kan* size, partly because the *ondol* system, which could not effectively heat rooms any larger.

In short, the principle of maintaining separate living spaces for the opposite sexes while ensuring individual spaces for the head of the household and his eldest son, and the need not only for a great number of rooms but also for expandable spaces, all played important roles in determining the sizes and structures of traditional residences.

(3) Space usage in relation to family relationships

The relationship between a husband and wife during Chosun Dynasty demanded the maintaining of an exceptional harmony, at least in appearance, as that tie served as the source of strength and peace for all other relationships. When the husband died, remarriage was forbidden. Even if she remarried, because her offsprings would be barred from becoming members of the literati (ruling class), the widow feared

anbang and remained there. But in some cases, if she lived long enough to see her grandson's marriage, she occupied a room in the *konno-ch'ae*, the quarters across from the *an-ch'ae*. Thus taking the route from a small, "new" room or *konnobang* where she started out in her own parents' home all the way to the *anbang* of her husband's family required a lot of patience and time (illustration 27).

Because the traditional family system was based on direct lines and extended familial circles, most families were large. Furthermore, to ensure plentiful labor force for the family's agricultural base, solidify the family lineage, and perpetuate and expand family wealth and fame, women bore a great number of offsprings, particularly sons. These factors contributed to the expansion of families.

remarriage. Therefore, only by remaining in her late husband's household, and serving the in-laws unto death could the widow receive adoration as a *yollo* (dedicated wife) and be considered as not having dishonored her in-laws' family heritage.

The Chosun period's patriarchal, extended family system meant that in some cases three or even four generations lived together, and if one counted married sons and their wives who did not set up separate households, a family could have two to five married couples and their children residing in one large compound. As discussed earlier, because of the separation of the living spaces of the sexes, women lived in the inner quarters and men lived in the outer quarters. The lady of the house lived in the *anbang* of the *an-ch'ae*, the eldest daughter-in-law in the *konnobang*, the head of the family in the master study, the eldest son in the junior study, and the rest of the family shared rooms. The grandfather lived with his grandson; meanwhile, daughters, and their sisters-in-law all shared spaces.

Married couples slept together only on the day identified as a good-omen day by the man's father or grandparents. Once such day was determined, the servant was ordered to heat a room in the *an-ch'ae* for the couple. This room went by the name of a *saebang* (new room) or *moritpang* (side room). Then the man was sent for to join his wife. The *an-ch'ae* and *sarang- ch'ae* with their separate entrances, courtyards, and servants' wings, were connected with an official *chungmun* (middle gate) door. In addition, separate quarters came with small side entrances. These were not official entry ways and were installed in the back of the living quarters off a small side ledge or stood low inconspicuously against a wall. Servants relayed official messages through the *chungmun* gate; unofficial messages

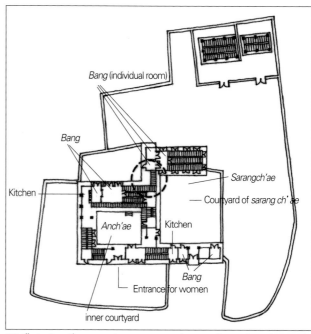

28. Illustration: The connecting passageway between the men's and women's quarters of the Yangjin-dang Estate. The dotted circle shows the section of the *maru* bridging the two quarters-which, according to Confucian principle of keeping men's and women's quarters divided, were expected to be built independently of each other. This device gave the impression of having followed the Confucian rule, but in actuality the two quarters were connected to increase convenience.

travelled through side gates. Women carrying night time snacks and wine to the *sarang* also took these informal passage ways, so that they would not cross the *sarang* courtyard. These entrances remained open when even after the *chungmun* was closed.

The layout of the Yangjin-dang estate in Hahoe is the epitome of functional efficiency. The *chungmun*, leading to the *sarang* stood under a *tarak* (annexed storage space) at the *mo-ch'ae* (corner structure). Thus, the gate conveniently connected the male quarters with that of the women. At first glance, the *an-ch'ae* and *sarang-ch'ae* look to be entirely separate structures; but, through the ingenious connective use of a *maru*, both quarters remained separate yet joined. Also, this way, both quarters faced the ideal southerly direction, even if from slightly off-angles. Instead of connecting the two main living spaces like a *t'oi-gan* or *t'oi-maru* Yangjin-dang made use of a set of cleverly dovetailed wooden floors as connecting devices. Through such a layout, the Yangjin-dang residents observed the moral principles expected of them by Chosun society, yet maximized functional efficiency (illustration 28).

The relationship between parents and children during Chosun Dynasty could be defined by one word: *hyo*, filial piety. At the death of a parent, husband, or parent-in-law, the son, wife, or the daughter-in-law set up a temporary tent by the grave site, lived there for three years, and shunned all forms of comfort. When they observed the *hyo* to this degree, they became objects of adoration and were praised as a *hyoja* (pious son), a *yollo* (pious wife), and a *hyobu* (pious daughter-in-law). Thus, even though Confucianism taught in (mutual benevolence between the parent and child), the morality of showing *hyo* overruled all else, and a total submission to parental authority was the only acceptable form of relating to the elders. The relationship between a mother and her daughter was unique. They occupied same living spaces until the daughter's marriage. Through these years, a type of sisterhood formed between them as fellow travellers taking the same road through life. But the relationship between a woman and her daughter-in-law acquired a competitive edge, as the older woman was required to pass on to the daughter-in-law her right to occupy the *anbang*, and depending on the type of inheritance rules their family might be following, the mother-in-law's *anbang* and the daughter-in-law's *konnobang* differed in sizes and quality of furnishings. Such differences or the lack thereof have already been noted in earlier pages in the discussion of the layouts of the Kims at Chongup, who

observed at-death inheritance, and of the Chongs at Hamyang, observing the at-retirement inheritance custom.

As for the relationship between a man and his son, the son's identity as the man's blood line and heir caused the formation of a unique bond. In the case of the eldest son in particular, by giving him the responsibility of receiving important guests from early on, the father taught him skills in public relations. By requiring the son to participate in ancestral rites, the father also educated the heir on moral principles, precepts of propriety, and the significance of the family lineage. He also trained the son on the art of managing the entire clan in preparation for his eventual succession. Thus, mutual support and interdependency characterized the relationship between a man and his son. The layout of the men's quarters reflected the nature of this relationship. By differentiating the size of the father's study and that of the son, the young man's training as future head of the family and his education on humility began. In some instances, a separate *sarang* quarters was built for the eldest son to allow him more independence, but in general, the eldest son's study was located next to the master study, or in a room facing a slightly different direction from the master study.

As seen thus far, the central focus of Chosun family life was not on a married couple, but on the entire household. The man and his son, the essential perpetuators of the family lineage, were destined to share the same living quarters in order to build the critically important father-son relationship, but because of the rule of respecting the hierarchy, the two men's respective studies differed in size and furnishings.

The relationship between a woman and her daughter-in-law was clearly the most strained. The daughter-in-law was required to live the life of patience and continual service to others. And because through the bearing of children, particularly males (and only through this route could she gradually strengthen her position), she had to keep sharp vigilance over her behavior and had to labor late into each night. Owing to the Confucian rule of paying attention to the separate functions of men and women, her husband behaved like a stranger to her and vice versa; yet, her submission to and caring for him was expected to be total and unconditional. The fear of disapproval from her in-laws was extremely intense. Such emotion and the difficulty of a daughter-in-law's life found expression in a song, in which a woman laments, "Work, work, work, round and round, tear out my sleepy eyes and hang them on a support stick, to stay open, so I can work, work, work, round and round."

Rather than mutually earned respect, caring and warmth, an absolute subjugation to the authority of her husband and in-laws characterized a young woman's relationship with them. She was taught that even sitting across from the mother-in-law at the same table and holding conversation with her was to be avoided. Thus, understanding of each other through verbal communication was not possible; only the assertion of the in-laws' authority and the daughter-in- law's obligations to submit to them counted. Therefore, the principle of respecting familial hierarchy might have served to maintain order in the household, but it definitely produced negative effects between mother-in-law and her daughters-in-law.

The lady of the house, as discussed before, occupied the *anbang*. But she had taken a long course of migration from the "new room" after marriage, via the *konnobang*, and finally to the *anbang*. Now, at some point, she would be required to relinquish the *anbang* to the wife of her eldest son. In this fashion, a woman's position and power was symbolized by the room she occupied.

For the lady of the house who carried out her duty of overseeing the operation of the entire household in meticulous compliance with the rules of hierarchy and separation of the opposite sexes, the expression of her affection for her sons and husband had to be realized through the sewing of their clothes and preparing of their meals as well as through the sacrificial spirit and dedication she brought to these tasks. Public display of affection between a husband and wife and between parents and their children signified a breach of the Confucian rule of propriety.

Studies of ancient artifacts reveal that the most highly developed and frequently utilized layout of traditional residencies was the square shape of a letter (ㅁ shape). Among the populace, this shape was preferred for security purposes. But in the ruling class houses, the *an-ch'ae* was constructed in this design, it seems, as a part of the overall endeavors by the Confucian society to restrict women's sphere of activities and interactions. The fact that while all the various living quarters, complete with separate servants' wings and accompanying walls, were still connected to one another within one walled compound, the women's quarters was the only one enclosed on all four sides in a square shape seems to support this theory. Also, the fact that the square-shaped *an-ch'ae* design was found most often in the North Kyongsang Province, specifically Andong, Hahoi, Yang-dong, and other towns, where the custom of restricting women's living space was enforced more vigorously than elsewhere, seems to indicate the relationship between the square (ㅁ) layout and the motive of restricting women's activities.

3 Space arrangement

Previous sections of this chapter have noted that the arrangement of various spheres of activities and the differentiation of sizes and decorations in a traditional house reflected the Confucian principles of observing the hierarchy among men and women. Each space reflected the occupant's status and place in the hierarchy. The *an-ch'ae* and *sarang-ch'ae* were the space of high level which served to the master and his family. *Hangrang-ch'ae* (servants quarters) was the space of lower level which served to the servants; and the *chungmunkan* (middle gate) *hangrang-ch'ae* was the space of middle level which served to middle level such as *chongjigi* (steward).

Traditional homes thus consisted of several quarters, which were divided by low walls or servants' wings. This layout created several courtyards, each of which had its own unique atmosphere. Next follows a close look at the arrangement of each space from the entry way to the interiors of a traditional house. This study bases its findings on the historical artifacts still remaining.

(1) The front gate and servants' quarters

The upper class houses occupied the center of a village surrounded by beautiful mountains and streams. However, the front gate always opened to a narrow, winding path. Such an arrangement, called *kosat*, sprang out of the belief that having the front gate face

29. Photo: The *kosat* (alleyway) leading to the front gate of residence. It was not customary to have the front gate open to a main roadway with its heavy traffic. One reached this extra lofty front gate after taking a narrow path.

30. Photo: The extraordinarily high front gate (left) of the head (heir's) family of the Chongs from Hadong and their *sarang* courtyard. Servants and their families lived in the servants' quarters built into both sides of the gate structure. A storage shed (right, back) could be seen from the *sarang*, and beyond the shed sits the master's outhouse.

a protected alleyway increased the security of one's home (photo 29). Thus, considerable effort went into developing the front gate area and its vicinity in a way that would generate a sense of peace and security.

Some walls and front gates functioned simply as walls and gates, but often they contained rows of built-in storage rooms or servants' wings. A *sosul* gate signified an entrance constructed with an extra high roof which allowed the passage of single-wheeled carriages. In some cases, the roof of an existing gate was raised and an opening was made into the gate to accommodate single-wheeled carriages.

Passing through the front gate, one stepped into the courtyard of *sarang*, or sometimes that of the servants' quarters (photo 30). In the case of the Yongyong-dang (illustration 31) of the Ch'angdok Palace (Kum-won), beyond the front gate one entered the courtyard of the servants quarters. It had a carriage house and a stable or barn, where cattle feed was kept and porridge for the cows was cooked. The front of these structures was open sided.

The servants quarters also included rooms for servants. Generally each servant and his family received one separate room and a small kitchen with a fireplace.

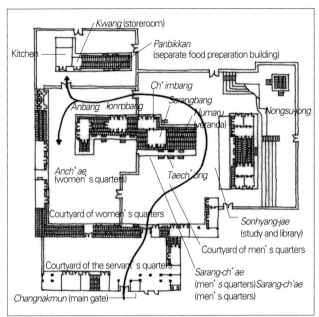

31. Illustration: The layout of the Yongyong-dang Estate. Once inside the Changnakmun Gate, one passed through the courtyard of the servants' quarters, stepped into the courtyard of the *sarang* and faced the *sarang-ch'ae* (men's quarters) and Sonhyang-jae (study and library). The path then led to the back courtyard and a small gate, which opened to the back courtyard of the *an-ch'ae* (women's quarters). To the right stood the *panbikkan* (separate structure for food preparation and storage).

(2) The *Sarang-ch'ae* and *an-ch'ae*

The *sarang-ch'ae* consisted of the *sarang*, the *taech'ong* (wood-floored main hall) and a veranda, bedroom, library, and courtyard. The *sarang* served as the living room of the head of the household, as well as an area of receiving guests of the lady of the house or dignitaries staying for meals. Because the *sarang-ch'ae* symbolized the status of the household, it sat on the highest foundation in the whole house and was decorated with much care in order to assert the dignity and position of the family. At the center of the main hall hung a large framed wooden scroll that properly symbolized the social standing of the household. The bedroom of the master of the house was attached to the *sarang*. This custom came into practice among upper class house-

32. Photo: The Sonhyang-jae Study and Library of the Yongyong-dang Estate. Scholars used to gather here to study. A plaque reading Sonhyang-jae hung above the door frame, and the wooden awning displayed a distinctive construction.

holds since the reign of King T'aejong when the rule of maintaining separate sleeping accommodations for married couples was instituted. The *sogo* (library) was sometimes called a *ch'aekpang* ("book" room). The *sogo* was sometimes a space where books were stored, or it doubled as a reading room if it was large enough (photo 32).

Going outside, one saw trees and a few uniquely shaped stones or stone chests placed along the walls gracing the courtyard. Sometimes the courtyard featured a pond with flowering water lilies. Also favored were stone fountains. A *hamasok* (stepping stone used when a person dismounted from a horse) stayed near the front steps leading up to the main hall. Some *hamasoks* came in stair step shapes; others were square. A flower garden occupied one corner of the courtyard or a space along a wall. The *sarang* courtyard accommodated important events like marriages,

33. Photo: The outhouse of the ancient Yun Ko-san estate. This outhouse featured a section for servants and a raised section reserved for the exclusive use of the master.

for which tents were pitched.

The *ch'ukkan* (outhouse or privy) of the *sarang*, was also of significance. The outhouse was situated outside the front gate or in one corner of the courtyard (photo 33). At the ancient home of Yun Ko-san in Haenam, the class hierarchy operated even in the outhouse. As one stepped into it, the first thing coming into sight was a dirt-floored toilet for the servants. Two boards lay parallel across a hole and after using the toilet, the servant was to scoop ash from the ash mound and spread it over his deposit. Off to the left, a few steps up stood a wooden-floored toilet set on a higher platform for the master.

The *chungmun* (middle gate) led one from *sarang-ch'ae* to *an-ch'ae*. But one had to go around a *nae'oe* wall, built at the edge of the *an-ch'ae* courtyard in order to prevent eye contacts between men and women. The existence of such a wall, and the men and women going to great lengths to avoid eye contact while moving about within ear-shot of one another, demonstrates how strictly and literally the code governing the behavior of men and women was enforced.

The *an-ch'ae* consisted of the *anbang*, *konnobang*, main hall, kitchen, and storage room. At night, the *anbang* functioned as the bedroom of the lady of the house. This room was deemed the most private living space in the whole house, and men, other than immediate family members, were forbidden from it. The *anbang* featured an adjacent room. Four-paneled, rice-paper-covered sliding doors separated the two rooms, but generally they remained open. The main hall served many purposes. It functioned as an entry way to *anbang*, as a living room in the summer, and as the site of ceremonies during special occasions. The *konnobang* was often used by the daughter-in-law. It featured a veranda, providing a cooling space in the summer. In the case of the Ch'unghyo-dang, a veranda was installed on top of the kitchen, to take advantage of or compensate for the relatively low level of the *an-ch'ae* courtyard (photo 34). One reached this area, often used during the women folks' break time, by taking three steps from the main hall of the *an-ch'ae* up to the roof of the kitchen.

The Kim residence in Chongup was equipped with two kitchens, one on each side of the *anbang* and *konnobang*. The *anbang* one was the main cooking area. The other was a supplementary cooking area, used for boiling water and similar tasks. In some upper class households, a detached kitchen facility was constructed, but in general kitchens were attached to the *anbang* and *konnobang*. Kitchens always faced east. Such a design took advantage of the morning light as well as the rays from sunset needed to provide light for food preparation.

The *an-ch'ae* and the middle gate servants quarters faced the *an-ch'ae* courtyard, which was surrounded by low walls. The dirt in the yard was packed down. Sometimes trees were planted in the courtyard, but to save space, families often went without trees. The kitchen and the servants quarters opened into the

34. Photo: The courtyard of the women's quarters of the Ch'unghyo-dang. Landscaped in the middle with trees and flowers, the courtyard elicited a sense of comfort and security. The kitchen, where women folk spent most of their time.

35. Photo: The back yard of the *an-ch'ae* with a cluster of earthenware jars used for the storage of sauces and other foods. The chimney, as well as the grove of pines trees surrounding the back wall, added much to the comfortable atmosphere of this yard.

courtyard, and because the servants quarters featured numerous small fireplaces—for the heating of the rooms and for cooking—this courtyard was an ideal space for preparing food for large events. At a marriage, for example, the ceremonial table sat in the center of the main hall serving as the focal point, while a flurry of activities occurred out in the courtyard. A back yard of the *an-ch'ae* was usually surrounded by low walls. It had a well and a raised platform where earthenware food jars and containers were kept. Much of the activity related to food preparation that could not be done in the kitchen was done in this open space. Along the walls stood trees, and some times a vegetable garden stretched along one side.

Stacks of fire wood also took up courtyard space,

and men split fire wood there. During festivals, folks laid out a large board for making rice-cake. A *cholku* (mortar) was brought in for this task. The back courtyard sometimes led to a hill. Occasionally, this area featured a terrace. The southern corner often held a bamboo grove. Once in a while a platform for earthenware jars was placed there as were a green farm and women's outhouse. The outhouse of the Chong Yo-ch'ang estate had no door, because it faced away from the path leading to it, and before reaching it, people gave a coughing signal to ascertain its occupancy. A final feature of this area that offered an aesthetic quality was a chimney, built as a separate structure. Stone chests or a *tolhwak* (decorative stone water basin) along low walls completed the back courtyard (photo 35).

(3) The *sa-dang* (family shrine) and *pyoltang* (annex)

The *sa-dang* was built behind the main hall of the *an-ch'ae* or behind the *sarang-ch'ae* at the most elevated spot. The *sa-dang* came into existence among the upper class after the institution of the family shrine law. The *sa-dang* structure measured about three *kan*s and its courtyard was surrounded by walls. Inside a shrine and against the north wall was a platform, upon which ancestral tablets rested. The first from the west side was that of the great, great grandfather. Next came that of great grandfather. The third was that of the grandfather. The last place was taken by the tablet of the father. A screen or curtain partitioned this area. Outside the screen, each spot corresponding to the location of each tablet held a small end table. A table for an incense burner stood by the place of highest honor. The incense burner was set to face the west, the incense box the east (photo 36). In homes without family shrines, niche for the ancestral platform was made at the north side of wall in the main hall.

In addition, upper class homes featured a *pyoltang* (annex) and *sanjong sarang* (separate *sarang* built at a spot with superior natural beauty). The annex belonged to the *an-ch'ae*, if the lady of the house used it; if used by the man of the house, it belonged to the *sarang*. *Sanjong sarang* was built inside the family's living compound or outside the walls on a nearby mountain. This structure was used exclusively by the head of the family, so it was a part of the *sarang* and was equipped with the four most necessary tools of a scholar– rice paper, brushes, ink stick, and ink stone (Photo 37).

36. Photo: The interior of a family shrine. Four generations of ancestors were worshipped in this shrine. A table was set at each station designated to the spirit of the ancestor to be memorialized. The incense table was set in front of the eldest ancestor's station only.

37. Photo: A *pyol-dang* stood far from the *sarang-ch'ae* (men's quarters). The annex consisted of an *ondol* room and *maru*s. The upward swinging roof line gave a lively appearance to this structure.

2. The *minga* (homes of the common people)

The broader definition of *minga* signified all residential structure excluding royal palaces and public buildings. But the more commonly used and narrower definition refers to the homes of men without government office positions. But even members of the literati or *yang-ban* lived in *minga* if they couldn't afford upper class homes; meanwhile some farmers, if they were rich, could live in middle class housing. The middle class housing meant the residential structures built for the *chungin* class or simply lower class houses that were larger than average. The *minga*s were built within the specifications established by government rules for both sizes and building materials. The government did not allow *minga*s to have a *sosul* (extra-high-roofed) front gate.

A discussion follows on the *minga*s as the houses of the lower classes and their regional variations in building materials as well as architectural designs. A variety of architectural designs sprang up because of variables such as differences in climates, surroundings, area business and social activities, and available building materials.

In general, the houses of the lower classes were small because the owners were of humble means, and depending on the geographical and climatic factors specific to different regions, the space arrangements and layout designs differed. For example, in cold climates with long winters, residences tended to consist of one large structure where many living spaces were crowded together in order to conserve heat. In warm climates with long summers, a number of buildings spread out for more efficient air circulation comprised one residence.

1 Types of *minga*

Regarding the space arrangement of rooms, the mingas fell into two types: single-row and double-row houses. But depending on the building materials and their shapes and functions, houses could be divided into many more types.

(1) Types of homes in relation to space arrangement

A *hotchip* (single-row house)

A single-row house, sometimes called *oet'ong-jip*, showed rooms set in a single row under the main beam. This type of house was widely used throughout western and southern regions. Because these plains were not mountainous, and therefore heavily populated, building materials were scarce. This resulted in small-sized single-row houses. Such layout allowed for a lot of light and ventilated efficiently. This type of house proved to be suitable for extreme climatic conditions and was popular in other parts of the peninsula as well.

The single-row houses divided into two types: straight-line (—) and kiyok or bent-line (ㄱ) houses. When additions were made to a straight-line house, various shapes occurred: ㄷ, ㄴ, ㅁ, and so forth. When additions were made to the bent-line (ㄱ) house, ㄷ, ㅁ, or ㄴㄱ shape houses showed. A look at a few examples of the single-row houses follows (photo 38 and illustration 39).

The straight-line form of the single-row houses consisted of a kitchen, the *araebang* (front room) and *wuibang* (back room). Although commonly seen throughout the peninsula, this type of architectural

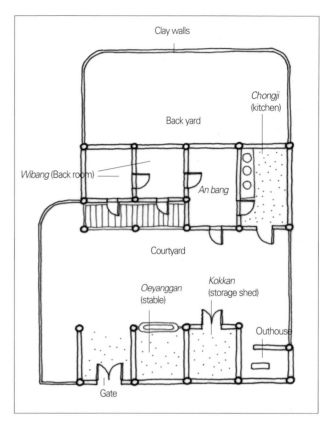

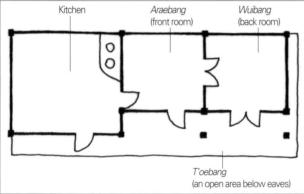

38. Photo(top) and illustration: The exterior view and floor plan of a single-row house. In this type of a house, rooms lined up in a single row. Generally, single-row houses in cold regions such as the P'yongan Provinces omitted *maru*s, whereas those in warm climates featured *maru*s.

form prevailed more in the southwestern plains areas of the North and South P'yongan Provinces (illustration 38).

In a double-straight-line house, the *an-ch'ae* (women's quarters) and *pakkat-ch'ae* (outer structure) stood side by side. Walls surrounded the house on the left and right sides, and the structuring of the *kan* spaces of the two quarters took a similar form (illustration 39).

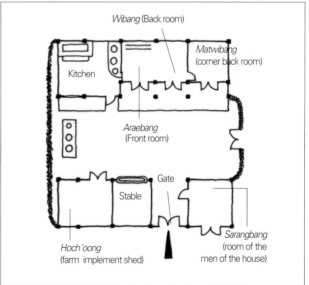

39. Illustrations: The layouts of double-row houses (二). Double-row houses (二), which consisted of two single-row houses, were appropriately called the twin houses. The sizes of rooms of double-row houses were similar to those of single-row houses.

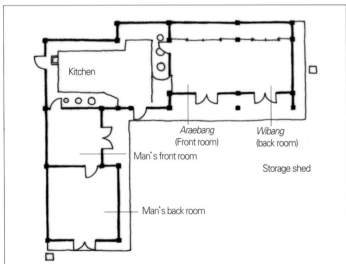

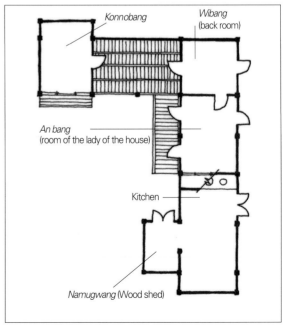

40. Photo(top) and illustration: The exterior view and floor plan of a *kiyok-* (ㄱ) or bent or L-shaped house. Some L-shaped houses, as seen in Seoul, featured south-facing *maru*s. L-shaped houses, seen mainly in the mid-region of Korea, featured *maru*s running east to west.

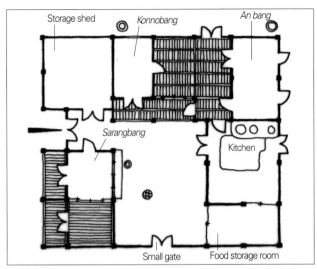

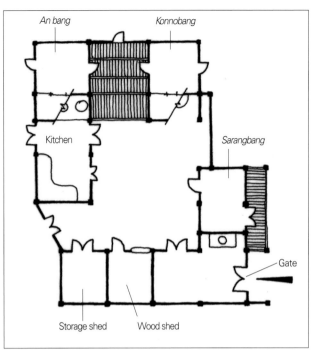

41. Illustration : The layout of a *tigut*-shaped (ㄷ) house. Generally this floor plan was formed by adding a straight-line unit to a *kiyok*-shaped (ㄱ or bent-shape) main unit. The roofs for the two units were not connected. The *sarang-bang* was usually situated in the straight-line addition close to the gate.

The bent-line houses of the middle regions, including Seoul and Kaesong, featured the main halls while those in the P'yongan Province had the kitchen at the corner of the building and generally did not have a main hall. The bent-line houses in *Kang*won Province showed a barn by the kitchen of the main house (photo 40 and illustration 40).

In the *tigut*- (ㄷ) shaped house, which was a type of the *kiyok* (ㄱ) or bent-line style, the *anbang* and the main hall were situated in the center, and other secondary spaces such as the kitchen, storage room, gate, and lower room formed the wings. In the Kyonggi Province, such design acquired the name *malgup* (a horse shoe) (illustration 41). A *kiyok* (ㄱ) or bent-line house resulted in *niun-kiyok*- (ㄴㄱ) shaped one when a *niun*- (ㄴ) shaped outer living quarters was added on to *kiyok*- (ㄱ) shaped inner quarters as the family fortunes improved. The inner quarters consisted of the *anbang*, *maru*, and kitchen. The outer area consisted of the gate, *sarang*, and a barn (illustration 42).

42. Illustration : The layout of a *niun/kiyok*-shaped (ㄴㄱ, double-bent-shape) house. A *niun*-shaped unit added to the *kiyok*-shaped main unit completed this floor plan. The front entry and a sarangbang rounded out the new

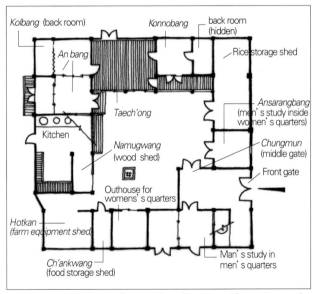

43. Illustration : The layout of a *mium*-shaped (ㅁ, square) house. Because the roofs joined at several corners, this layout required sophisticated architectural techniques and was considered the most advanced. Generally, people did not adopt such a floor plan from the beginning of the construction. Rather, they started with a *tigut*- (ㄷ) shaped house, and then added the last component when improved finances made such remodeling possible.

The *mium-* (ㅁ) shaped house was a variation of the straight- and bent-line designs. The most advanced of all types, this shape was the last to emerge. Some *mium-* (ㅁ) shaped houses were constructed in that design from the beginning, but more often the shape occurred as the result of later additions made as the family's fortunes improved. For the most part, more well-to-do families used this type of design and thus were classified as middle class. These people attempted to follow the Confucian codes of behavior embraced by the upper class by constructing separate gates for men and women or building the *nae'oe* wall to prevent them from making eye contacts (illustration 43).

A double-row house

These are houses featuring two or three rows of rooms under the main ceiling beam with pillars in the middle. They populated the northeastern regions, including the Kwanbuk region, mountains along the Amrok River in the North and South Pyongan Provinces, both sides of the T'aebak Mountain Range in the eastern

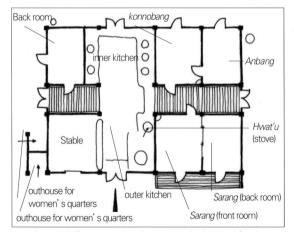

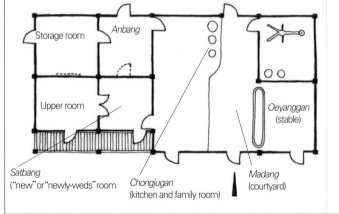

44. Photo and illustration: The *chongju-gan* (kitchen and family room) and the floor plans of double-row houses. The *chongju-gan* was a very large area where cooking, eating, and entertaining occurred, particularly during the winter (top photo). The houses in the Kangwon Province featured inner and outer cooking areas, which functioned a little differently from a *chongju-gan* (left illustration). In the case of double-row houses in the Hamgyong Provinces, the *chongju-gan* served as a large multi-purpose room where families cooked, ate, entertained, and even slept (right illustration).

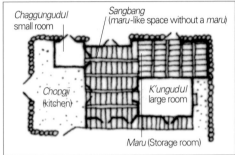

45. Photo and illustration: The exterior view and floor plan of a Cheju Island house. On Cheju Island a condensed version of the double-row house prevailed. A kitchen, storage room, individual rooms, and *sangbang* (*maru*-like space without a *maru*) composed the floor plan. In general, the houses of the common class consisted of only one *ch'ae* (structure with interconnected rooms); however, some houses featured inner and outer structures.

Chaggungudul small room

Sangbang (*maru*-like space without a *maru*)

Chongji (kitchen)

K'ungudul large room

Maru (Storage room)

Kangwon Province, and even down to the middle region of the North Kyongsang Province. In regions where the two styles of the single- and double-row houses came together, the double-row houses eventually took over.

Some double-row houses had a *chongjugan* (dining and family entertainment area), and some did not. Those with *chongjugan* were found in Hamkyong and the North P'yongan Provinces; those without existed in the southeast area of the North Hamgyong Province. The *chongjugan* came with an *ondol* (heated floor) and opened into the kitchen in cold regions. Because *chongjugan* was a warm space next to the kitchen, it served as a dining room as well as a space for the family to spend time together. In a double-row house with a *chongjugan*, a square-shaped *chongjugan*, courtyard, and kitchen occupied the center of the house, and bedrooms were placed on either side of the central space.

The rooms were arranged either in a *chon* (田) or *il* (日) configuration. In the case of the former, the lower room and upper rooms were placed to the front off of the *chongjugan*, and the lower and upper storage rooms were set up to the back off of the *chongjugan*. In the latter case, a barn was built directly across from the front of the *chongjugan* and a mill was set up to the back of the *chongjugan* (photo 44 and illustration 44).

Double-row houses were widely used in insular regions such as Cheju Island and southern coastal areas. The Cheju double-row houses had a *chongji*, unheated storage room, heated rooms, and a *sangbang* (central room or space) (photo 45 and illustration 45). A unique characteristic of this type of house lay in a *sangbang*, which occupied the central space. Generally *sangbang* referred to a *maru*, but when there was no wood floor, that space was called *sangbang*. This was a

Floor plan labels:

Tojangbang (a lady's sitting room)

Anbang

Chongji (kitehen)

Saetbang (new or newly weds' room)

Maru

T'ongsi (outhouse)

Sarangbang

Magu (stable)

46. Photo and illustration: A *ch'ukip* type of a common class house in Samch'ok. To conserve heat during long winters and to cope with the climactic factors specific to a mountainous region like Samch'ok, people opted for the floor plan of a *ch'ukip* house where all rooms were built close together under one side of the roof.

multi-purpose area serving as a space of ancestral worship ceremonies and meetings, but also as a living room, dining room, and reception area for guests (illustration 45).

The double-row type houses were seen all along the east of the T'aebak Mountain range, down the plains to Andong and even in a section of the west coast. One of the most unusual styles of housing along the Tae-back Mountain Ridge was *ch'ukip minga*. In this type, facade of the house was placed in one slanting side of the roof. The *ch'ukip minga* found in Samch'ock-kun in Kangwon Province had an *anbang*, *sarangbang*, *tojangbang* (woman's sitting room), *saetbang* (spare room), *chongji*, stable, and *maru* (photo 46 and illustration 46).

(2) Types of houses in relation to building materials and their shapes and functions

Houses consisted of three elements: flooring, walls, and roof. Particularly in the lower class houses, the roof was the most important element; and depending on the materials used or the shape of the roof, roofs fell into several categories. Houses also fell into different types according to the materials used for walls or the special functions of the structures. An examination of several of the representative types follows.

Types of houses according to the roof
materials and the shapes of the roof

The shapes and functions of roofs varied a great deal as they were built in response to natural surroundings and cultural demands. Depending on the materials used for the roofs, there were the tiled- or thatched-roof houses, the *satchip* (the "weed" house), *nowajip* (wood- or stone-shingled house), or the *kulp'ijip* (oak- bark

house). In terms of the shapes of roofs, there were *matpaejip* (boat-shaped), wujingakjip (trapezoid- shaped), and *p'alchakchip* (raised-roof-cornered houses).

The tiled roof used commonly among the middle and upper classes symbolized wealth. It was an expensive investment; only a person with enough means, namely, at least 1,000 *sok*s (sacks) of annual rice production could afford such a roof. In order for the house to support the weight of a tiled-roof, the size and structure of the building itself needed to be substantial.

A thatched roof was made of the dried rice stalks, the most easily available material. Because the stalks were empty inside, they helped deflect the summer heat and in winter functioned as insulation. The soft curve, muted color, and gentle texture of thatched roofs imbued a feeling of comfort, softness, and warmth. A new layer of thatch laid each year added a clean and bright look. In addition, because the thatched roofs did not slope sharply, in autumn red peppers could be spread on the roof to dry. It also provided extra space to grow pumpkins and gourd plants, which climbed up the wall and to the roof. A typical autumn view of thatched roofs covered with drying red peppers and various sizes of pumpkins and gourds formed a mellow harvest scene (photo 47).

A woven straw covering laid on the roof and another piece of woven straw mat placed along the peak roof line completed the roof. In regions with strong winds, a large net made of braided straw ropes covered the entire roof and provided protection. Sometimes people even tied stones to the thatch. In general, the top of the thatched roof took the shape of a pyramid, and the thatch draped over the eaves, but in double-row houses, builders shortened the peak ridge of the roof and tucked under the straw hanging over the eaves at the left and right sides of the roof, leaving

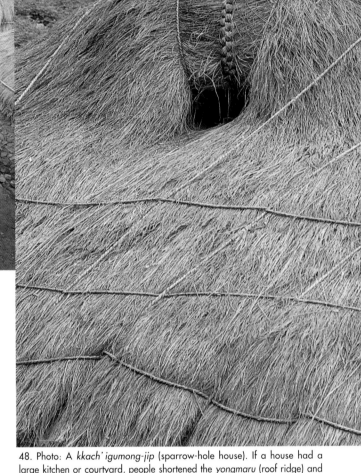

47. Photo: A *wujingak* type of thatched-roof house. Blending well aesthetically with stone walls and trees, thatched roofs elicited in viewers a sense of soft comfort.

"sparrow holes", openings big enough for sparrows to go in and out of the eave line. This opening allowed more sunlight into the house and let smoke escape (photo 48).

Thatch made of wild weed straw went on the *satchip* roof. Because this type of thatch lasted 20 to 30 years, a new roof went on only once in every new generation. As this type of roof had significant weight, it necessitated an extra strong structure. If the house stood in a shadowy area, the straw rotted and required at least a partial replacement. *Nowajip* was also known as stone-shingle, board-shingle, or *nosaejip* house. If pine shingles were used, a roof lasted about five years. Stone shingles were very durable and lasted almost forever.

48. Photo: A *kkach'igumong-jip* (sparrow-hole house). If a house had a large kitchen or courtyard, people shortened the *yongmaru* (roof ridge) and tucked under the thatch strands in order to make openings for ventilation. The holes were large enough to allow sparrows to fly in and out, thus the name *kkach'igumong-jip*.

For the *kulp'ijip*, people used bark taken off the stumps of roughly 20-year-old oak trees. The bark shingles were laid in double layers. The *kulpi* roof cut summer heat and winter cold; however, this type of roof did not render a neat appearance. The bark pieces contracted during cold weather and left openings that

49. Photo: A *wujingak* roof. This type of roof sloped gently; and, to prevent wind damage, a net of straw ropes was placed over the entire roof

50. Photo: A *matpae* (tiled) roof. This style presented an intricate dovetailing of A male and A female tile pieces.

were big enough to allow a person to see the sky, but in humid weather, they expanded and filled up the openings. This type of roof lasted about five years.

As to the shapes of roofs, the boat-shaped had the simplest design; in this case the length and width of the house were the same. The two sides of the roof seen from the ends of the roof line formed the shape of the character 八. In the Kyongju area, out of the belief that its geographical configuration resembled the shape of a boat, the residents of this region built their houses in the figure of a boat (photo 50).

The width of the *wujingak* style house was shorter than the length of the building. Therefore, seen from the front of the house, the roof took a trapezoid shape,

but from the sides, the roof lines formed triangles. Nearly all thatch roofs looked this way (photo 49).

In the *p'alchak* (the raised-roof-corner style house), the width of *maru* was shorter than that of the house. The side roof planes formed triangle shapes, and the four corners of the roof were raised high. This type of roof generally was characterized by tiled roofs, but occasionally shingle roofs as well (photo 51). Among these three types, the first form to appear was the boat-shaped house. In the upper class residences, the roofs of servants' quarters or storage structures featured this shape, but the *an-ch'ae* or *sarang-ch'ae* roofs followed the *p'alchak* style.

51. Photo: A *palchak* (tiled with uniquely shaped roof ends) roof. The two *hapkak* (triangular shaped roof ends) required a special roofing treatment called *pakkong*. Such a roof created a neat, dignified appearance.

Types of houses in relation to the material used for walls

The two main categories of houses classified according to the materials used for walls were: *t'obyok* (mud) and *kwitul* (log) houses. The majority of lower class homes were of the former type and went by the name of *t'odamjip*. To build these walls, one filled the wall space with small tree branches laid in a criss-cross fashion. Then one made mud "tiles" by mixing materials found in nature—namely, dirt, wood, straw, and stone chips. One chopped straw into short pieces, mixed it with mud and finely crushed stone chips, filled a mold with the mixture, pressed it down with a pestle or a wood piece like a rafter, removed the mold, and set the "tile" in the wall space. When the piece dried, the next piece went in. As this type of wall was not very water-resistant, it necessitated long eaves to protect the walls from rain (photo 52).

52. Photo: A *t'obyokjip* (clay house). People built the walls of *t'obyokjip*s with materials found in nature, including clay, wood, straw, and stones. To built a wall, a checker-patterned support structure was placed between two posts, and the openings in the framework were filled with a mixture of chopped straw, water and clay. For the finish, a layer consisting of a fine clay mixture was applied .

To build the *kwitul* (log) house, builders searched mountainous areas for material. The work required no special tools. This type of house was known in Wullung Island by various names, such as *t'obangjip*, *t'umakjip*, *tot'umarijip*, or *mokch'aejip*. When the crevices between logs were filled with mud, the house was called *hwat'ongjip*. These log houses were prevalent in mountainous regions near major mountain ranges. Logs of about a 10-inch radius were laid one on top of the other to build the walls, leaving openings for windows and doors. Then the roof went up (photo 53).

One of the log houses, known as the *t'ubangjip* of Wullung Island, known for heavy snows, featured a *wudaegi* (secondary) wall as protection against wind, rain, and sun. This wall was formed of wild weed or bush clover stalks. Sometimes corn stalks were used for the side of the wall.

53. Photo: A *kwit'uljip* (log house). Logs were piled one on top of the other as the spaces between them were filled with a clay mixture. Log houses were prevalent in remote, mountainous regions.

House types categorized according to their function

A *maksari* ("rough" house) served as a small, temporary farm house meant for a rough living. The prefix "o", meaning "small", was sometimes added to the name, making it *omaksarijip*. It was a dirt-floored, one-room place with a portable stove and sleeping area (photo 54).

Another type of shelter was a *wummakchip*, a dugout. A shelter for the poor and easy to build, this also went by the name *wumjip*. After digging a hole in the ground, one set poles into the corners to support the roof. Artifacts found at the sites of these shelters in the northern region, such as large stones and strata of clay and ashes, seems to indicate that an *ondol*, a hypocaust heating system, was in use. This type of shelter had a *kop'ang* (cross between a *chongji*, a dining room, and kobang, a storage room), and a sleeping space. A portable stove was placed in the middle of the *chongji*. The dirt sides served as walls (photo 55).

A *Odumakchip* (tree house) was also called a *wondumak* or *darak* house. It was built high above ground in protection against the humidity of the ground and the forays of animals. The flooring was made with woven tree branches. Sometimes these shelters were used as residences, but more often, they were located near rice or other fields and were used as storage for fruits such as cantaloupes, watermelons, or grapes to protect them from frost. This type of shelter served many functions: a fruit stand, a place to take a break from summer heat, and a spot for general relaxation during less busy periods of farming. An awning shaded the place and allowed pleasant breezes to cool the interior (photo 56).

A unique type of shelter called a *haemak*

54. Photo: A *maksarijip* (makeshift house). A humble form of dwelling, a *maksarijip* provided the barest minimum accommodation: a one-*kan ondol* room with an adjacent *maru* and kitchen.

(birthing house) existed in the coastal regions of South Ch'ungch'ong Province. Facing away from the village and built at the foot of a mountain, such housing accommodated pregnant women. The idea for such a house seems to be associated with folk beliefs dealing with taboos and the desire to avert individual as well as community disasters. Even following delivery, the woman could return to the village only after a *tongje* (village-wide festival and ceremony for peace and safety). A *haemak* usually consisted of two rooms of one *kan* each and a one-*kan* size kitchen. A servant couple

55. Photo: A *wummakjip* (dugout shelter). Half buried underground, this type of shelter afforded space for only a minimum amount of domestic activity, such as rudimentary cooking.

56. Photo: A *wondumak* (outdoor shelter). Generally built on the shoulder of a field for the storage of farm products and/or as a farmers' break room, the *wondumak* retained traces of earlier forms of shelter, like the *odumak* (hut) or *tarakjip* (attic house).

lived there and assisted with the delivery. The fact that this particular type of house existed along coastal areas seems to indicate that the strict taboos were observed among fishermen and sailors. If his wife gave birth to a child, the returning sailor had to wait until three weeks after the child's birth to enter his house. If this rule was breached, he was not allowed to sail. People sometimes went as far as to bar sailing for a certain period after a birth occurred in the community.

2 Space arrangements and sizes of lower class homes

Because of the mountains and jagged coastal lines, the sizes and shapes of building sites varied a great deal. So, even in the same general area, differing shapes of houses such as *kiyok-* (ㄱ), *tigut-* (ㄷ), parallel (二), and *mium-* (ㅁ) shapes emerged.

Generally, additions were made within the courtyard in the home's center. New structures surrounded this central space. When a poor family made enough money to build a house, they constructed the *an-ch'ae* first. This took on the simplest housing type of an *il* (一), the Chinese character meaning the number "one". As the family gained more financial security, they added onto the *an-ch'ae* to reduce some of the limitations of the simple, single-line layout. Additions were made in a separate single-line layout, giving the whole house a parallel floor plan.

Sometimes a connecting structure was erected, forming a U-shape, or similar structures were built to fill out a square layout. In lower class homes, owners made layout decisions as they went through the construction process, making adjustments that would maximize convenience and functionality. There were regions where, taking the economy of the area into account, houses of simpler layouts were built. In such areas the *sarang-ch'ae* was attached to the *an-ch'ae* and served as an area for storage, accommodation of guests, and education of children. This type of a house featured a square layout with a small courtyard at the center.

There were many variations to the square layout design. Some were open-sided, characterizing the "wing" layout; some had only one open side. Hwang-

hae or Yon*pyong* Islands yielded yet another variation known as a "*ttwari*" (ring-shaped) house (illustration 57). A *ttoesae* style house was constructed of a square layout. Its characteristics lay in its square courtyard, which was so small that only about a palm-sized section of the sky could be seen and in the fact that the house featured both main and middle gates.

In general the layout of lower class houses fell into two types: an enclosure type and a scattered type. In the former, structures were connected to one another, forming a large square layout. In the latter structures were scattered.

Because the residents of the lower class houses were small-scale farmers, they made improvements on their property as time went by. Structures such as a barn, ash storage shed, animal pen, or *kimch'i* storage shed were built as temporary, supplemental buildings (photo 58).

From the layout of the house and the size of its inner courtyard, the size of the house could be estimat-

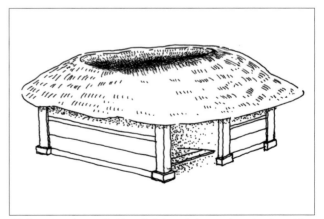

57. Illustration: A *ttwarijip* (donut-hole house). A type of a *mium*-shaped (ㅁ, square) house reduced in size, the *ttwari-jip* featured a tiny courtyard in the middle, which allowed only a limited view of the sky. The shelter took its name from the shape of the *ttwari* (a small cushion women placed under a heavy item, such as a jug of water, when carrying it on their heads).

ed. In the lower class homes, the courtyard played an integral role in the maintaining of family relationships and in the building of a family-centered life. This was a space where much of the conversation among family members occurred and such crucial interpersonal interactions as observing others' facial expressions could be achieved.

In the inner courtyard daily routines as well as traditional seasonal activities that enriched lives, such as the *tano* festival, were carried out. Such special occasions marking the rites of passage, marriages, funerals, and ancestor worship, occurred in this space. From this focal point, the various rooms in the whole house could come into view.

At the same time, from any of the surrounding enclosed rooms, one could tell who was in the courtyard. The entire floor space of a *minga* was rectangular, and in general, the longer wall was viewed as the frontal plane.

A study of the three basic spaces—the kitchen, individual enclosed rooms, and *maru*—in *minga*s and their relationship to climate and geography of different regions follows.

In double-row houses, which were designed to withstand cold climates in the Hamgyong Province region, individual enclosed rooms were arranged in a *chon* (田) or a grid pattern layout, so that the number of walls directly in contact with the outside would be minimized for heat conservation.

58. Photo: A *kimch'i-gak* (*kimch'i* shed). This was built to protect from the elements an assortment of large earthenware jars filled with enough *kimch'i* (spicy, marinated cabbage) to last throughout winter months. The *kimch'i-gak* consisted of roughly constructed straw coverings placed on an A-frame structure.

These homes did not have wood-floored main halls. A barn and mill were annexed to the kitchen, and the house sometimes included a storage room. In P'yongan Province, which is also a cold region like Hamgyong Province, a single-line house was popular with the kitchen and enclosed rooms all in one row with no *maru* in between.

Moving to the south, houses that could ensure warmth in winter and coolness in the summer were built in a *kiyok* (ㄱ) or bent-shape layout.

Facing south, the kitchen and rooms received a maximum amount of sunlight. (Illustration 57) The layout of a *kiyok* (ㄱ) or bent-shaped house in Kyonggi Province area. The single-line houses in the North and South Kyongsang Provinces and South Cholla Province were similar in their layout to those in P'yongan Province. The only difference was that the former featured a *maru*.

The houses in Cheju Island had the single-line, double-row layout, but when a secondary structure was figured in, the layout formed a *kiyok* (ㄱ) or bent-shape. The *an-ch'ae*, which consisted of a kitchen, small heated room, *maru*, and large heated room laid out in this order, measured four *kans*.

As discussed earlier, the shapes and space arrangements of these relatively small commoners' houses showed a great variety, reflecting factors such as climate, geographical characteristics, and the availability of building materials. Even though the size of the total living space was small, spaces were arranged according to their functions; and prudence was employed to maximize convenience and practicality.

In summary, the upper class were required to conform to government-imposed regulations on the size and decorations of their residences in a national effort to discourage excesses in the building and decorating of homes. Also, as Confucianism controlled the ethical behavior of Chosun people, the living spaces of houses were designed to suit the moral principles governing the daily lives and the special rituals to be performed. Because of the Confucian ideal of distancing the males from females, separate living quarters for men and women emerged.

In addition, as ancestor worship gained increasing importance, worship spaces, such as the family shrine and special areas for performing ancestral rites, were worked into the overall design of houses. Furthermore, the Confucian rule of maintaining a hierarchy according to the ranks of individuals necessitated separate spaces for the upper and lower level individuals.

On the other hand, in housing for the commoners there was no significant difference between the early and later Chosun periods. Since these shelters were small and used wood, clay, and common stones for building, not many of these structures remain today, and even those remaining have suffered from lack of proper maintenance. One point can be made about these houses with certainty: because climates played essential roles in the construction of these shelters, a great number of regional variations occurred. Also, as the owners of these houses were farmers of modest means, in most cases the houses did not even reach the regulation size of "ten-*kans*, including three-*kan*s of storage space." A discussion of the various finishing techniques of the interiors of upper class houses follows.

CHAPTER 3
Layout and Design Elements

Traditionally, Koreans favored using nail-free joining techniques and allowed seams and parts of the frames and support beams to remain exposed, even after applying finishing touches. As a result, finished products gave a somewhat rough, uneven appearance. In this sense, Korean sensibilities and techniques differed somewhat from those commonly seen in Western culture.

The upper class residences exhibited more uniformity in their structures, as well as joining techniques and finishing treatments, than those of lower classes. At the same time the upper class retained basic characteristics of traditional architectural elements. The reason for the difference lay in the fact that the elevated financial and social standing of the members of the upper class allowed them to afford homes built with more uniform building practices, standardized to meet the criteria set for their class. This chapter deals with issues of interior spaces in relationship to the structure of upper class homes. Specifically, a discussion follows on such basic structural elements as the walls, floors, ceilings, and windows, as well as the finishing techniques used on them.

1. The layout of upper class residences

One of the most basic concepts required to understand the arrangement of interior spaces in traditional Korean homes is a *kan*. This measurement unit refers to the square space created by four posts. So, a house of ten *kan*s meant that it had ten such spaces. However, the distance between the posts was not always uniform. It ranged from six (180 cm) to ten (300 cm) *ch'ok*s. However, the average was about seven or eight *ch'ok*s. Such variance resulted from the differing sizes of the most commonly available building materials of the day. If the spacing between posts was increased to produce a larger *kan*, then longer pieces of *po* (cross beams) had to be found.

Thus, the *kan* was not only a unit of measurement, but also was a basic building module. The *kan*s were added to form various floor plans such as *kiyok* (ㄱ),

niun (ㄴ), and *mium* (ㅁ)-shaped. A discussion follows on the structure of houses built with such modular units and an examination of the layouts of the main hall, rooms, and kitchen.

1 The structural forms of residences

Traditional upper class houses were built on granite foundations of about three - (90 cm) to four-(120 cm)-*ch'ok* heights. Depending on the social status of the master of the household, the material used for the foundation, the extent to which stones were sculpted, and the height of the foundation varied. Before setting the frame of the house on the foundation, builders placed well-shaped granite *chuch'udol*s or *chusok*s (base stones) on top of the foundation at even intervals. *Komegi* (filler) stones filled the spaces between base stones. Large posts of seven-*ch'i* (20 cm) thicknesses-- the posts used to create *kan*s– went on top of the base

59. Photo: The *kidan* (foundation) of an upper class residence. The height of the foundation of upper class houses was often in proportion to the status of the master of the household.

stones. Generally four-cornered–square-shaped– pillars were used. Round pillars were used on palaces and temples, but sometimes on wealthy upper class homes as well.

The height of pillars, along with the spacing between them, determined the size of the house. These pillars contrasted with the horizontal lines of the foundation cross beams, lintels, and the eaves, creating aesthetically pleasing design elements.

A post divided into the sections of pillar-root, pil-lar-waist, and pillar-head. These were the areas where supporting timber, called *sujangjae*, rested. These support pieces lay at predetermined heights on the walls, or fit into door frames, or floorings. The wall spaces referred to here are not support walls. They are spaces that filled the area left by the support beams and posts. Door frames were formed by the vertical and horizontal beams and posts. (Photo 59 and 60)

To form a square *kan* space, at the "head" positions of the pillars, *tori*s (cross beams) fit horizontally

60. Photo: The round pillars, symbolizing a high status, used in a private residence. Contrasting with square pillars, which were considered less stately, round pillars bespoke of the grandeur and lofty status of the master of the house, as well as serving as a heightened decorative element .

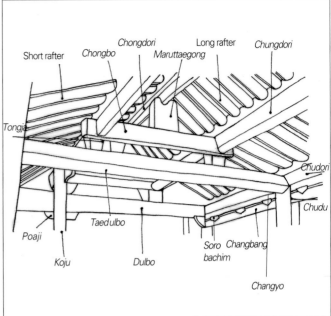

61. Illustration: The structure of a *oryang* (five-cross-beam) house. For the *oryang* ceiling structure, builders first made a frame with *tori* and *po* cross beams. They then fitted *tongja* support posts on top of the *po* cross beams before placing the next set of cross beams called *chungdori* and *chongbo*. Another set of support posts, called *maruttagong*, was set on top of the middle level *po* cross beams. At last, the placement of the final ridge beam at the highest spot completed this highly intricate ceiling structure.

along the width of the house. Next, *po*s (also cross beams but fit from the front of the house to the back) went in. Square cross beams were used for low class houses, and round ones for the upper class or palaces. Square, narrow, and long pieces of wood called *changyo* fit on top of another set of beams called *ch'angbang*, which strengthened the joints and *changyo*s. *Tori*s rested on top of *changyo*s. In the space between the *changyo*s and *changbang*s, square pieces of wood called *sorobach'im* dovetailed at even intervals. These *sorobach'im* pieces prevented the warping that could occur when two different types of wood were used for the *changyo*s and *ch'angbang*. *Sorobach'im*s also lent a festive element to the frontal view of the house (illustration 61).

In traditional houses, no empty space existed between the roof and ceiling. The shape of the roof seen from the outside and the view of ceiling from the inside corresponded to each other. The structure of the ceiling was formed with the *pos* (cross beams running from the front of the building to the back) the *tori*s (cross beams running the length of the house from side to side) and rafters. On the central beam laid across the tops of supporting pillars, short posts called *tongja*s were set to support the *chongbo* (the highest cross beams running from the front of the house to the back) and *chungtori*s (two mid-level cross beams running the length of the house from side to side). Builders fastened another type of short posts, called *marudaegong*s, on top of the *chongbo* in order to support the *chongtori*s or *marudae*s (the highest cross beams crossing the building from side to side). Long rafters were placed between the *chongtori*s and *chungtori*s; between *chungtori*s and *chutori*s (the lowest beams crossing the building from side to side) short rafters were fitted to complete the framing of the ceiling. These wooden beams determined the height and slant of the roof. Builders installed the rafters at varying pitches of 30 to 60 degrees, depending on the slope desired to deflect the amount of precipitation received in their region. The pitch between the lowest cross beams and the next level was gentle, and the roof height between these two horizontal beams was short. But the slant between mid-level beams and the highest ones was steeper and formed the highest point of the ceiling.

In general the highest point of the roof measured

62. photo: The various wood pieces of *tori*, *changyo*, and *ch'angbang*, all intricately fitted to form a magnificent eave supported by the *chudu* (pillar cap piece). The *soros* (photo bottom) fitted between the two long horizontal beams of *ch'angbang* and *changyo* (which supported another long cross beam called *tori*).

ten *ch'ok*s (300cm) from the floor. In other words, since Koreans' median height was five *ch'ok*s (150cm), the height of the house was about twice the height of most people. In wealthier homes, the ceiling reached thirteen to fifteen *ch'ok*s. (390-450cm high) A house that featured five *tori* cross beams was known as an *oryang* house (photo 62). Such a structure evolved from a more basic, lower class residential structure, known as a *samryang* (three-tori-cross beam house), described above. The *oryang* houses generally came with average-size frontal and back pillars. However, most *oryang* houses of the upper class population featured one additional pillar called *koju* (extra tall pillar) which accommodated the addition of an *apt'oi* (frontal spare *maru*). People called this type of a house a *kojuoryangjip* (five-*tori*-cross-beam house with an extra tall pillar). The grander houses of the literati class even came with two additional *tori*s, making them

63. photo: The ceiling structure of an *oryangjip* (five-cross-beam house) built on *koju* (extra high posts). For increased head room, people built five-cross-beam ceilings using extra tall posts on which the *chongbo* (mid-level cross *po* beams) rested.

64. illustrations: Various types of roof structures. Usually, the houses of the general population ranged from *samryang* (three-cross-beam) to *oryang* (five-cross-beam) houses with extra tall posts. Only grand estates featured seven-cross-beam roofs.

ch'ilyangjip (seven-*tori*-cross-beam) houses (photo 63 and illustration 64). These residences had both an *apt'oi* and *tuit'oi* (back spare *maru*).

Regardless of the status of the owners, the walls of traditional houses were built with a *simbyok* (core wall). Frequently, walls had plaster finish and some featured fire proofing. Usually two or three out of four walls had windows and doors, thus little open wall space remained, but what was left was finished with wallpaper.

Lower beams were installed at the bottom of walls between the roots of pillars. Top beams ran between the tops of pillars. Sometimes, middle beams were added. The walls between rooms were made with clay mixed with chopped hay. This surface was then plastered and wall papered, leaving it smooth and white. When doors were placed in a wall, the door was wallpapered in the same manner as the wall to make the two surfaces nearly indistinguishable.

One could distinguish windows from doors by the existence of a *morum* (sill). Even if the two openings were of the same form and size, if one was set above a sill, it was a window; otherwise, it was a door. Builders constructed a sill as one of the means of protecting a room from heat loss. Also, the sill served as a device for privacy and comfort that kept people outside a room from easily seeing those inside. The sill was formed by setting rib-shaped posts on top of the base boards at even intervals, then covering the whole section with a top board, and filling the space in between with more boards (photo 65). The height of a sill was about 1.5 *ch'ok*s (45 cm). The top of a *morum* was at a comfortable height for a person sitting on the floor to rest his elbow on and look outside.

65. Photo: A window built above a *morum* (sill). The heights of the *morum*s differed from house to house, but generally did not exceed 1.5 *ch'ok* (45 cm), a height considered ideal for a person sitting on the floor to rest his elbow on. An opening constructed above a sill was not intended to serve as an exit or entryway.

2 The *taech'ong* (wood-floored main hall)

The *Taech'ong* (main hall) was symbolic of the status of an upper class household. Generally facing south, it also served as a space that connected individual enclosed rooms. There were two types of main halls—those of the *an-ch'ae* and *sarang-ch'ae*. In each case, the main hall served as its central space. In terms of size, down to the middle period of Chosun, the main hall of the *sarang* (men's quarters) tended to be higher and larger, but in the later period, as the main hall of the *an-ch'ae* became the central family space, its size was expanded, and it began to serve as a place of important ceremonial and other functions. Without any obstructions, such as pillars, across the entire front of the main hall, a person could enjoy a full view of the courtyard and outside.

Facing the *Taech'ong* (main hall) from the courtyard, the first step that leads up toward the main hall was *kidan* (the foundation). On this base, a rectangular stone called a *taettol* (stepping stone) was laid. From this step, one alighted onto the floor of the *taech'ong*. Generally, off to the side and front of the

66. Photo: A view from inside a *taech'ong*. Without any obstructions, except pillars, across the entire front of the main hall, a person could enjoy a full view of the courtyard and outside

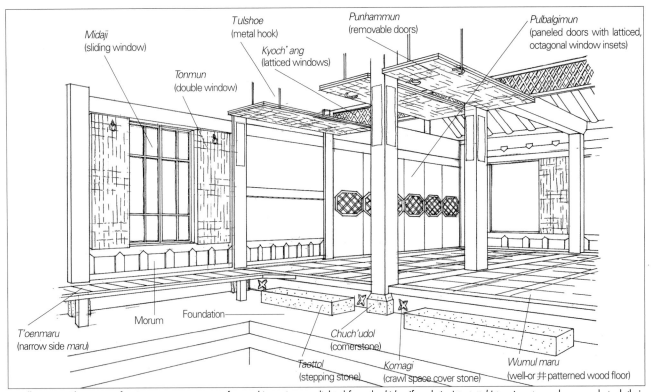

Midaji
(sliding window)

Tulshoe
(metal hook)

Punhammun
(removable doors)

Pulbalgimun
(paneled doors with latticed,
octagonal window insets)

Kyoch'ang
(latticed windows)

Tonmun
(double window)

T'oenmaru
(narrow side *maru*)

Morum

Foundation

Chuch'udol
(cornerstone)

Taettol
(stepping stone)

Komagi
(crawl space cover stone)

Wumul maru
(well-or ⌗ patterned wood floor)

67. Illustration: The names of various component parts of a *taech'ong*. As one alighted from the *kidan* (foundation) to *tattol* (stepping stone where people took their shoes off and left them), one faced the *wumul*-shaped (⌗ -shaped) *maru*. Once all the *punhammuns*, door panels of individual rooms on either side of the *taech'ong*, were lifted and kept open by way of hooks looped around rings set above the door frames, a very large communal area was created. One could estimate the size of the *taech'ong* by the number of panels in the *pulbalgi* (with latticed octagonal mid sections) doors installed between the large individual room and *taech'ong*.

68. Photo: A *taech'ong*. This open space served as the center for various domestic activities, particularly during summer. Festivities such as weddings, as well as ancestral worship ceremonies, were conducted here. The *taech'ong* functioned as a symbol of the status, authority, and heritage of each household. The wooden floor of the *taech'ong* was laid in a *wumul* (井 - well) pattern. This design was widely used for *taech'ong marus* and storage room floors in both upper and lower class houses.

69. Photo : A *yondung* (exposed-rafter) ceiling. Favored as the finish for *taech'ong* ceilings, the *yondung* ceiling allowed the natural wood color of the rafters and the color of plaster to contrast sharply and create a distinctively pleasing interplay of lines and planes.

70. Photo: A *nunsop* (eyebrow) ceiling. A *wumul*-patterned (井) wood ceiling was installed where the ceiling lines came together in triangular shapes on either end of the roof. The name of this style ceiling, *nunsop* (eyebrow), came from the slightly rounded shapes of the lines showing above the rafters.

taech'ong was a wooden ledge or a secondary *maru*. The size of the *taech'ong* varied a great deal, depending on the number of pillars used. In general, *taech'ong*s ranged from two to eight *kan*s (Photo 66 and illustration 67).

The wooden floor of the *taech'ong* was laid in a *wumul* (井 - well) pattern. This design was widely used for *taech'ong maru*s and storage room floors in both upper and lower class houses. This floor was constructed first by laying two or three *changgwit'ul*s (long floor board props), at the bases of pillars from the front of the house to the back in the same direction as the *taedulpo* (the main ceiling beam). Then *tonggwit'ul*s (short floor board props) were fitted onto the *changgwit'ul*s at even intervals. Short and wide filler boards dovetailed into the *tonggwit'ul* pieces (photo 68).

The ceiling of the *taech'ong* left all the rafters, *tori*s, and *po*s exposed. This style of ceiling finish was called a *yondungch'onchang* (exposed-rafter ceiling).

The spaces between the rafters were filled with white plaster, which contrasted sharply with the natural beauty of wood, creating a visually stunning whole (photo 69). Sometimes, a side portion of the *sarang taech'ong* ceiling, where boards joined in a triangular shape and the rafters fanned out, was finished with an *wumul* style ceiling. To construct this ceiling, a frame in the pattern of the *chong* (井) character meaning a well was fashioned and the spaces filled with boards (photo 70).

The front side of the *taech'ong* featured many windows. Windows were framed in between the vertical framing posts and horizontal beams. A wide *kyoch'ang* (clerestory) was placed above a beam. A *sabunhapmun* (four-paneled) *ttisal*-type lattice-worked door was built under a top lintel. In winter this door was kept closed, but in the summer, the door was pulled upward and propped open by hooking the metal handle placed at the bottom of the window around the metal hook hanging from the rafters above the *apt'oi*

71. Photo: the view of a *taech'ong* in winter. The paneled doors were kept closed in cold months, leaving individual rooms protected from winds.

(front spare *maru*) section of the *taech'ong*. In large upper class houses, a *misegimun* (second door treated with very thin rice paper) was built on the inside next to the four-paneled door.

At the entrance from the *taech'ong* into a room, beams and posts framed a doorway. Depending on the size of the *taech'ong*, the door contained four to eight panels. Both sides of these panels were finished with rice paper, but the middle sections, at about the height of a person sitting on the floor and looking out, *pulbalgi* (latticeworked) windows were inserted to allow in more sunlight. The *pubalgi* windows came in square or octagonal frames, which were filled with various types of latticework. A rice paper coat went on the interior side of

72. Photo: A *taech'ong* in the summer. The doors of the *taech'ong* remained open in summer months with hooks looped around rings fastened onto ceiling rafters, allowing the enjoyment of fresh air and the natural surroundings of the house. The *pulbalgi* doors between the *taech'ong* and individual rooms were also lifted up, leaving the *taech'ong* an area open on all four sides.

73. Photos: The exterior (left) and interior (bottom) views of an enclosed *numaru* (veranda). In this veranda off a *sarang-bang*, the window panels were lifted up and kept open in the summer to allow in fresh air and scents of various flora. In winter, the windows were lowered and the enclosed interior provided a space partially insulated from the harshness of winter.

the *pulbalgi* windows. These uniquely designed windows gave the *taech'ong* a strikingly decorative appearance. In the summer, these windows were propped open by hooking the handles around metal hooks hanging down from the *taech'ong* ceiling, allowing the rooms to remain open to the main hall, improving ventilation and increasing coolness throughout (photos 71 and 72,73).

The doorways of individual enclosed rooms opening into the *taech'ong* featured low thresholds. But the doors opening toward the back were built on top of high *morum*s (sills) for increased insulation. The back doors were generally chess-board patterned double doors or *kolp'an* (framed wooden board) doors. *Numarus*—a place of relaxation and enjoyment of the exterior spaces of the house – were built around *sarang-ch'ae*, but in some cases, if the kitchen was a structure detached from the *an-ch'ae*, a *numaru* was built onto the *an-ch'ae* in the space where a kitchen would have been located. The *numaru*s of the *sarang* or a *munbang* (small study) were built one *ch'ok* (30 cm) higher than the main floor. *Numaru*s were done in strip flooring and the ceiling featured either the *yondung* (exposed-rafter), or *wumul* (井 patterned) finish. Since three sides of the *numaru*s were opensided, wainscot-high railings were installed in order to build in a sense of an enclosure and some privacy. Fashioned in a variety of intricate designs, the railings and their lattice work provided an important aesthetic dimension to the appearance of the entire mansion. These railings went by the names of *rangan*. Sometimes, instead of a railing, a *morum* (sill) was constructed. In this case, four-paneled doors were installed above the *morum*, and in the summer, these were kept propped up like the other doors in *taech'ong*; however, in winter they were lowered and remained closed, and the *numaru* area served as an enclosed room.

3 *Pangs* (Individual enclosed rooms)

Unlike an open space such as a *maru*, individual rooms were enclosed, multi-purpose spaces, accommodating various activities including sleeping and eating. The interiors of rooms were finished with wallpaper and ceilingpaper, covering up building materials such as pillars and beams. Windows received rice paper finish on the interior side; and a thick paper materials covered the floor.

The size of the larger of the two rooms composing each of the *anbang* and *sarangbang* measured fifteen (450cm) by twenty-seven *ch'ok*s (810cm). A *satchangji-mun* (removable sliding door between two rooms) increased the utility of both areas, but also set the larger inner room apart from the other as a symbol of its occupant's authority. At night, the door was closed, turning both areas into sleeping rooms. In the day time, visitors other than close family or friends, were not allowed beyond the dividing line into the inner area. Thus, the sill between the two rooms served as a distancing device and a status indicator (photo 74).

The smaller room of the *anbang* that was further away from the front of the house was called the *yuit-pang* (upper room). Two- or three-tiered dressers and other pieces used for storage furnished this area. In the *sarangbang*, the room that was farther away from the front of the house functioned as the bedroom of the master of the house. A set of doors divided the upper rooms from the lower ones.

The floors were *ondol* (hypocaust-heated) and finished with *changpanji* (thick, oiled paper). An *ondol* was a heating system in which heat produced in the fireplace located in the kitchen travelled through a sub-floor flue that warmed the stones under the floor. The floor covering material was thick, tough, oiled

74. Photo: The *changjimun* (sliding doors) between individual rooms. These doors functioned as room dividers between the *anbang* and adjacent upper room or between the *sarangbang* and *ch'imbang* (bedroom). In this photo, the second sliding doors are the *changjimun*.

paper. Those favoring extra fancy floor used silk. Oiled cotton was also employed. Taking into account such factors as durability and water-resistance, people experimented with various techniques, including incorporating into the floor covering a thin layer of mashed pine cones or ginkgo leaves.

The *chongibanja* (rice-paper-covered drop ceiling) was the most commonly used for finishing ceilings of individual rooms. The ceiling height measured seven (210 cm) to eight (240 cm) *ch'ok*s, roughly one and a half times an average person's height. One fashioned the rice-paper-covered drop ceiling by constructing a wooden frame to fit the circumference of the ceiling at

a desired height. Fitted boards were placed into the space created by the frame. The paper covering applied to the drop ceiling consisted of three layers: the *ch'obae* (first layer), the *chungbaeji* (thick middle layer), and the final *chongbaeji*. This type of drop ceiling helped conserve heat as well as cover up posts and beams.

The doors of individual rooms faced the *taech'ong* and provided a uniquely decorative element to that side. The number of panels varied depending on the size of the *taech'ong*, but generally four to eight panels formed these doors. In the summer, sets of two panels each were lifted and kept propped up by handles secured around hooks protruding from the ceiling. The second sets of paneled, sliding doors finished with what was called a *myongjangji* (single-layer of rice paper) went on the interior side of the regular doors for extra insulation in winter time.

There were two types of *ch'angho* (applying rice paper) techniques used for windows and doors: a *myongjangji* (single-layered and semi-transparent) and *maengjangji* ("blind," or multiple-layered).

The windows opening toward the front or back of the house were built above *morum*s. Double windows, consisting of two panels each, with *ttisal* style lattice-work, overlaid the exterior of regular windows. The windows set on the interior side were called *ssangch'ang* (twin) windows. These were sliding windows finished with a single layer of rice paper. On the interior side of the room, sliding window pockets were constructed, so

that when the window slid open, the panels disappeared into the pockets to allow one to see out without anything blocking the view. Sometimes, on the interior side of the sliding window, a gauze window was added for better ventilation and to keep insects out.

On the baseboard of the sliding windows, grooves were made to facilitate the sliding motion. Each sliding window required only one groove, but when equipped with another set of sliding windows, like silk or double-layered Korean rice paper windows, two grooves were fashioned. Paintings or calligraphy scrolls decorated the sliding window pocket panels, particularly the second set.

In some houses, the *apt'oe* (small side *maru*) off to the front of the *anbang*, was enclosed with a *sabun-hapmun* door toward the front of the house and a slid-

75. Photo: A small *apt'oe* (wood-floored ledge) used for washing the hands and face. Added onto the *anbang*, the *apt'oe* was a half-*kan* in size. The door provided privacy to people washing themselves.

76. Photo: The attic door and the doors of built-in cabinets. The attic was built above the kitchen ceiling, while built-in cabinets occupied the space above the cook-top counter in the kitchen. The doors were usually finished with wallpaper. For an added decorative effect, pictures were hung on the doors.

ing door toward the *taech'ong*. Women sometimes used this space to keep wash basins and chamber pots. This enclosure functioned as a buffer against the cold weather outside and helped keep the *anbang* cozier (photo 75).

The doors leading to a *pyokchang* (small built-in cabinet) and a *tarak* (attic) were framed into the wall on the *aranmok*-side (fireplace-side). The built-in cabinet was an essential storage space for various domestic items used daily. The cabinet measured about 1.5 *ch'ok*s (45 cm) high--a convenient height for a person sitting on the floor to reach by turning around. People made the cabinet door non-transparent by applying rice paper on both inside and outside. The door leading to the attic was positioned next to this and was given the same finish as the cabinet door. Sometimes, these doors featured a *kapch'ang* (blind door) which came with exposed rims (photo 76).

A *tarak* served as storage for household items. Because this addition went on top of the ceiling of the kitchen, its size came in proportion to that of the kitchen. Generally, the floor of a *tarak* was built with wood, but sometimes oiled paper was laid over the wood. A *kyoch'ang* (horizontally wide window) kept the *tarak* bright. The ceiling was finished in the *yondung* (exposed-rafter) style. Some *sarang*s also featured *tarak*s. In this case, the *tarak* was built above the fireplace room.

As mentioned earlier, houses often came with two small side *maru*s: one in the back of the house and another in front. Sometimes, a *tchongmaru* (narrow ledge) substituted the back *maru* (photo 77). The ledge was fashioned in *changmaru* (strip flooring) style, and a *rangan* (railing) was installed for safety. Railing designs differed from house to house, or even in the same house depending on the location of the railing.

4 The kitchen

The kitchen, a food preparation and storage space, was a women's activity area and a part of the *an-ch'ae*. The agricultural (non-dairy) and sea food products, mainstays in the Korean diet, affected not only Koreans' dietary life, but also the food preparation space arrangements, the equipment, and utensils.

The direction of the kitchen depended on that of the front gate and *anbang*, but generally the kitchen faced the east or southeast. Attached to the *anbang*, the kitchen was arranged mainly for the convenience of the lady of the house, the administrator of the household, rather than for the workers. Supporting structures

77. Photo : The *tuittoenmaru* (narrow back *maru*) enabled people to walk from one room or area to another without having to put on and take off their shoes. Railings were installed around the *maru* for safety as well as decorative effect.

78. Photo : The fireplace in the kitchen. Pots of varying sizes were set on the cook-top counter built over the fireplace. A china cupboard hung on the wall .

such as the well, the platform-style cellar, and storage room were scattered, offering less than optimum efficiency to the workers. Generally, the kitchen floor lay 2.5 (75 cm) to 3 (90 cm) *ch'ok*s lower than that of a room, owing to the hypocaust type of heating whereby heat from the fireplace travelled through the sub-floor flue and warmed the stones below the floor covering. The *puttumak* (cook-top counter) was constructed above the *agung-i* (fireplace), about 1.5 (45 cm) *ch'ok*s from the floor, and leaned against the wall of the *anbang*. Two or three slots of varying sizes cut into the cook-top counter accommodated the cooking of rice and soups, or boiling of water. Thus, the fireplace and cook-top counter formed one structure, providing heat to the room as well as counter space (photo 78).

Next to the kitchen was a *ch'anggan* (space for food storage and preparation). The floor of the kitchen was dirt, but the floor of *ch'anggan* came in either *ondol* or *maru*. The walls of the kitchen featured three horizontal beams and the spaces between them were finished with white plaster. Often the lowest sections of the walls were built with stone for fire prevention. Above the cook-top counter and to the right toward the courtyard was a *salch'ang* (vertically lattice-worked window). Toward the backyard, a horizontal chess-board-style lattice window was installed for ventilation. The front and back doors of the kitchen showed a clapboard style. As for the finish of the kitchen ceiling, if there was an attic above the kitchen, a wooden-board type of a flat surface, much like that of a narrow side

maru, was fitted into the ceiling space. If there were no attic, then the ceiling was completed in the *yondung* (exposed-rafter) style with exposed *tori*s and *po*s.

Rural upper class houses were often equipped with two kitchens: the large one was used for food preparations, while the other with only a fireplace and cook-top counter was used mainly for boiling water.

In some upper class households, a separate kitchen structure called a *panbikkan* was built. All the kitchen and *ch'anggan* (food preparation room) equipment and tools were set up in this detached kitchen, and kitchen maids and housekeepers took charge of food preparation and inventory (photo 79). When a house had a detached kitchen, a *numaru* rather than an attic was built over the space that would have been taken by a kitchen. The *numaru* served as a space for cool relaxation in the summertime. In the place that would have been occupied by an attached kitchen, builders put into a special fire chamber called a *hamsil -agung-i* (fireplace without a cook-top counter) deep into a heating box under the foundation of the *anbang* to heat it. When a house had a kitchen attached to the *anbang*, the floor of the kitchen was set lower than that of the *anbang* to facilitate the heat's course through the floor of the room. This also left extra space above the kitchen. An attic addition went into this space with an entryway made through the *anbang*.

79. Photo: A *panbikkan* (free-standing kitchen structure) of the Yonkyong Estate. Unlike kitchens, which were usually attached to the *anbang*, *panbikkan*s stood independently of the *anbang*. Here, kitchen maids had charge over the management of foods and goods, and they prepared meals in this structure, which consisted only of a room and *maru*. The room in a *panbikkan* differed from other individual rooms in that the ceiling in the *panbikkan* room featured a *yondung* (exposed-rafter) rather than *panja* (drop) ceiling.

2. Elements of interior spaces

A study of interior spaces and their arrangements and decorations reveals not only a great deal about Chosun people's life styles, but also the degree of architectural sophistication and aesthetic considerations given to the finishing techniques. A discussion of the design elements, their forms and finishing techniques used by the upper class Chosun population follows.

1 The floor

The functions of the two basic forms of flooring, the *ondol* (heated, enclosed area) and *maru* (cool, well-ventilated, and open space) are at opposite ends; yet, both are the byproducts of climate-sensitive forms of flooring designed for multi-purpose uses and complement each other in creating a comfortable and visually pleasing environment.

(1) An *ondol* (hypocaust-heated floor)

The *ondol* is a uniquely Korean system of providing warmth to rooms by way of heat produced in the fireplace, travelling through a sub-floor flue. The heated stones laid above the flue warmed the floor above. The dispersement and circulation of the heat was fairly efficient. The precursor of the *ondol* was *changgaeng* of the Koguryo Period (37 B.C. - 668 A.D.). Because the *ondol* warms the surface where people sit, it provides a direct tactile experience, and has continued as a favored heating system.

The *ondol* consists of two main elements: the *agung-i* (fireplace) and *korae* (flue). The heated air from the fireplace travels upwards and over a raised fire entrance into the flue which pulls the heated air and smoke out through the chimney. Depending on the type of the flue constructed, the amount of fuel required and heat produced varied.

The interior of the fireplace featured a very steep incline in the front, which relaxed a bit over a hump that led to the flue. This hump was designed to prevent the heat and fire from moving backwards. The flue leading from this hump to a *kaejari* (ash collecting dip) at the base of the chimney rose gradually, and the *kuduljang* (stones) laid over this area were also often arranged with a gradual incline to facilitate the radiation of the heat from front to the back of the room. Thus, the stones floor generally shows a slight upward slant. This was why the space closer to the fireplace was called the *aranmok* (lower section) and the side near the chimney the *wuinmok* (upper section).

At the junction between the flue and chimney, a dip was fashioned to allow ashes and smoke to settle a bit before flying out the chimney. Depending on the designs of the grooves carved into the floor of the flue, *korae*s (flues) fell into several types: *hot'ungorae* (no grooves), *chulgorae* (straight-line grooves), *puch'aegorae* (fan-shaped grooves), *massongorae* (parallel-lined grooves), and *kubungorae* (sectioned grooves) (illustration 80 and 81).

The lower class folks could not afford special finishing materials for the *ondol* floor. Therefore, they placed a bamboo or reed mat directly over the dried clay floor of the room. But the upper class population opted for fancy, aesthetically pleasing and convenient coverings, including oiled paper or cloth, and layers of pine cones or crushed ginkgo leaves.

The oiled paper floor finish

Oiled paper finish was the most widely used technique. First, one evenly spread clay over the sub-floor stones. Over the dried clay, one pasted the first layer of low quality Korean rice paper over the entire floor. Next came good quality paper. Because pieces were overlapped, the seams showed slight raises, creating a pattern of square shapes throughout the floor. Also, because the oiled paper itself consisted of two layers of paper glued together, the brush strokes made when applying paste between sheets showed through slightly, producing a unique, brush stroke designs on the floor.

The next step was oiling of the floor with soy bean or wild sesame seed oil. This step gave the floor a smooth and shiny surface. For coloring, one added the liquid from gardenia seeds to the oil, producing a rich amber hue. This process also provided water-resistance to the floor covering.

The cloth finish

In this process, one chose silk from a variety of beautiful colors and patterns, and after oiling it, laid it on top of the first paper covering. The colors and soft texture of silk added to the warmth and comfort of the room. Sometimes cotton, which provided more durability than oiled paper, substituted silk.

The pine cone finish

This method makes use of the resin of pine cones. After one applied a layer of clay over the sub-floor stones, and while the clay was leather hard, the ends of young pine cones, still a bit green, were cut and pressed into the clay to form a pine-cone covering. Then the fireplace was lit. With the heat, resin released from the cones, formed a thick, transparent, and light corn-colored layer of flooring.

With use and much wiping and polishing, the floor smoothed out, and with more wear, the coloring turned a deep pumpkin color. Along with the fragrance from the cones, the patterns of cones showing through the transparency of the floor created the most pleasing type of finish.

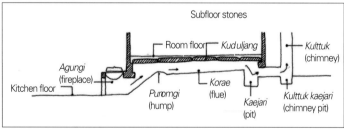

80. Illustration: The structure of an *ondol* (hypocaust-heated floor). The heat generated in the fireplace in the kitchen helped cook food in several pots set on the cook-top counter. The heat then traveled to and over the *punomki* (hump), designed to keep fire from rushing backwards into the kitchen, and then proceeded to the *kaejari* (pit), which caused the heat to linger a while before escaping up and out the chimney. This process kept the subfloor stones heated, which in turn warmed the *ondol* floor of a room.

81. Illustrations(right): The types of *korae*s (flues). The various names of the types of *korae*s originated from the shapes of the flues. All were designed to maximize even and effective heat distribution.

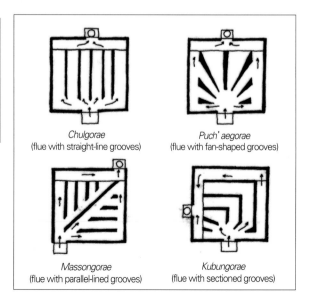

Chulgorae
(flue with straight-line grooves)

Puch' aegorae
(flue with fan-shaped grooves)

Massongorae
(flue with parallel-lined grooves)

Kubungorae
(flue with sectioned grooves)

The ginkgo leaf finish

For this method, after straining out stems and other undesired material, one mashed in a mortar a large quantity of ginkgo leaves collected in the fall. One kneaded the remaining smooth, green substance into a dough-type mixture and evenly spread a layer of this substance about three centimeters thick over the dried clay flooring. The hypocaust heat dried this, and the end result was a thick, hard, and smooth surface with green and brown tints. This made a very durable floor, but the process was labor intensive.

The pine-bark powder finish

For this flooring, one powdered pine barks and added to it a glue made by boiling Indian mallet flour and water. A thick coating of this mixture went over the clay flooring. When polished with wild sesame seed oil and dried with heat from the fireplace, this process produced a hard, pumpkin-colored floor.

As seen above, Koreans showed ingenuity by utilizing natural materials and taking care to produce not only durable, practical floors, but also aesthetically pleasing surfaces that were smooth to the touch, warm and appealing visually, and even fragrant.

(2) A *maru*

The floors finished with wooden boards were called *maru*s. The boards had various names of *marunol*, or ch'ungp'an. The frame into which these boards were fitted was called *marutul*s or *maruguitul*s. Such an wooden-board floor was sometimes called *maruch'ang* and the room featuring such a floor was called *maruch'ong*. An extra large *maruch'ong* was called a *taech'ong*. When framing boards were long, the floor was called a *chang* (strip flooring) *maru*; when short, a *tongmaru*; when thick, *nolp'anmaru*; and when the filler boards were of irregular widths a *magnobinolmaru*. Connecting boards together to make a wide piece was called *tchongmae*; and, depending on the types of boards used, the methods of *tchongmae* (joining) varied.

As seen earlier, a variety of names were used for floor boards. But the methods of laying the floor and the resulting patterns, generally fell into two types: a *changmaru* (strip flooring) or *wumulmaru* (well - 井 shaped) floors.

A *changmaru* (strip flooring)

This type of flooring method was used mainly for a *numaru* (veranda) or the floors of a storage room or attic. To lay this type of floor, one made a subfloor foundation using joists and sleepers and then lay strip flooring boards. This created a floor with mostly parallel lines, with a few cross lines showing between boards that were pieced together. Today, this method is more widely used than the *wumul-* (well - 井) pattern (illustration 82).

A *wumulmaru* (well - 井 - shaped wood floor)

Both the upper and lower classes favored this flooring technique and used it widely on the *taech'ong* and storage floors. The *changguit'ul* (long framing boards), and *tongguit'ul* (short framing boards) formed the frame and *ch'ongp'an* (filler boards) completed the space inside the frame. The long boards lay at the bases of support pillars across the length of the house (from the front to the back) paralleling with the main roof beam. The *tongguit'ul* board went in in the middle of the frame. *Ch'ongp'an*s (short and wide boards) fit into the *tongguit'ul* boards and filled out the *maru* space. The *ch'ongp'an*s were cut in increasingly short lengths, so that the shortest pieces fit near the door. The tongue and groove joining method was used, but the last board placed by the door was nailed down .

Upon completion of the flooring, for the finish, red coloring was added to a glue-like substance and applied to the wooden surface. Or, one mixed the coloring from gardenia seeds with bean oil and polished the floor to a yellowish sheen with this substance (illustration 83).

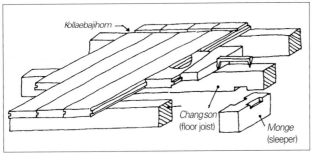

82. Illustration: The structure of a *changmaru*. Generally the floors of storage sheds or attics featured this type of *maru*.

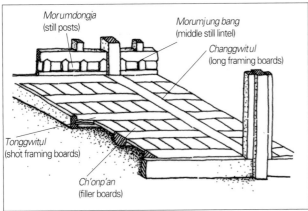

83. Illustration: The *wumul* (井 or well-patterned) *maru*s were laid in storerooms or *taech'ong*s. Short boards were fitted onto longer framing boards by a tongue-and-groove method, resulting in a *wumul*-patterned floor.

(3) *Rangan*s (railings)

Railings were installed for safety in elevated spaces like *numaru*s, narrow side *maru*s, staircases, or corridors. But in traditional houses, railings featuring a wide variety of shapes and forms also served as decorative elements.

The *rangan* (railings) around *numaru*s were called *nuran*s. Those around a narrow side *maru* located outside the pillars were named *honham*. Depending on their shape, the railings could be divided into plain or curved. The plain railings fell into two types according to the shapes of the posts: *keja* and *kyoran*.

The *keja* railing

The posts of the *keja* railing jutted out like chicken shape. These posts were thick and wide and the top sides were carved, so that the outside edge extended outward.

To build *keja* posts, first, one laid a base board over a base frame. Next, one fitted *kejagak*s (sculpted top boards) on the base boards and placed a long, thin board across the tops of posts and filler boards carved with *ansang* (cloud-like swirls). Wood pieces carved in water-lily shapes topped the *keja* posts. The cover boards with rounded backs were then fastened into place. The newel posts were called *omji* (thumb) posts. The decorative pieces placed on top of these end posts were called popsus. One kind of the *popsu* was the *poju* (wooden balls with a pointed top). It symbolized the beads treasured in Buddhism (photo 84).

Because the top edge of *keja* posts and the cover boards jutted out, this type of railing lent an airy appearance.

84. Photo: A chicken shaped railing. The carved wood posts of this type of railing jutted outward, creating an overall sense of ease and humor.

The *kyoran* railing

This type of railing featured various types of lattice-work between the posts. Depending on the configurations of the latticework, there were *a*-shaped (亞), *wan*-shaped (卍), and *pissal* (slanted-grill shaped) *kyoran*s. Sometimes latticework was fitted over wide base boards. On the top edge of the railing, under the cover boards, various carved shapes, including those of lotus blossoms, vases, animals, or cows, were arranged (photo 85 and illustration 86).

The *kongran* railing

The cover board of this type of railing curved in a decorative arc. Sometimes the end of the cover board curved upward like a wing (illustratioon 87).

85. Photo: A *kyoran*-style railing. Simple latticework, formed of thin strips of wood in the pattern of the *a* (亞) -shaped character inserted at even intervals between posts, enhanced the modest, neat appearance of this railing.

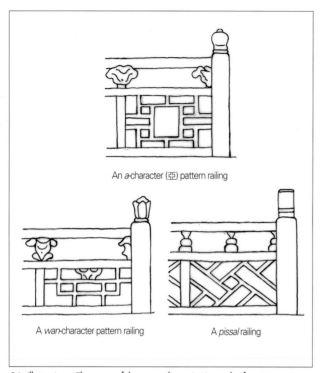

An *a*-character (亞) pattern railing

A *wan*-character pattern railing

A *pissal* railing

86. Illustrations: The types of *kyoran* railings. Latticework of various patterns filled the spaces between posts, and the wide variety of decorative pieces supporting the top boards or the pieces that topped the posts all contributed to the different appearances of the railings.

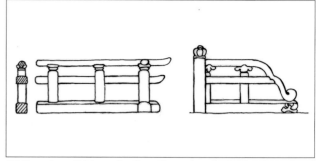

87. Illustrations: *Kok* (curved) railings. The top boards of railings were carved in such a way that they would bend upwards or downwards to generate graceful and lively lines.

2 *Byoks* (walls)

In traditional houses, various posts, windows and doors divided the wall surfaces, leaving little unbroken space. There were two types of walls: a *simbyok* and *panghwajang* (fire-resistant). When walls were not wallpapered, pillars, posts, door frames, and other building materials remained exposed. With the *panghwajang* finish, parts of the posts remained covered.

(1) A *simbyok* (core wall)

The *simbyok* refers to the filling of the area created by lintels. To build a *simbyok*, one first erected pillars on top of granite bases. Next, one laid the upper lintels on the tops of the pillars and fitted the middle and bottom lintels at appropriate heights. The builder set small reinforcing studs vertically at even intervals between the pillars. The next step required laying horizontal support posts between the vertical studs. Pieces of bamboo, Indian millet, or other branches woven in a crisscross fashion were laid close together to the spaces created by the studs. He mixed clay with chopped hay and spread it over the entire surface. Over this went the wallpaper, cloth, or plaster finish (illustration 88).

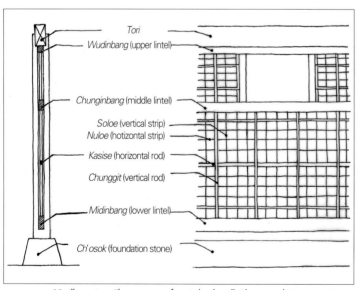

Tori

Wudinbang (upper lintel)

Chunginbang (middle lintel)

Soloe (vertical strip)
Nuloe (hotizontal strip)

Kasise (horizontal rod)

Chunggit (vertical rod)

Midinbang (lower lintel)

Ch'osok (foundation stone)

88. Illustration: The structure of a *simbyok* wall. The space between posts was filled with a clay-and-straw mixture over crisscrossed sticks.

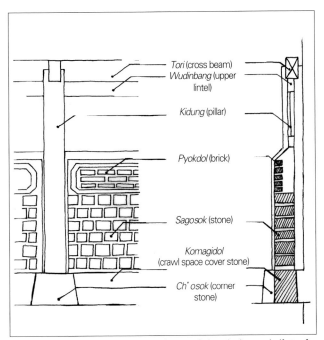

89. Illustration : The structure of a wall fire-proofed on the bottom half. For fire prevention, particularly in wood houses, walls were fire proofed with bricks from the bottom up to the middle-lintel level.

Tori (cross beam)
Wudinbang (upper lintel)
Kidung (pillar)
Pyokdol (brick)
Sagosok (stone)
Komagidol (crawl space cover stone)
Ch'osok (corner stone)

90. Photo: Completed fire-proofed walls. Areas near the fireplace received particular attention with this fire-proofing method.

The wallpaper finish

Generally, one applied three layers of paper. With very thick paste, one coated the clay surface with the first layer. The next layer was a bit thicker, and after it dried the final wall paper went on. The general populace used *takji* for the final layer, and for the *anbang*, they chose printed, colorful wallpaper while opting for plain, white Korean rice paper for the *sarangbang* walls. For the rooms of unmarried young women, people chose more colorful wall paper.

The cloth finish

Records show that this finishing technique existed during the Koryo Period. Just as people sometimes completed floors with silk, they treated walls with silk as well.

The plaster finish

For this treatment, people chose a limestone plaster, which was made with equal parts of limestone plaster, white clay, and sand. When finished, the walls showed the coloring of white ceramic pottery, thus earning the name of *punbyok* ("powder" wall).

(2) A *panghwajang* (fire-resistant wall)

These were walls made for fire prevention. Formed of brick and stone, they lined the exterior of certain rooms and covered up sections of beams. Often seen in kitchens, the fire-resistant walls generally covered the entire exterior surface, but in some cases, they reached only up only to half the height of walls (illustration 89 and photo 90).

3 *Ch'onjangs* (ceilings)

While some ceiling finishes left beams and other building materials exposed, the drop ceiling technique covered them. For this technique, one first crafted the frames and then covered these with paper coating. Men fashioned sturdier frames if they were to be completed with boards. However, a paper finish was more widely used than the wooden board finish. There were three types of ceiling treatments: the *yondung* (exposed-rafter), *panja* (drop), or *satkat* (cone-shaped) ceilings. The types of drop ceilings ranged from paper, plain board, well-shaped, and *pitpanjas*. *Panjas* (drop ceilings) were generally finished with paper, and served the dual purposes of rendering decorative surfaces while providing heat conservation.

(1) The *yondung* (exposed-rafter design) ceiling

People chose this style of ceiling, which leaves the rafters and beams exposed, mostly in the *taech'ong*. Unlike the plain papered ceilings of *panjas* in *ondol* rooms, in *yondung* ceilings, their aesthetically pleasing element came from the contrast between the natural wood and white plaster.

To form this ceiling, one applied two coats of clay before spreading interwoven wood pieces over the space between rafters. A plaster covering finished the surface. The surface completed with two coats of clay was called a *ch'akkolmagi*, *tanggolmagi*, or *tanggol* wall. Boards sometimes filled the spaces between *puyons* (flying rafters) and square-shaped rafters.

(2) The *panja* (drop ceiling)

There were paper, plain board, and well-shaped ceiling finishes, but the paper finish was the most popular. People favored the paper ceiling especially for the *ondol* rooms. For this style of ceiling, one crafted a frame to fit the ceiling space at a desired height. One pasted three layers of paper stretched over the frame. This treatment covered the lantern style ceiling and served to conserve heat. At first, people used white paper for the final layer, but as time went on, they opted for pastel colored paper with or without subdued patterns (photo 91).

One installed the *p'yongbanja* by filling the drop ceiling framework with boards across the frame, much like the boards arranged like those of the *changmarus* (strip flooring). People either left the wood exposed or covered with clay. This type of ceiling dominated in cold climates as it helped cut drafts (photo 92).

91. Photo : A *chong-i-banja* (drop ceiling finished with paper). Used mostly on the ceilings of individual rooms, this term referred to a drop ceiling finished with paper.

92. Photo : A *p'yongbanja* (drop ceiling finished with wood boards). Using a technique similar to that of installing a *changmaru* (*maru* laid with long boards), builders fitted long pieces of boards across the ceiling. *P'yongbanja*s that served as drop ceilings for kitchens also worked as the *maru*s of the *tarak*s (attics built above kitchens).

93. Photo : A *wumulbanja* (drop ceiling finished with wood boards laid in a 井 pattern). To install it, one fashioned a framework and then filled the space in the middle with boards. The process resulted in a neat and rather solemn-looking ceiling. This method was generally not used in private residences. However, some examples could be found in the *nunssop* (eyebrow) style dropped ceilings fitted into small, triangular shaped areas under either end of certain types of tiled roofs.

The *wumul* (井 - well-shaped) *panja*, also called *soranbanja*, was the fanciest form of ceiling treatment. One crafted the frame for this by repeating chess-board patterns with boards. People sometimes covered the square space left in the center of the ceiling with paper, but more often, they filled it with a square piece of board. Decorative metal fixtures accented the border between the frame and boards, or the frame and boards were painted in *tanch'ong* (multi-colors).

Generally, however, the natural wood was left alone, or stained with smoke. When the roof lines came together in a triangular shape and the rafters fanned out, people usually put in a *wumul* (井 - well shaped) ceiling (photo 93) In this case the ceiling was called a *nunssop ch'onjang* (eyebrow ceiling).

(3) The *satkat* (cone-shaped) ceiling

This ceiling sloped down and outward from the highest center point. The lower class people favored this method because the beams they used were short, and drop ceilings would not have left enough overhead clearance. So, they kept the contour formed by the rafters to serve as the ceiling. Thatched roofs generally featured this type of ceiling. Instead of clay, people used fine meshes of willow branches to cover the entire ceiling, which created a neat, orderly surface.

94. Photo (left): A *pongch'ang* (small, frameless window). Generally put in along side a kitchen door, this window, formed by making a hole in the wall and laying lattice sticks across the opening, let in more light on the cooking area and facilitated kitchen ventilation. This window was the precursor of windows installed in lower class houses.

95. Photo (bottom): A *kwangch'ang*. Small and installed high up on a wall or above a door, this window helped allow more light into a room. This example shows a *ttisal* (vertical) style latticework.

4 *Ch'angs* and *Muns* (Windows and doors)

Muns (doors) allowed for the accessing of people and objects, while *ch'angs* (windows) were for letting in light and air. But, in traditional houses that featured a great variety of accessing devices, sometimes the strict differences between windows and doors were not always clear. This is the reason an inclusive designation of *ch'angho* applied to both windows and doors. The vestige of this usage still remains in the word "*ch'angmun*" ("window-door" in literal translation). As the only movable elements set into immobile. But, because they were not constructed to fit perfectly, one could see cracks around the frames. So, to cut drafts, people glued strips of rice paper along the cracks. To a degree, these strips also functioned as a temperature control device.

(1) *Ch'angs* (windows)

If openings were installed over *morums* (sills) and were of smaller size, they were considered windows even if they were framed and finished in the same way as doors. Because windows were for allowing in light and air, generally they received only one layer of Korean rice paper coating. In the upper class homes, windows not only displayed an array of lattice work, but also came in various shapes: square, rectangular, round or half-moon-shaped; but, perhaps because the latter two shapes clashed with rectangular structural lines, they were rarely used.

Bongch'angs (frameless windows)

These were frameless fixed windows, formed basically by making holes punched into walls. The designation

bongch'ang denotes the act of drilling and a fixed state. *Bongch'angs* were the precursors of windows. In earlier times, people made *bongch'angs* and laid a few sticks across them for light and ventilation. Areas like the kitchen, which required maximum ventilation, featured long horizontal opening across which lattice pieces were inserted closely together (photo 94).

96. Photo (bottom): A *kyoch'ang*. This type of a window was installed over the paneled doors of a *taech'ong* or in a *tarak* (attic). The example in the photo features a *kiyok*-letter (ㄱ) crosshatch pattern latticework.

97. Photo : A *nunggopchegich'ang* (peeping window). This small window was put into a larger window or door, so that one could peek out without opening the window or door. The example shown in the photo was set in a window of a *yong*-character (用) patterned latticework.

98. Photo : A *salch'ang*. A window designed to facilitate ventilation used especially in kitchens. The sizes varied depending on the efficiency of ventilation desired. Vertical wood strips partially screened the opening.

*Hwach'ang*s (exhaust windows)

*Hwach'ang*s were placed in the upper section of the kitchen wall close to the *anbang*. They served mainly to ventilate smoke from the fireplace and the steam from cooking. When a *hwach'ang* faced the courtyard, it came in a larger size. Just under it, people placed grooved tiles or a stone to function as a type of a platform, and a pine knot fire was built on it to help ventilate the odor of smoke and food. This fire also shed extra light on the cooking area and worked as a fire starter.

*Kwangch'ang*s (fixed windows)

Evolved from *bongch'ang*s, these windows did not open and were placed in the upper section of walls or above the doors of rooms. For decoration, some featured straight lattice pieces inserted vertically and close together or in intertwining patterns (photo 95).

A *kyoch'ang* (crosshatch lattice window)

These windows appeared on kitchen or storage room walls or in an horizontal direction above the front-facing paneled windows or doors of rooms. The shapes were rectangular and thin wooden lattices decorated the window frame at 45 degree angles in a cross-hatch pattern. The various types of lattice designs used on *kyoch'ang*s included the cross-hatched; *a*-character-shaped (亞), *wan*-character-shaped (卍), and *chong*-character-shaped (井) (photo 96).

A *nungopchaegich'ang* (peep-hole window)

This was a very tiny window constructed next to a door for the purpose of peeking out. Later, any piece of glass fitted into a door, *bongch'ang*, or *kwangch'ang* to look out acquired this name. Even a window formed of different shapes of holes bored into the clap board door of a kitchen was considered a peep-hole window (photo 97).

A *salch'ang* (straight-line lattice window)

For this window, used mainly for ventilation in the kitchen, one fitted thin lattice pieces into the frame vertically at even intervals. The shapes of lattices varied: triangular, square, hexagonal, and octagonal and so forth. The pottery of the Kaya Period reveals that this type of window existed even at that time (photo 98).

A *kapch'ang* (double-window or door)

These double windows or doors increased the efficiency of heating and went on the inside of a window or the sliding attic door. These windows or doors featured exposed wood rims. The lower sections were wood while the upper sections were finished with paper. Calligraphy art works hung on top of these openings provided an aesthetic element.

(2) *Mun*s (doors)

The structures and shapes of doors differed a great deal depending on their locations and functions. The kitchen door and back door of the *taech'ong* were formed of thick wooden boards while the doors to individual enclosed rooms opening to the *taech'ong* had a rice-paper covering and could be lifted and propped up. Doors generally came with *tonmun*s (double doors), which functioned as protection against cold and intruders. Between rooms, *satchangji*s (removable

sliding doors) worked as dividers. Sometimes a *kapchangji* (door with a thick paper finish or "blind" door) replaced a *satchangji*. The sliding doors were finished with Korean rice paper to allow light in, and the most typical lattice work used were the *wan*-character shape (卍), or *a*-character shape (亞). All the doors, decorated with short lattice pieces, took the form of double or single sliding doors. An interesting pattern shown by the different lattice styles points to the fact that the farther one travelled to the north, the simpler (well- 井 -shaped) was the lattice work. This relates directly to the shorter daylight hours of the north; peo-

99. Photo : A *p'anjangmun*. Used as a kitchen door or front gate, this door was made by fastening thick, long boards onto a pair of cross boards and installing locking devices.

100. Photo : A *kolp'anmun*. For this door, a frame was constructed and boards were fitted inside. Doors of this type were used as back doors of *taech'ong*s to cut drafts.

101. Photo : A *mangjangji*. Several layers of paper were applied to the inside as well as outside of the door, causing its surface to look similar to that of a wall.

ple designed windows and doors for maximum reception of sunlight. On the other hand, in the south, with more dense lattice design, residents attempted to reduce exposure to light and heat. The types of doors varied a great deal and included *p'anjangmun*s, *kolp'anmun*s, *maengjangji*s, *todummun*s, *pulbalgi*s, *punhapmun*s, and *tukkoptaji*s. The description of each follows.

A *p'anjangmun* (plain board door)

Wide vertical boards steadied with thin cross boards formed this type of door. It generally equipped kitchens and storage rooms, and functioned as a double door of individual enclosed rooms (photo 99).

A *kolp'anmun* (framed board door)

One filled the space inside a frame with boards to form this door. It generally served as a double door for individual enclosed rooms or storerooms (photo 100).

A *maengjangji*
("blind" or non-transparent window or door)

Several layers of paper coated both the interior and exterior sides of this door, and its finished look resembled the surface of walls. One used this method on doors leading from the *taech'ong* to the individual rooms or on the dividing doors between rooms (photo 101).

A *todummun* (extra fancy, decorated door)

This was a type of a non-transparent door. Only the more visible side of the door received a fancy finish. Attic doors, sliding door pockets facing a room, or the double doors that slid into the pockets featured this style.

In the upper class homes, the frames of these doors came in ordinary wood, but a thin layer of fancy material such as sandalwood was added to the borders for fancy appearance. Calligraphy scrolls hung on the doors completed the decoration (photo 102).

A *pulpalgimun* (door with latticed mid section)

This was a non-transparent door, but in the middle, at about the height of a person sitting on the floor, a square, octagonal, or other shape opening was made. After a frame was fitted into the opening, lattice of various designs such as cross-hatched, *chong*-character-shaped (井), or *wan*-character-shaped (卍) forms, filled the frame. Only one layer of Korean rice paper coated the frame to allow in light. This treatment was typical of those used on doors between the *taech'ong* and individual rooms in middle to upper class houses, palaces, or Confucian shrine schools. These doors were multi-paneled and, when needed, sets of two panels each were lifted up and hung from hooks (photo 103).

A *changjimun* (sliding room divider door)

This door was finished with rice paper and *ttisal* (lattice work of close vertical lines with several horizontally densely latticed sections). This type of door deflected strong sun light and also, if used as a room divider, provided visual privacy. In middle and higher class houses, lattice designs including *wan*-character (卍) and *a*-character (亞) shapes were favored (photo 74).

102. Photo : A *totummun*. After a frame was constructed, thin wood strips were fitted into it at wide intervals. Then the entire surface was covered with paper, and a separate border paper was applied. An oriental painting mounted on the surface completed this door.

A *punhapmun* (paneled, removable door)

This door functioned as a room divider, but when lifted up, opened rooms into one large space. Generally installed between the *taech'ong* and rooms, the door panels ranged from four to eight. When lifted up, the *ondol* rooms and *maru* became one large area. To allow the penetration of sunlight, the middle sections of the panels were treated with *pulpalgi* (lattice) windows.

A *tukkoptajimun* (pocketed sliding door)

These were pocketed sliding doors. Structurally, these consisted of frames and panels with a thick rice paper finish, like that of *maengjangji*. Paintings or calligraphy hung on these doors, which were installed only if there were wainscots (photo 104).

103. Photo : A *pulbalgimun.* The octagonal insets received only one layer of rice paper while the rest of the paneled doors were covered with several layers. The octagonal insets allowed daylight into the room and at night indoor lighting shone out, creating a decorative effect.

104. Photo: A *tukkoptajimun*. This door featured pockets into which another set of sliding doors could remain out of view. These were usually not removable.

(3) The finishing materials of windows and doors

Wood, cloth, and paper were used to finish windows and doors.

Wood finish

The frames of windows and doors were made of strips of wood cut along the grain. Craftsmen usually chose red pine, big cone pine, or wood of broad-leaved trees. In the case of a *p'anchangmun* or *kolp'anmun*, the sides of wood showing the most beautiful grain were placed facing outward and craftsmen made efforts to have the wood grain on the panels match symmetrically.

Cloth finish

Between sliding and double doors, a gauze door, similar to today's window netting, was installed to allow the circulation of cool air in the summer. Silk of a coarse weave or ramie cloth was used for this type of window to provide maximum air circulation and to keep out insects.

Paper finish

Almost all windows and doors were treated with a rice paper finish. Paste was applied to the paper in areas beyond the lattice lines, and the paste brush strokes showed when it dried. With the passage of time, the glued areas extending beyond the lattice lines turned brown. The excess edges of rice paper were not cut away in order to allow them to help cut drafts. When the window or door was used as a double window or door, oiled or otherwise treated paper was used for durability and to keep it from getting dirty. For the latter, a mixture of glue and alum was sprayed onto rice paper, creating transparent and tightly stretched surface that was water-resistant and allowed effective penetration of sunlight.

As discussed in this chapter, the interior spaces of traditional Korean houses might appear somewhat Spartan with large empty-looking spaces, but upon closer look, one would find aesthetic richness in a variety of fine details.

s in architecture, societal elements also played a role in the craftsmanship that went into the creation of such practical objects as furniture and accessories. As these items were designed to fulfill the dual objectives of serving functional purposes and satisfying man's need for artistic expression, they were exceptionally good examples for revealing the culture in which they were produced.

Profoundly affected by nature, traditional Korean furniture expressed uniquely Korean sense of aesthetics as well as spiritual and philosophical ideologies. Naturally, Korean furniture differed significantly from that of China and Japan both in form and technique. One of the distinguishing characteristics of Korean furniture involved the use of wood—namely, the art of highlighting the beauty of the natural texture and grains, using nail-free joining techniques, placing emphasis on producing a functionally strong rather than decorate structure and favoring unexaggerated, simple yet graceful decorations. The very first precursor of furniture seems to have been basket-type containers during the period when the foremost function of furniture was storage. Particularly because Korea produced an abundance of seasonal products throughout the four distinct seasons, creating a great many types of storing devices to accommodate the accumulation became an issue of survival. *Chang, nong, ham, kwe, pandaji,* and so forth were containers, all of which varied in their size, form, structure, and decoration.

Compared to the Buddhist-influenced furniture of the United Silla and the fancy and artistic upper-class-oriented furniture of Koryo, those of Chosun displayed a simplistic, natural beauty. Emphasis was placed on utilizing the natural textures of materials while striving for beauty arising from well-developed proportions.

However, despite the tradition of creating furniture of superior quality, the art of furniture making in Korea never developed to its full potential. The reason lies in the fact that the makers of furniture were classified and treated as *ch'onmins* (lowest class citizens), and with such lack of support, the art eventually petered out. In addition, because the furniture was made mainly of wood, a majority of it was lost to various wars, not leaving enough for posterity to learn from and perpetuate the tradition. Therefore, the remaining pieces of furniture are from the latter period of Chosun, about 100-200 years ago.

1. Traditional furniture

1 Types and uses of furniture

Traditional furniture can be divided into those items used in the *anbang, sarangbang,* and kitchen. The *anbang* furniture included several types of wardrobes called *chang* (wardrobe), *nong* (stackable chests), *pandaji* (clothes/blanket chest), *ham* (top-opening deep chest) and *kakkaesuri* (safe) and *pitchop* (small comb box with no mirror), and *chwagyong* (small mirrored vanity). The *sarangbang* furniture included various tables, bookcases, *yonsang*s (end table where ink stones and other writing tools were stored), *mungap*s (writing supply boxes) and *soan*s and *kyongsang*s (desks), *munsoham*s (document boxes), and *kwe*s (chests) for books. The kitchen furniture included *ch'anjang*s (food storage cabinets), *ch'ant'ak*s (shelves for prepared foods and dishes), *soban*s (tables), *twiju*s (grain bins) and various types of vats.

(1) *Anbang* furniture

A *chang* (wardrobe)

The four distinct seasonal changes necessitated many types of clothing and bedding along with a great deal of storage space for these items. Therefore, a majority of

Korean furniture was used for storage. *Chang*s, *nong*s, *ham*s, and *kwe*s are examples. *Chang*s especially crossed all class boundaries and were utilized in every Chosun household. As for the structure of wardrobes, one thick, wide and long board served as the back of the *chang*, which featured several compartments or levels. *Chang*s ranged from one to five levels.

The top board, middle section, and legs formed the structural frame of *chang*s. Four posts of sturdy quality framed the middle section. Each level came with a door and compartment, where women's clothes were folded and laid flat. The building material for wardrobes was mainly wood. For decoration, craftsmen chose materials including bamboo, paper, silk, and mother-of-pearl. The *hwagak* (decorative technique of painting the surface of thinly sliced ox horns) with bright colors and attaching them to furniture pieces was also popular.

105. Photos: Several types of wardrobes or cabinets. A single-level cabinet (right), generally placed at the head of a bed, was used to store important documents or small accessories. Bi- and tri-level (middle and left) cabinets functioned as wardrobes.

106. Photo : An *uigorijang* (right). This wardrobe featured a clothes hanging rack much like modern day wardrobes.

107. Photo : A *nong*. A *nong* (set of stacked chests) consisted of two or more chests of same size and construction stacked together. A *nong* had an appearance similar to that of a wardrobe or cabinet, but a *nong* lacked the special cover board that hung over the top rims of a chest or cabinet.

The *chang*s ranged from single- to tri-level (photo 105), and, less commonly, quadruple or quintuple types. The *posonjang* (storage for *poson*s — white cotton-padded socks) was also a kind of a *chang* and acquired the name "baby" wardrobe because of its small size. A single-level wardrobe generally stood at the head of a person in bed and was used for the storage of valuables and keys, thus earning the name "headside" wardrobe. Wardrobes went by various designations depending upon their uses: *uigorijang*s (tall wardrobes with clothes racks) (photo 106), *silchang*s (for threads), *posonjang*s (for socks), *ibulchang*s (for bedding), and *somjang*s (for cotton battings). The number of tiers in *chang*s and their decorative metal fixtures came in a wide variety. The *wonang*s (wardrobes with a level divided into two side by side compartments), for example, had three tiers. Butterfly wardrobes were also tri-level, but featured butterfly-shaped metal decorations. Depending on the materials used for decorations, various wardrobes had different designations. Examples are *chijang*s (with

paper), *pidanjang*s (with silk), *hwagakchang*s (with a veneer of sliced ox horns), *chukchang*s (with bamboo), *chagaejang*s (with mother-of-pearl), *yongmokchang*s (with the wood grain in the shapes of dragons from zelkova tree roots), *hwaryujang*s (with the reddish tinted, beautiful wood grain of sandalwood), *mokgamnamujang*s (with dark wood grain of persimmon tree), and *hwach'ojang*s, (with glass pieces pained with designs of flora and attached to the wood surface). The latter type, considered the most fancy, was used exclusively by the upper class.

A *nong* (stackable chest)

A *nong*, one of the necessities of the *anbang*, consisted of two or three stackable chests of equal sizes. Each was equipped with a door to the front. As seasons changed, without disturbing the content of each chest, one simply switched the order of the stacks in order to get to the clothing and other items needed for the season.

A *nong* looks similar to a *chang*, but one of the differences was that each *nong* piece was separate and complete by itself. Even legs were detachable so that they could be used under another chest as needed. Also, *nong*s were smaller than *chang*s. In most cases, *nong*s came with handles on the sides for easy handling, and double-stack *nong*s were the most popular. Material used for *nong*s, however, was the same as that for *chang*s. As with *chang*s, materials used for decoration on *nong*s included bamboo, paper, reed, and mother-of-pearl. Depending on these materials, *nong*s could be classified into several types: paulownia (dark persimmon wood chosen for its decorative property), mother-of-pearl, bamboo, and reed mat *nong*s. (photo 107).

A *pandaji* (clothes/blanket chest)

For this storage chest, craftsmen chose a sturdy and thick wood like zelkova. The upper section of the front panel opened downward. While *pandaji*s were used in place of *chang*s or *nong*s to store clothes in the *anbang* among lower class households, in upper class houses *pandaji*s served as multi-purpose storage chests for books, documents, implements used for ancestor worship ceremonies, and other household goods. In Cheju Island in particular, these chests gained more importance, by accommodating not only clothes, but also books and valuable documents. Therefore, each family owned and made use of several of these storage chests.

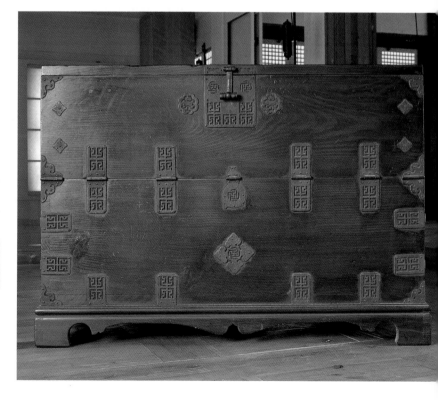

108. Photos: Several types of *pandaji*s. The *pandaji*s (chests) from Kyongsang Provinces generally featured bottle-shaped front hinges (left) while those from the Kyonggi (right) Province boasted neat and well-proportioned decoration. Their beauty outshone *pandaji*s from other regions. *Pandaji*s from Pakch' on area came in larger sizes and were covered with metal fixtures showing sevral designs made by tiny holes punched into the metal pieces.

109. Photo: A *pitchop* and *chwagyong*. A *pitchop* (comb box) was used when combing hair or applying makeup. Women's comb boxes were usually painted or decorated with mother-of-pearl. After mirrors were introduced, the comb box (left) evolved to the popular *chwagyong* (mirrored cosmetic box). It was equipped with a folding mirror mounted on the underside of the box lid. When the box is opened, the mirror stayed propped up at an angle perfect for personal grooming (right).

The top, the body section, and legs formed *pandaji*, which was rectangular in shape; and its height and size were designed to serve people using it while sitting on the floor. People utilized the space on top of the chest for a variety of purposes, including the placement of bowls or jars, small knickknacks, or folded bedding. Large and thick wood boards of distinctive wood grain used for these chests created fetching contrasts with their large and bold cast-iron decorations, producing simplistic yet stylish appearance.

*Pandaji*s enjoyed popularity throughout the peninsula; however, they showed regional differences in their material composition in the ways they reflected the life styles of the users. *Pandaji*s from Pakch'on, Pyongyang, and the provinces of Kyonggi, Ch'ungch'ong, Kyongsang, and Cholla typified some of these regional variations as will be discussed here (photo 108).

The Pakch'on style *pandaji*, also known as a *sungsungi pandaji*, was formed of linden wood.

Cast-iron ornaments of punched-hole or very rough filigree design accented the piece. The Pyongyang *pandaji* stood tall with its frontal plane almost square; and, because its large tin or white bronze fixtures covered nearly the entire frontal surface, this chest stunned viewers with its luxuriant brilliance. In contrast, *pandaji*s from the Kyonggi Province featured more modest proportions and less pronounced decorations. The Cholla Province style *pandaji*s sat low and wide. Simple spool-shaped cast-iron fixtures rounded out the decoration of these unassuming chests.

A *chwagyong* (mirrored vanity)

Known today as a *kyongdae*, a *chwagyong* was one of the most important items a bride took with her to her husband's household. Therefore, in general, these vanities came in very fancy and colorful forms. Designed for the convenience of a woman using it while sitting on the floor, they were portable and were often moved

110. Photo : A *kakkaesuri*. A type of a safe, *kakkaesuri*s were used mostly in the *sarang*s of wealthy upper class households, but began to be seen in women's rooms as well during the latter period of the Chosun Dynasty.

A *kakkaesuri* (safe)

Equipped with several drawers behind a door, this single-level chest held valuables and was a necessity in both the *anbang* and *sarangbang* (photo 110).

Because it functioned as a safe, its makers designed it to be large and structurally strong, with sturdy planks and metal fixtures. Immediately behind the door of the middle section was a drawer; the lower and upper sections contained shelves, or sometimes even drawers.

Makers of *kakkaesuri*s, also known as *kapkaesuri*s, or *kakkisori*s, modeled them after small Chinese chests called *kakpisuri*s.

to sunny spots. When not using the vanity, a woman kept the mirror folded down. A *chwagyong* came with a door in the lower section, which contained a drawer for cosmetics. To use the mirror, a woman propped up the top lid which had a mirror on the interior side (photo 109). While a *chwagyong* and pitchop shared similar forms and sizes, unlike a *chwagyong*, a *pitchop* did not feature a mirror and consisted strictly of drawers for the storage of combs and other objects.

A *ham* (chest)

This is a deep chest with a shallow top-opening lid that came with a metal lock and lock plates. Because valuables were kept in it, it was equipped with a hook on the lid and another on the box, so that a padlock could pass through them. For larger size chests, handles went on the sides for easier handling.

Even today these chests are used to send to the bride a marriage agreement document and gifts of silk fabric. The types of *ham*s included *honham* (bride's clothes), *uibokham* (daily clothes), *munsoham* (documents), *posokham* (jewelry), and *panujil* (sewing) chests. Generally accented with mother-of-pearl designs, the chests used in the *anbang* enjoyed prominent placement on top of a *chang* or *nong*. As families had these chests custom made to their differing specifications, these containers exhibited a great variety of forms and sizes (photo 111).

When people stacked two *ham*s, they called them *hamnong*s. These came in large sizes to accommodate the clothing of all the family members. The *hamnong* lids opened to the top like those of *ham*s.

111. Photos: Various *ham*s. Used for the storage of personal possessions, many different types, sizes and shapes of boxes became popular. Generally the entire top portion opened.

A *kwe* (storage box)

A *kwe* is a box whose function was similar to that of the *ham*. The difference was that while the entire lid of the *ham* opened, on the *kwe*, about half of the lid was fastened to the box and only the other half opened upward. Thus, a *kwe* was distinguished by the hinges in the middle of the lid.

*Kwe*s also served as multi-purpose containers for such objects as books, documents, money, clothes, dried sea food, china, and ceremonial implements. Depending on the contents of these boxes, they were placed in various rooms, including the *sarangbang*, attic, storage room, and shrine. Every household owned several of these boxes, as they were sturdy and convenient. They were also in wide use in government offices.

(2) *Sarangbang* (study) furniture

A *t'akcha* (shelf) types

*T'akcha*s, shelves used by men in their *sarang*s to store and display their books and bric-a-bracs, were a uniquely male piece of furniture that defined and accented their spaces. *T'akcha*s had decorative rather than utilitarian purposes, though, and were used mainly by middle and higher classes. Featuring several shelves, *t'akcha*s stood tall, creating a vertical visual element and, when coupled with horizontal furniture like *mungap*s (writing supply boxes), an interesting asymmetrical or symmetrical dynamic emerged. Thus, *t'akcha*s stood out among Chosun furniture as one of the decorative pieces that interacted particularly well with the relatively uncluttered open spaces of men's studies.

*T'akcha*s, ranging from two- to five-level shelves, were opensided. However, some combined shelving with drawers or closed storage compartments, producing yet another type of visual effect. Serving as multi-purpose pieces of furniture, *t'akcha*s worked ideally for displaying books and accessories like vases and incense boxes on the top two or three shelves. Also various objects could be stored in the lower closed compartments. Thus, men considered *t'akcha*s to be one of their undisputed necessities.

*T'akcha*s came in several types, including a *sabang t'akcha* (open on four sides) (photo 112), a *changt'akcha* (horizontal and long), a *chaekt'akcha* (with a back board), and a *t'akchajang* (with a storage compartment).

112. Photo : A *sabangt'akcha* (open-sided shelf). Well-proportioned, this open-sided shelf features drawers or cabinets in the lower compartment.

A *ch'aekchang* (bookcase with doors)

As the upper class population of the Chosun Period considered the *sarang* (a man's study) to be the center of learning and art, a *ch'akchang* was an essential piece of furnishing for any *sarangbang*. The interior of the *ch'akchang* consisted of two or three compartments with extra-wide shelves for convenient storage of books of varying sizes, and each compartment was equipped with a two-paneled door.

Carpenters generally chose paulownia wood for the front panels of the bookcase while they preferred strong pear tree wood for the posts. Craftsmen usually kept metal accessories of bookcases to a minimum and used them only where needed for structural strength (photo 113)

A *mungap* (writing supply box)

People used this furniture piece in both the *anbang* and *sarangbang*; however, when used in the *sarangbang*, it stored men's necessities such as writing supplies and documents. Generally, *mungap*s occupied a space along a side wall or under a window that faced the back courtyard. To fit the *mungap*s in the latter space, cabinet makers built them lower than the wainscots under the windows. Most often, people positioned a set of two *mungap*s side by side along a wall. A *changmungap* (extra-long horizontal box) usually sat by itself. Because of its low height and extended length, this piece lent a larger, open appearance to an otherwise small, closed-looking space. Items such as pencil boxes, well-shaped rocks, or potted oriental orchids placed on a *mungap* rounded out the decoration.

113. Photo: A *ch'aekchang* (enclosed bookcase). The interior of this small cabinet contains four shelves, and its skillfully crafted appearance leads one to believe that rare books were stored in it.

114. Photo: A *mungap* (writing supply box). This well proportioned *mungap* contains many drawers and open spaces to store writing supplies and documents.

115. Photo: *Pomsang* and *kyongsang* desks. Common class people used the more simply designed *pomsang*s with straight top panel (top), while *kyongsang*s (bottom) were used in Buddhist temples when reading prayer books. The legs and drawers of *kyongsang*s which has top panel with curved end were elaborately carved.

During the early Chosun Period, craftsmen used mostly plain wood like pine that produced a simpler texture on these writing supply boxes, but later they turned to higher quality woods like the Chinese red sandalwood, especially on pieces used in the *anbang*.

The contents stored in the *mungap*s kept in *anbang*s were similar to those in *sarangbang*s, but the *anbang mungap*s displayed ornate elements such as mother-of-pearl inlays, red sandalwood bodies, lacquer finish, and various other accenting techniques, like embossing. In some cases, the decoration became so excessively complex and intricate that they even earned the name *nanmungap* ("complex" design box). The *tukkoptaji mungap*s, also called *pong-ori* (mute) boxes, owed their names to their uniquely constructed doors. The first door panel had to be lifted out before the next door could be slided open. The interior of these boxes consisted of drawers and shelves where important documents were stored (photo 114).

A *soan* (desk)

*Soan*s (desks) used for reading and writing came in two forms: the *pomsang*s and *kyong-sang*s (photo 115). The former featured straight lines and a simple structure. Influenced by Chinese models, the latter displayed more decorative elements such as scrolled ends and were used in Buddhist temples at readings. Only later, did they gain popularity among the laity as well. Portable tables with folding legs developed out of this style of table.

In general, people chose the more austere types of *soan*s for their *sarangbang*s, as they considered this piece of furniture to be one of the most visible symbols of the scholarly environment reserved for males.

116. Photo: A *yonsang*. A box for the storage of ink stones, yonsangs also served as ink stone stands. They were one of the most prized possessions of scholars and favorite piece of furniture used in sarangbangs. Yonsangs came in a wide variety of shapes and received a great deal of attention from the craftsmen decorating them.

117. Photo: A *salp'yongsang*. This portable wooden daybed was used in a *taech'ong* or *numaru* (veranda).

A *yonsang* (side table)

This small table came with a drawer in the upper section where writing tools, such as the "four writer's friends"--the ink stone, ink sticks, paper, and brushes--were stored. Other items such as seals and small books in scroll forms were also kept in the *yonsang*, which usually came with top opening lids. The inkstone and ink sticks went in the upper compartment; letters in the middle, and books, paper, and *yonjok*s (small water pitchers for ink) in the lower. *Yonsang*s came in a great variety of shapes and types depending on materials and decorations. Craftsmen used mostly paulownia, pine, or dark persimmon wood for *yonsang*s; decorations were of bamboo and mother-of-pearl inlays (photo 116).

A *p'yongsang* (wooden recliner)

The *p'yongsang* was a type of a wooden bed or recliner used for sitting or lying and was placed in the *taech'ong* or *numaru* (veranda). In the summer, a straw mat was laid on it. Sleeping there using a bamboo pillow and hugging a bamboo wife was a men's popular and cooling way of spending muggy summer nights. The *salp'yongsang*s referred to those constructed with closely joined lattice work while *nuhl-p'yongsang*s referred to a more crudely structured piece. The former commonly furnished the *taech'ong* (photo 117).

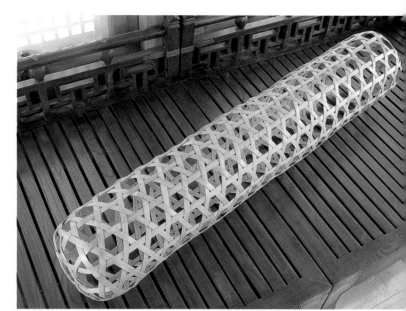

118. Photo : A *chukpuin* (bamboo wife). In summer time, sleeping with their arms around *chukpuin*s helped men to keep cool through sultry nights. When not in use, the *chukpuin*s were hung on walls.

119. Photo : A *kwesang*. A person sitting up on a *poryo* (large cushion) on the floor rested his arm on this device. Made of wood, the armrest was designed so that the ends of the top board rose slightly higher than the middle section.

A *chukpuin* (bamboo wife)

Also called *chukkwe*, a bamboo wife was, along with a bamboo pillow, one of the summer time necessities enjoyed by men in the *sarangbang*. Woven in a log shape with twelve long strips of bamboo, leaving an empty space in the middle for ventilation, the bamboo wife made cool sleeping possible in the summer. According to records, the bamboo wife owed its name to the fact that it came in about the size of a woman, just right to hug and sleep with. Because of the tradition of never leaving bamboo wives to the next generation, few examples remain (photo 118).

A *kwesang* (armrest)

Also called an *uich'im*, a *kwesang* supported the arm of a person sitting on a *poryo* (large cushion or futon). The edges of a *kwesang* rose a bit, leaving the middle sagging slightly to fit the contour of the arm. Once in a while, a *kwesang* doubled as a *mungap* and had a drawer attached to it. (photo 119).

A *t'oech'im* (napping pillow)

The men of the literati class generally used these pillows when taking naps in their *sarang*s. The material composition as well as shapes of *toech'im*s varied and included *mokch'im*s (wood), *chukch'im*s (bamboo), *najonch'im*s (mother-of-pearled), or *chagich'im*s (ceramic).

The spot where the head would rest was built with material like paulownia wood, which was soft to the touch, and sometimes that section was also curved. The four corners were formed with more durable wood such as locust or red oak. A very hard wooden surface was believed to exert a finger-pressure type of therapeutic effect on the user; therefore, this type of pillow gained popularity among the elderly (photo 120).

120. Photo: *T'oech'im*s. Used at nap times, these pillows generally came in simple shapes, but some were elaborately decorated.

(3) Kitchen furniture

A *ch'anjang* (food storage/china cabinet)

A storage cabinet for prepared foods and china, a *ch'anjang* occupied a corner of a food storage or food preparation room. To support the weight of china and foods, the wood used for the cabinet had to be of a dense texture and durability, such as zelkova, pine, or big cone pine.

Generally containing three levels, the structure of the *ch'anjang* was similar to that of wardrobes. Thick posts formed the framework that supported deep shelves for convenient storage. The cabinet was equipped with a door, and a drawer was placed in the upper section.

Metal accents used on *ch'anjang*s included plain, round cast-iron hinges, *appat'ang*s (metal front panel

121. Photo: A *ch'antak* was built with very sturdy boards to withstand the weight of the heavy earthenware and brass dinnerware stored on the shelves. This *ch'antak* contains a cabinet under cupboard shelves.

piece) and *hwandulsoe*s (bow shaped handles). The *chanjang*'s strong joints gave the piece a solid appearance (photo 121).

A *ch'ant'ak* (cupboard shelves)

Women stored china and prepared foods on these two- or three-leveled shelves. Because the china pieces in the Chosun Period were made of heavy glass or ceramic and a large quantities of these were used daily and stored, the *ch'antak*s accommodating such weight required a strong construction with thick posts and planks as well as extra sturdy joining techniques.

The shape of a *ch'ant'ak* was similar to that of an open-sided *sarang t'akcha*s (shelves), except that *ch'ant'ak*s were wider and of thicker materials. They were generally simple shelves, but sometimes a doored compartment was installed for the storage of foods. A *ch'ant'ak'*s strong lines, and thick and solid boards give this item a visually bold appearance, and when equipped with a closed compartment, the proportion between the shelves and the enclosed sections was well balanced, creating an aesthetically please product (photo 121).

A *soban* (meal table)

Soban was one of the most unusual wood furniture pieces in Korea. Because of the nature of the floor plans of the Chosun Period houses, and because of the Confucian life styles and values, meals were prepared and set on numerous, separate tables upon which the food was transported to various rooms. Therefore, an enormous variety of serving tables emerged.

Each type of *soban* displayed distinctive characteristics reflecting the nature of its material composition and a style specific to its region of origin. According to where they were developed, *soban*s were known as Haeju-*ban*; T'ongyong-*ban*; Naju-*ban*; Anju-*ban*,

122. Photos: Types of small meal tables. The names of the tables varied depending on the shapes of legs, regions of origin, and types of use. The tiger-leg-shaped table called *hojok-ban* (top). A small meal table serves only one person(bottom).

Ch'ungju-*ban*, and so forth. Some were named after the shapes of their legs: a *hoban* (tiger-legged), or a *kujokpan* (dog-legged). A *myojokpan* refers to a cat-legged table. This differed from the tiger-legged in that the *myojokpan* legs were shorter and thinner.

Another type of table was called a *konggosang* developed to be used when serving lunches to government officials at their work places. Its top was twelve-sided; and, while the legs were either eight- or twelve-sided, the contour of the legs nevertheless paralleled that of the top. The table came with flame-shaped openings carved between the legs and small holes made on two sides. This design enabled a woman to balance this table on her head and hold onto it. Often a drawer came attached to the table for the storage of spoons and chopsticks. After loading the table with food, covering it with an oiled paper or cloth wrap and closing the wrap behind the table, a woman placed the table on her head and walked while watching her steps through the opening between the table legs (photo 122).

A *twiju* (rice or other grain bin)

A storage bin, the *twiju* held either rice or other grains. Measuring 100 cm in height and width, the rice bin was designed to store up to two *kama*s (woven straw sacks) of rice. Bins made for other grains were smaller at 30-50 cm.

The lid came without any hinges and opened from the top. Craftsmen used zelkova wood for rice bins while choosing pine for other grain bins. The *twiju*s featured few accessories, except for a tin lock and lock plate.

In upper class households, a *twiju* was kept in a food storage/preparation room adjacent to the kitchen,

123. Photo: A *twiju* (rice or grain bin). Top-opening rice and other grain bins were built to last along time and had no hinges.

whereas in middle and lower classes the bins occupied a corner in the *taech'ong*. Small jars filled with spices or simple pre-made side dishes lined the tops of *twiju*s. The thick, simplistic appearance of *twiju*s lent a sense of warm, unassuming familiarity, much as did large wooden Korean vats (photo 123).

2 The characteristics of Korean furniture

Many unique features–simplicity of lines, clean planes or surfaces, graceful proportions, sturdy structures, discreet use of metal accessories, and nail-free joining techniques-characterized traditional Korean furniture. The unassuming, modest yet graceful aesthetic sensibility Korean artisans displayed in their craft grew out of the values and philosophy of a life style they developed over centuries.

(1) Composition of aesthetic planes and proportions

As mentioned above, the most distinctive characteristics of traditional Korean furniture lie in its simplicity of lines and planes. The former refers to the beauty created by using only a few, choice, straight lines as compared to using curvy lines or an excessive number of detailed lines. Simplicity of planes reflect the orderliness and uncluttered look produced by square or rectangular planes that are not overly decorated.

Simplicity of planes can best be observed in *chang*s (wardrobes). Consisting of a top board, upper and lower compartments, door and legs, and paralleling the design patterns found in the linear elements shown by windows and doors, the *chang* panels displayed clean, straight lines in symmetrical check patterns, exemplifying sublime sense of proportions. For example, for a large *chang*, taller legs were installed to create a harmonized look. On a wide *chang*, shorter legs were attached to generate a sense of security.

As seen above, while traditional Korean furniture displays a diversity in sizes and shapes, it also exhibits a high degree of uniformity in terms of the way surfaces are composed and constructed. For example, in the case of a double- or tri-level *chang*s, the rectangular spaces created by vertical posts were redefined by smaller square shapes appearing on either side of the lock plates, all of which collectively contributed to the creation of an aesthetically pleasing whole.

Koreans carried a well-developed sense of proportion and a unique way of handling the planes on craft work into their layout of living spaces (illustration 124).

A study of traditional Korean furniture reveals several typical proportional patterns. They include the golden ratio (rectangular proportion of 1:1.618), the double ratio(1:2), and the square ratio(1:1). Among these, Koreans considered the golden ratio to be the most aesthetically pleasing and adopted it most often. However, while proportional patterns provided the basic consistency and uniformity seen in Korean furniture, they did not function as rigid rules. Rather, the proportions of individual pieces received adjustments, as needed, in the context of their variables.

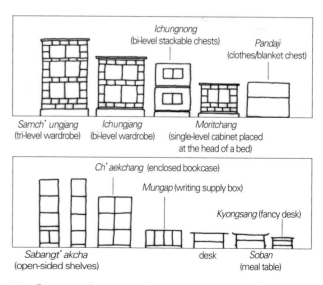

124. Illustrations: The proportional dimensions adopted for the making of Korean furniture. Korean furniture displayed a wide array of heights and sizes; however, furniture was always built to accommodate the average heights of Koreans and fit within common ceiling clearance.

(2) Structure and joining techniques

Traditional Korean furniture pieces show that wood was selected on the basis of its strengths as well as its decorative elements. Structurally, a piece of furniture consisted of the top, body, and legs. A board used at the top forms the uppermost portion; and support posts, a back board, doors, and drawers comprise the middle section.

The identity of each part of a furniture piece is shown in (illustration 125).

In modern furniture making, various types of nails and affixing substances are used, but during the Chosun Period a great variety of joining techniques that did not require the use of nails were employed. With these methods, Koreans produced furniture of outstanding durability and smooth, nearly invisible seams.

The purposes of joining methods fell into two broad categories: one was to connect smaller pieces in order to create larger ones; the other was to fit pieces for structural composition. For the latter, one took into account considerations such as to the nature of wood, including its ability to bear weight, and its decorative elements.

The joining techniques included the *sagaetcha'im* (finger joint), *matcha'im* (butt joint), *yonguitcha'im* (miter joint), *t'oktcha'im* (lap joint), and *changbuch'oktcha'im* (mortise and tenon joint). In the finger joint method, without the use of posts, pieces were dovetailed by way of teeth that were cut into the wood, allowing the seams to show like interlocked fingers. This joining method lent internal strength to the joints, so it was widely used and was a popular technique, particularly for the joining of panels of *pandaji* (blanket chest) and *mungaps* (writing supply boxes). In the butt joint, pieces were connected at 90-degree angles, while the miter joint was formed by parts meeting at 45 degree angles. To the latter, a mortise and tenon joining method was often added for increased strength.

In joining posts, depending on the finished exterior look desired, craftsmen utilized the miter, semi-miter, butt, or lap joint. But, they reinforced the joints with hidden tenons. In general, a mortise and tenon method was chosen if the posts' surface was slightly rounded; miter for those prominently rounded; and miter or butt for flat posts. The higher the quality of furniture, the more likely it was to feature the miter joint craftsmanship. In such pieces, even the side posts received the same the technique. Through the use of such a wide variety of techniques, craftsmen strove to achieve a perfect mix of visual balance and diversity.

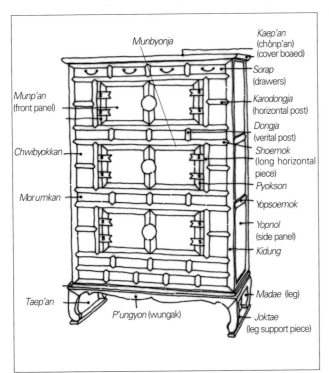

125. Illustration: The structure of a traditional tri-level wardrobe and the names of various component parts. This piece consisted of the top cover board, body, and legs.

When attaching a board to a post—for example, a front panel of a wardrobe to the center post—furniture makers used a method called chehyotchongmae technique. Namely, they made grooves into the side of the post and tongues on the board side. They used the same tongue-and-groove method to the doors or back panels, but miter joint to the frame . Using all these basic joining techniques, furniture makers produced a great variety of goods (illustration 126). Upon completion of a project, furniture makers reinforced the structural strength and functional utility of the furniture by attaching simple metal accessories.

126. Illustrations: Traditional methods of joining wood pieces to build Korean furniture. Never using nails, Koreans used the various non-intrusive joining methods seen here.

sagaetchaim (finger joint)
Yongwitchaim (miter joint)
Matchaim (butt joint)
T'oktchaim (lapjoint)
Changbuck'-oktchaim (mortise and tenon joint)

The lap joint used on the corner of a Kyongsang table.

The miter joint used on a corner of a wardrobe.

2. Accessories

1 Lighting accessories

Lamps had been in use throughout Korea among all classes from before the Three Kingdoms Period. Bowl lamps were especially wide spread, and the reason lay in the fact that the oil used for this type of lighting was easily accessible and poor people did not need to acquire any special bowls for this type of lamp. They simply used wine bowls or other small bowls as containers for the oil.

With the establishment of Chosun, and as living standards improved, the demand for lamps increased; and as a result the production of lighting devices expanded and a wide variety of shapes and forms of lamps

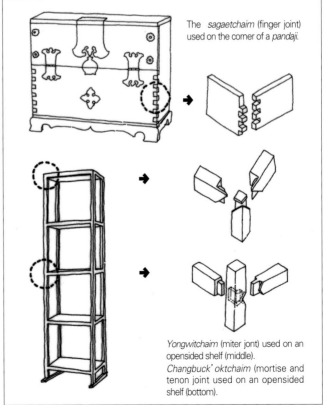

The sagaetchaim (finger joint) used on the corner of a pandaji.

Yongwitchaim (miter jont) used on an opensided shelf (middle).
Changbuck'oktchaim (mortise and tenon joint used on an opensided shelf (bottom).

emerged. The lamps during the Koryo Period displayed an appearance that was rather simple but stylish in a subtle, folksy way. But due to the scarcity of fuel, the lamps did not become popularized among the general public. With the introduction of imported candles, however, lighting accessories changed from a relatively exclusive upper class commodity to something accessible to the general public. According to their shapes, lighting devices came in several types, including *ch'oktae, tunggyong, chwadung, ch'orong*, and *tungrong*. A look at these different lighting accessories follows.

(1) Everyday lighting

Of various types of lighting accessories, the *tunggyong*s (lamp stands), and *ch'oktae*s (candlesticks) were the most popular. Mainly the upper class used the latter, while the lower classes favored the lamp stands since the oil for the lamp was easily accessible.

A *ch'oktae* (candlestick)

A *ch'oktae* was the Chosun Period name for today's *ch'ottae*. During the Chosun Period, because the cost of candles was high, the government restricted their use exclusively to ceremonial or interior lighting in upper class houses. A candlestick used for daily lighting consisted of a square or round bases and a support post. A wax catcher, which varied a great deal in shape, was set on top of this post.

The candlestick support posts came in 40-50 cm heights and featured carved bamboo or water lily designs. Some back boards were decorated extensively, often showing embossed Chinese characters meaning "wealth, fame, and many sons." Candlesticks were often used for a wedding ceremony which is depicted in folk paintings of the Chosun Period.

A *tunggyong* (lamp stand)

The common classes used this type of lamp stand. It consisted of a square, octagonal, or round base, upon which a post with two or three different notches was set. One adjusted the height of the light by using different notches to hang the lamp bowl (photo 127). People stored matches or tongs in the base, which sometimes doubled as an ashtray. Once in a while the base came in the form of a drawer, where small lighting accessories were kept. Generally constructed of wood, the lamp stand ranged between 40 and 90 cm in height for the convenience of a user sitting on the floor. Lower class folks often made lamp stands themselves.

*Tunggyong*s and *tungjan*s were used interchangeably, but strictly speaking, *tunggyong* was the stand on which the *tungjan* (lamp bowl) would sit. The latter were bowls made of materials including clay, blue and white ceramic, stone, or jade. Unlike other accessories, lamp bowls remained relatively constant in their shape throughout history; however, the exceptionally tall pieces made specifically as lamp bowls were used exclusively by the upper class. The general populace fashioned their own wooden lamp bases, which eventually developed into stands that earned the name *tunggyong*.

(2) Occasional lighting

In addition to everyday lighting devices such as a *cho'ktae* or *tungrong*, members of the upper class also favored decorative lighting accessories such as a *chwadung* (lantern with silk covered sides), portable *ch'ongrong*, and *tungnong* (outdoor lantern) hung on a wall.

127. Photos: Various lighting devices. A *tunggyong* was a lamp stand onto which a lamp bowl could be hung. The height of the lamp could be adjusted (right). A *ch'oknong* was a portable lamp in which a candle could be placed, lit and carried (left, middle). A *chwadung* was a lamp covered on three sides with rice paper or silk. The fourth side in the back functioned as a door (left, left).

A *chwadung* (lantern with silk-covered sides)

A candle set on a stick or in a bowl was placed inside a *chwadung* (lantern, often hexagonal) for indoor lighting. The interior of the four sides of the lantern was finished in silk or rice paper. One side was crafted to open (photo 127).

The precursor of the *chwadung* can be found in Koryo Period artifacts. During the Chosun Period, people inserted even kerosene lamps into lanterns. About one meter in height, the lantern came in four-, six-, or eight-sided forms and featured a drawer at the base where items such as candles and fire-making flint pieces were stored.

Because of their striking, decorative appearance, these lanterns were popular among the upper class. Today, the same type of lanterns are used with electric lights as a decoration.

A *ch'ongrong* or *ch'orong* (portable lantern)

Sometimes referred to as a *cho'rong*, this portable lantern was used to hold a candle light. The *sach'ongnong* was for ceremonies; *chich'ongnong* for lighting paths at night; and *choch'oktung* for night security guards on their rounds.

Coming in four-, six-, or eight-sided forms, some *ch'ongnong* was a folding lantern. Often decorated with the four typical brush painting motifs of iris, bamboo, plum blossoms, and chrysanthemum and landscapes or birds, the *ch'ongnong*s came in a wide array of shapes and decorations. Craftsmen made the handle with braided strings, bamboo branches, or carved wood. Some handles were hollow, so people stored spare candles inside (photo 127).

A *tungnong* (outdoor lantern)

Exterior lighting devices, these lanterns came in several types including *yanggaktung*s (two-sided), *sabangtung*s (four-sided), *yuritung*s (glass-sided), *ch'ongsa*s (covered with blue-silk), or *hongsa*s (covered with red silk) lanterns. Generally made of stone, these lighting implements symbolized the social status of the owner or held religious significance. Those finished with blue and red silk, or with painted glass, were highly decorative and were reserved for palaces or households of the literati.

2 Other accessories

Because of the Korean tradition of sitting on the floor, most furniture pieces were low, which left wall spaces largely exposed. People filled them with accessories including oriental paintings, most commonly showing landscapes or flower and bird designs, and decorative brush holders, and mail holders. However, it was of supreme importance to avoid giving a cluttered appearance while allowing undecorated spaces to interact with the few well-chosen and aesthetically placed accessories to create an atmosphere of beauty and order. Functional yet decorative objects, such as *byongp'ung*s (folding screens to cut drafts or to divide space), and *pal*s (woven screens used for privacy), and ceramic pottery pieces used for storage of food stuffs, served as accessories that, by harmonizing with the shapes of spaces left unadorned, added a sense of movement, change, and liveliness to a room.

(1) Functional accessories

A *kobi* (mail holder)

This was a flat, wooden wall hanger that doubled as a mail holder. People stored important documents or letters in the sideway slots. Like other accessories that needed to match the furniture as well as reflect the taste of the occupant, mail holders came in an enormous variety of shapes and types (photo 128). These holders came in paulownia wood that was smoke-stained, so that the natural and humble beauty of the wood shone. Some featured oriental brush paintings of iris, bamboo, plum blossoms, chrysanthemums, and flowers and bird combinations. Also displaced were embossed calligraphy of poems, brightly colored

128. Photo: A *kobi* (mail holders doubling as wall hangings). Koreans hung *kobi* on walls and used them to store scrolls. Wood with fine grain, such as paulownia or bamboo, was favored for this attractive accessory.

paper cutouts of flower and bird shapes, and thinly shaved or bent bamboo slats through which colorful paper or the colors of the mail could be seen. In general, the mail holder/wall hangings for *anbang*s were fancier, while those for *sarangbang*s bore a simpler and more solid look.

A *byongp'ung* (folding screen)

This screen or room divider served multiple purposes: to cut drafts, to maintain privacy, to add a decorative element to the wall, and, on occasion, to be used in sorcery. People covered the wooden framed rectangular panels with many layers of paper and then mounted paintings, calligraphy, or embroidery work. One could fold the sections, which came in even numbers from two to twelve panels and connected with hinges. Two-paneled screens were called *karigae* or *kokbyong*, while those set at the head of a person sleeping were referred to as *moribyongp'ung* or *ch'imbyong*. Often, to facilitate transportation, the twelve-paneled screens came in two sets of six panels each. The width of each panel ranged from 36 to 45 cm, while the height measured from 60 to 180 cm. The sizes of the sections were determined in relation to their desired decorative and other functions.

Generally accented with paintings, calligraphy, or embroidery, screens fulfilled aesthetic more than practical needs. The screens in the *sarangbang* were resplendent with calligraphy of renowned poems or moral axioms, paintings of Kumgang Mountain (Diamond Mountain) and its 12,000 peaks, or the eight famous sights along the East Coast of the Kangwon Province. The *byongp'ung*s in elderly parents' room featured paintings of stylized characters of *su* (long life) and *pok* (blessings), flowers and birds, or the ten

objects symbolizing immortality—oceans, mountains, streams, rocks, clouds, pine trees, *pulloch'o* (herb of eternal youth), turtles, cranes, and deer. Water color figures or brush paintings of *sagunja* (the four cardinal subjects of oriental orchids, bamboos, plum blossoms, and chrysanthemums) adorned the screens in young women's rooms. Pictures of children at play, people in resorts, or lakes and streams accented the screens for wedding ceremony. Designs of flowers, birds, butterflies, or other similar objects appropriate for the mood of a specific room highlighted the screens placed at the head of a person's bedding.

A *pal* (woven screen)

This screen woven with reed or bamboo hung over a window or in the *taech'ong*, generally in the summer time to serve as an awning and a ventilation device. It also provided some privacy to rooms where windows and doors remained open. In sultry Korean summers, these *pals* helped maintain cool, shaded, and private spaces. Because of the patterns woven into the mat, its decorative metal hanger, and the texture-enhancing knots in the weave, the screens also served as wall hangings (photo 129).

Hung on the interior side of a room, these screens were designed to be rolled or lifted up from inside. This was to keep the view of the interior of the room almost invisible to outsiders, yet allow a person inside to see out. Sometimes, craftsmen painted the bamboo knots or worked various designs into the screen. Most favored motifs were the characters meaning double joy, long life, and blessings. The border design consisted of the repetition of the stylized wan (卍) character. A dark blue velvet border completed the decoration.

Compared to the Chinese woven screens, the

Korean examples were more finely detailed, yet executed in simpler and more modest taste with color and texture of the bamboo.

A pottery

Koreans began firing clay pottery and utilizing it in their daily lives as early as the Stone Age. Gradually pottery took on more artistic elements and became expressions of spiritual and aesthetic satisfaction, culminating in the world-renowned Koryo blue and white celadons. But, even before the Koryo Period, Silla and Backjae Kingdoms produced outstanding ceramic works of art as well.

In Koryo blue celadon pottery, one can find traces of the inner life and hopes of Koreans. The willow branches stooping over a pond, a pair of love-birds careening in water, the relaxed and carefree clouds, and the cranes pictured on the pottery form a spiritual parallel to the inner life of Koreans.

The types of pottery seen in Korea were diverse: jars of all sizes, crocks, portable room warmers, plates, incense burners, tea pots or wine kettles, wine bowls, pillows, ink stone boxes, large bowls, ink stones, seals, and spittoons. All of them served utilitarian as well as decorative functions.

When sunlight seeping through rice paper cast warm, milky rays on the decoration-free Chosun celadon pottery, the white color of the pottery glowed subtly, like the skin of a woman hidden under her clothing. With the creation of such understated art, Chosun people strove to create an atmosphere that exuded quiet and comfortable beauty. And, during that period, as pottery began to take simpler forms, strictly functional or semi-decorative pottery became popularized among the general public.

129. Photo(left): A *pal* (woven screen). A *pal* generally used in the summer time to serve as an awning and a ventilation device.

130. Photo: A *pangchang* (draft-blacker screen). These screens served as a draft- blocker, but they also fulfilled decorative purposes.

A *pangchang* (draft-blocker screen)

Because an *ondol*, a hypocaust system, warmed the floors of a room rather than the air in it and because of the numerous windows and doors in each room, in winter, rooms were drafty. *Pangchang*s were screens made of cloth that were set just inside the door in order to reduce the cold winds invading the interior. These screens served an important function, but they also fulfilled decorative purposes (photo 130).

In most cases, people made these screens with blue or black cloth made from arrowroot, although they sometimes substituted dyed cotton. As with other accessories, the decorations of these pieces exhibited a minimalist approach: the designs were limited to the graceful painting of one or two trees, flowering branches, or dark-colored butterflies, always giving only hints of the beauty of nature in tantalizing understatements. The design motif of the *wan* (卍) character highlighted the four corners. A brass ring was attached, so that the screen could be folded up.

People chose blue, black, maroon, and green for this type of screen, so that dirt would not easily show and for the feeling of warmth these colors produced. Sometimes, people filled the screens filled with a thin layer of cotton batting and quilted or embroidered them.

131. Photo: A *totchari* (woven mat). To sit on a mat spread out on a *taech'ong maru* was to experience coolness in the summer's heat.

A *hwaro* (portable stove)

In winter times, this small stove, generally made of cast-iron or earthenware, was a constant companion, especially for people of lower classes. It kept them warm and was used to maintain a starter fire. The stove was welcome in various spaces including the *maru, anbang, konnobang, sarangbang*, entry way by the front gate, and courtyard. The ceramic type was more popular among relatively well-to-do people. They also favored stone stoves, as they were well crafted and extremely efficient in preserving heat.

Stove accessories included *tong*s and small shovels, used to keep the fire alive by shoring up and patting the ash around the fire. The size of portable stoves ranged from very large (100 cm) to small (20 cm). Women enjoyed the small ones, especially while sewing, because these stoves helped keep small irons heated and proved handy for boiling tea water.

These stoves were one of the few household items everybody, regardless of social status or financial standing, could afford and enjoy. People observed a strict etiquette in the use of the *hwaro*s. For example, hosts offered their guests choice spots by the stove; and, when many people were sharing one stove, the eldest took the seat closest to the heat.

A *totchari* (woven mat)

Craftsmen wove traditional mats very finely with rush weed, showing no visible knots. Such mats are still enjoyed today. To sit on a mat spread out on a *taech'ong maru* was to experience coolness in the summer's heat (photo 131).

Mat makers wove fancy design patterns into ceremonial mats, which were called *hwamunsok*. Spreading such mats at coming-of-age rituals or weddings was a necessary element of observing Confucian propriety.

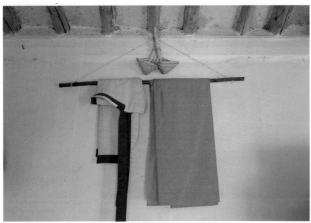

132. Photo: A *hwettae* (clothes rack). Hung on the wall, this rack was used for long pieces of often-worn clothing.

A *hoettae* (coat rack)

This was a long horizontal rod mounted on a wall where oft-worn clothes, full-dress attire, or coats could be hung. The makers of these long racks carved designs into them and decorated the ropes holding up the rack with fancy knots (photo 132). Such racks were also installed inside wardrobes used in the *sarangbang*. Often a beautifully embroidered cover went over the clothes on the rack for decorative purposes and in order to keep the clothing dust free.

A *poryo* (mattress-sized cushion), *pangsok* (small cushion), *ansok* (back rest), and *sabangch'im* (square arm rest)

A *poryo* was a futon-like mat filled with cotton or animal hair. Covered, quilted and bordered with cloth, the thick, sturdy, yet soft cushion always took a place at the *aranmok* (the warmest spot in the room) in the *anbang* and *sarangbang*. The cushion served for sitting or naps, but was generally not slept on at night. *Pangsok*s were made in the same way as the futon, but were square in shape and just large enough for one person.

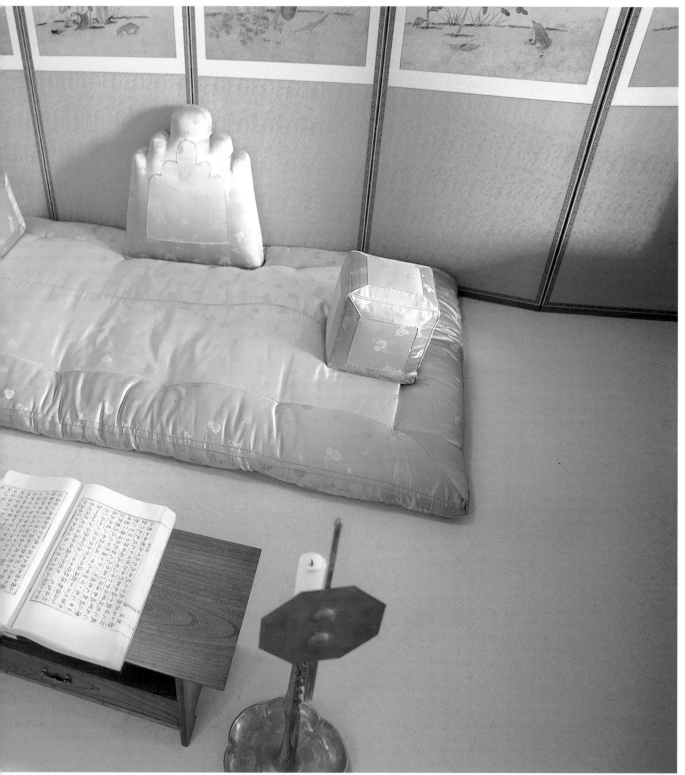

133. Photo: A *poryo* (large cushion), *ansok* (backrest), *sabangch'im* (square armrest), *changch'im* (long pillow) and *bangsok* (one-person-sized cushion). *Poryos* were necessities in *sarangbangs* and *anbangs*. The backrest was set to the rear of the piece, the square armrest lay to one side and a long pillow to the other. Individual cushions were arranged for guests.

An *ansok* was a cushion for the back, its top portion being shaped like a low mountain. Traditionally, stuffed with ox or pig hair batting, today, people have them filled with cotton batting and quilted. Various decorations accented it including embroidery of Chinese characters symbolizing long life, turtles, cranes, or *ponghwang* (a pair of mythical birds).

A *sabangch'im* was a six-sided pillow which served as an elbow rest for a person in a reclining position. A *changch'im* functioned in the same way as a *sabangch'im*, except the *changch'im* was longer.

Generally, a *poryo* was placed at the *aranmok* for the host to sit on while *pangsok*s (small cushions), were offered to guests.

The four items described above were used for greeting guests in the households of the *chinsa* class or higher (photo 133).

(2) Symbolic accessories

A *chokcha* (scroll)

Scrolls were hung on walls in a vertical fashion. This came about because traditional Korean homes came with many windows and doors, and did not leave many large empty wall spaces to accommodate paintings or calligraphy displayed horizontally. Therefore, scroll forms to hang vertically emerged. The fact that large-size antique paintings were very rare points to such limits in wall space.

In traditional Korean society, people viewed the display and enjoyment of calligraphic art as an essential part of daily life rather than mere decoration. With well-placed calligraphic artwork, Koreans sought to create cohesive, modest, yet warm interior spaces.

134. Photo: *Churyon*s. These were vertical plaques hung on pillars and featured carved designs of poems.

A *churyon* (vertical) and *p'onaek* (horizontal) carved
wooden plaques

*Churyon*s were decorative wooden plaques embossed with poems or carved with flower or bird designs. People usually mounted them vertically on the front posts of their house (photo 134).

    *P'onaek*s were silk, paper, or wooden plaques showing either paintings or calligraphy, hung horizontally inside a room or above the top of a door frame. Plaques reflected the personality or beliefs of the occupant of the room or professed something that offered spiritual comfort to the person. Thus, these plaques had a purely symbolic and decorative value.

3 | Household utensils

Although the primary function of traditional household tools and vessels was not decoration, many of them were crafted with such high aesthetic concern that they remain as folk treasures. A close look at them--roughly divided into kitchen utensils and those related to clothing or hobbies--is worthwhile.

(1) Kitchen utensils

A *mokp'an* (wooden tray)

Built with a thin bottom board and edges all around, these containers looked like square trays and came in a variety of sizes. The *mokp'an*s were generally used to transport foods, and their sizes depended on functions. When not in use, the containers were stacked according to size. Their utility was so general that they were used even in markets to display foods (photo 135).

135. Photo: *A mokp'an* (wood tray). Crafted in a great variety of sizes and decorative schemes, Koreans used these wood trays to store or transport prepared food or other edibles like nuts and fruit.

136. Photo: A *ch'anhap* (portable lunch box). These boxes, which had tight lids and could be neatly stacked, were used to store or transport prepared foods.

A *ch'anhap* (picnic box)

Equipped with a lid and many compartments, these boxes served as food storage containers or picnic boxes. They came in wood, lacquerware, or chinaware, in round or square shapes and in stackable sections (photo 136).

137. Photo: A *tasikpan* (cookie press). These were instruments used to make patterns on rice cookies.

A *hamjibak* (wooden vat)

Formed by scooping out logs of dense woods like paulownia, maple, ailanthus, and linden, these vats were deep vessels, like gourds without top lips. Women used vats to mix rice cake flour, to toss salted *kimch'i* cabbage with seasonings, or to prepare other kinds of food. Women folk also used these containers to store large quantities of food such as rice cakes or fruits. Vats came in two main shapes: the round and oval.

A *ttoksal* (rice cake stamp) and *tasikp'an* (cookie press)

These were instruments used to make patterns on rice cakes or cookies. The typically Korean designs used on these tools were simple yet unique (photo137).

*Ttoksal*s, in some cases coming in white celadon pottery, were used to make impressions into rice cakes, typical patterns being wheel or square shapes. Mothers, about to send their daughters to their in-laws' homes for her marriage, poured their hearts into the patterns they pressed into each and every piece of the rice cake to be offered as gifts to the in-laws into whose hands they were entrusting their daughters' lives.

The most popular pattern was the chrysanthe-

138. Photo: A *mattol* (hand mill). Used to grind or powder grains, this tool was a household necessity for all classes.

A *cholku* (mortar) and *maettol* (hand mill)

The grain-rich Korean diet necessitated the development of a variety of implements for taking the outer hulls off grains before grinding. Constructed of wood, stone, or even metal, a *cholku* served this purpose. Pestles or pounders that cracked grains came in numerous sizes in proportion to the size of the mortar.

A *maettol* (hand mill) cracked or powdered grains. Formed from two pieces of stone, grain was fed through the hole on the top stone. With the rotation of the wooden handle, the two pieces of the hand mill ground against each other in circles; processed grains squeezed out from the sides of the millstones. There were several types of hand mills including those producing fine or roughly ground products (photo 138).

(2) Tools related to clothing

A *tadumidol* (fulling block) and *pangmangis* (mallets)

These were instruments made of various hard stones, indigenous throughout Korea, and used by women to smooth out wrinkles on laundered sheets and clothes. Constructed simply with sturdy, natural materials, the pounding block was an essential household instrument. On it women laid starched clothes and pounded them with wooden mallets (photo 139).

mum, but a great variety of others were chosen as well, including the designs of peonies, cross-hatched check, the character *wan* (卍), water lily buds, butterflies or cranes (symbols of good luck), and characters signifying long life, many blessings, wealth, and fame. Even in these small, simple household objects, Koreans' sense of beauty shone.

Craftsmen carved designs into rectangular pieces of wild walnut boards to make *tasikp'an*s. Some cookie presses came in two pieces. A cookie mixture called *tasik* was pressed into the bottom piece while the top part made the imprints. In case of a one-piece press, cookie patterns were made by pressing the dough by hand. A great variety of flowers and characters served as patterns. The characters used were generally those signifying long life, many blessings, wealth, and fame.

139. Photo: A *tadumidol* (fulling block) and *pangmangis* (mallets). Women pounded starched clothes with wooden mallets.

Household items of the upper class were generally crafted with intricacy. The same applied to the fulling blocks, which often exhibited designs of fleeting clouds or delicate leaves on their sides as well as underside. Some smoothing blocks featured tiny holes about the size of hulled millet grains all along their underbellies. Symbolizing the bellies of animals, these finishing touches exemplified the amount of fine, detailed craftsmanship artisans applied to their work. Some blocks were made of hard woods such as persimmon, Chinese date, or birch.

A *panjiggori* (sewing box)

Women stored sewing items like thread, thimbles, fabric, and scissors in this box. *Panjigori* is an abbreviated word for *panujilkori*, which was a box woven with finely sliced reed and bamboo strips. However, some boxes were made of wood, in which case they were called *panjigurut* (sewing containers). Some were even crafted with paper (photo 140).

Sewing boxes were one of a woman's essential possessions because she sewed her own and family clothes and cotton socks. Women kept the boxes, along with a measuring stick, under wardrobes.

(3) Instruments related to hobbies

The tools and vessels used in pursuing recreational activities included tobacco boxes and pipes, musical instruments like a *komungo*, and game boards such as a *paduckp'an* (Korean chess).

A *tambaeham* (tobacco box) and *tambattae* (pipe)

A *tambaeham* was a small lidded box, sometimes with a side drawer, where tobacco was stored. Locust or paulownia wood were the typical materials for these boxes, and some featured work of fancy silver inlay.

The pipes consisted of three parts: the bowl, stem, and mouthpiece. Formed with bamboo, the stem was also called *changjuk*. It was believed that long stems enhanced the taste of tobacco because the substance got a chance to cool. Such long-stemmed pipes were widespread throughout Korea, China, and Japan.

Tobacco was introduced to Korea about 1618 A.D. By the 17th century, pipes had became widely prevalent. In famous 18th century paintings, men were often depicted with long pipes extending from their mouths. While the long pipes were called *changjuk*, shorter ones were named *gombangdae*. The long pipes served as status symbols for the upper class *yangban*, but later, as lower class folks began to use pipes, the symbolic significance dissipated and shorter stems appeared. Although rare, white ceramic pipes also existed.

As seen in this chapter, the evolution of traditional Korean furniture and accessories exhibited close relationship to their utility. Wooden furniture pieces served as particularly good examples that typified the integral inter-relatedness between them and external controlling factors such as the ceiling height, the size of the room, and the Korean custom of sitting on the floor. To sum up, Korean wood products exuded an elegance springing from aesthetically planned proportions and functional and structural integrity and strength. These were achieved through wise choice of materials as well as superb craftsmanship demonstrated in various ways, particularly joining techniques. To study traditional furniture and accessories is to steal glimpses of the complexity, richness, and splendor of ancient Korean philosophies, customs, and dreams.

140. Photos: Covered and uncovered *panjiggori* (sewing box). Sewing boxes were one of a woman's essential possessions because she sewed her own and family clothes.

During the Chosun Period, as in the modern era, people's life styles and personal preferences entered into the choice of furniture and its placement, particularly among the people of the upper echelon. Also, a variety of ways of placing furniture emerged as other factors — such as structural characteristics of the residence, the function and size of each room, the number of furnishings owned by the household, the need to satisfy both the aesthetic and utilitarian purposes, and, most importantly, the custom of not using chairs — all played roles in the arrangement of furniture. As the result, a study of traditional furniture arrangement yields a sense of rich diversity rather than uniformity.

Conducting such a study proves to be a challenge, however, as few sites of the Chosun Period exist. Only through the research of ancient articles and a few remaining upper class houses, where artifacts remain in their original locations and have been preserved fairly well, can one make a few observations about the characteristics of furniture arrangement.

1. The arrangement of furniture in *taech'ong*

The *taech'ong* was a space that connected enclosed rooms and served as a site for activities that were difficult to carry out in individual rooms. In other words, in addition to a structural function, the *taech'ong* fulfilled social functions. Particularly in the summer, the *taech'ong* served as a space for relaxation, the greeting and entertaining of guests, and the enjoyment of meals.

In the event of social activities such as greeting guests or holding meetings, workers set furniture and accessories such as meal tables and desks in the *sarang-taech'ong*. In other words, furniture pieces such as dining tables, or sometimes even desks, did not serve as fixtures of any specific rooms. Upon completion of an activity, workers cleared everything away,

returning the *taech'ong* to its usual, sparsely furnished space. Occasionally, shelves accented with antique artifacts remained on either side of the *taech'ong*, and often a desk remained at the center, which served as a reception area for visitors (photo 141).

Compared to the *sarang taech'ong*, the *antaech'ong* (the main hall in the women's quarters) served many more diverse functions, including Confucian ceremonies such as the ancestor worship rituals, folk ceremonies like weddings, a wide range of household events, and even meals and meal preparations. Therefore, a certain number of kitchen utensils and implements remained in the *taech'ong*.

According to *Sallimkyongje*, a book on domestic economics published during the mid-Chosun Period, domestic artifacts fell into several categories, including those for the kitchen, *anbang*, and *sarangbang*. Implements that were not used daily were divided into those

141. Photo: The *taech'ong* of a *sarang* (men's quarters). Furniture such as *sachungt'akcha* (open-sided shelf with cabinet), enclosed bookcase, and *p'yongsang* (portable *maru*) equipped the *sarang*, which doubled as the quarters for the man of the house and as a reception area for visitors.

used for agriculture, ceremonies, weaving, and miscellaneous purposes. The book does not clarify the items kept permanently in the *taech'ong*. But since men performed ancestor worship rituals in the *antaech'ong*, one may conclude that various ceremonial implements were stored there. According to the lists appearing in the domestic section of the *Sallimkyongje*, absolutely necessary ceremonial objects included candlesticks, *mosagi* (containers for bunched bands or belts and sand used at ancestral worship ceremonies), *chessang* (tables used at such ceremonies), *hyangsang* (incense tables), and platforms on which the ancestral tablets rested.

As for the types of *antaech'ong* furniture, some classic novels offer glimpses. The literary works making such references include: *Ch'unhyang-jon* (The Story of Ch'unhyang); *Onggojip-jon* (A Stubborn Man) and *Hungbu-jon* (The Story of Hungbu) appearing in the dramatic songs of *Yoltumadang* (Twelve Courtyards); the mask dance lyrics of the Pongsan Mask Dance and *Tongnaenorum* (Village Game), and *Songjupuri*, one of sorcerers' songs. However, because the lists of furniture described were wish lists for story characters, the referenced contents did not always reflect reality; and among various lists, discrepancies, though minor, occurred.

142. Photo: The *taech'ong* of the *anch'ae* (women's quarters). Furniture pieces designed for the storage of foods and kitchen utensils, including a *tuiju* (rice or grain bin) and *ch'anchang* (cabinet-style cupboard), were placed in the *andaech'ong*. Domestic implements also found their places in this space.

143. Photo: The ceiling of an *andaech'ong* (*taech'ong* of the women's quarters). Shelves were constructed across the ceiling to store portable tables used in serving meals.

From a passage contained in a prayer song offered to the Songju (the chief guardian spirit of homes), it seems that the permanent fixtures of the *antaech'ong* included a *twiju* (grain bin) and a *ch'anchang* (cupboard). Other items stored in that space included various types of wooden tables and sundry bowls and platters. At ancestor ceremonies, other implements made their appearance in the *antaech'ong* including a ceremonial table, incense table, high platforms for ancestral tablets, candlesticks, and special ritual containers.

In large size upper class houses, people often kept the *antaech'ong* free of furniture and equipment. However, in general, a *twiju* remained toward the back of the *antaech'ong*. Next to the *twiju* stood a cabinet-style cupboard where kitchen tools and dishes were stored (photo 142). Two types of *twiju*s (rice bins and bins for other grains, which were smaller than those for rice) sometimes stayed in the food preparation room or *maru*. For extra storage, people used racks and shelves installed under the *taech'ong* ceiling for tables, jars, and utensils (photo 143).

For important events like weddings, workers spread a mat woven in flower patterns on the *taech'ong* floor, set a folding screen decorated with peony designs toward the back, and placed a table in the center facing south. Two candlesticks went to the front. During ancestral worship ceremonies, platforms supporting ancestral tablets fronted the folding screen. The tablets and an incense stand flanked the central table.

144. Illustration: The layout of a traditional house. Upon entering the front gate, one faced a *nae-oe-dam*, a wall constructed to prevent eye contact between males and females and increase mutual privacy. Proceeding around the wall, the *anbang* (room of the lady of the house) came into view at the most secluded northeast corner of the house.

2. The arrangement of furniture in individual enclosed rooms

1 The *anbang* (room of the lady of the house located in the women's quarters)

The central space in the *anch'ae* (women's quarters), the *anbang* was a woman's space — therefore an yin space — and was tucked away from men's world and outside traffic. Because of the Confucian rule of "separate functions" for men and women, the women's sphere of activity was limited to the few rooms in the *anch'ae*. Events such as the delivery of babies, attending a death-bed, or reception of a bride, all of which signified the element of water, occurred in the *anbang*.

Water signified north in geomancy; therefore, it became the general rule to locate the *anbang* in the back north corner of the house became the general rule (illustration 144).

At the spiritual level, therefore, the location of the *anbang* served as a symbol, but on a practical level, it fulfilled a function as a multi-purpose area. Restricted by Confucian teaching on the role of women, the various activities occurring in the *anbang* never included learning and artistic endeavors for women, as they were banned from such male activities. Thus, the *anbang* served primarily as a domestic space where clothes and beddings were made and stored (photo 145).

In general, the furniture for storage during the Chosun Period came in fairly ample sizes. However, because they were designed to be used by people, who were not very tall, and who always sat on the floor, the furniture was low. Also, as the tops of furniture pieces became visually prominent planes, people lent them careful finishing touches.

Even relatively tall pieces, such as tri-level wardrobes or cabinets with clothes racks, were fairly short, five to six *ch'ok*s (150-180 cm), falling within reach of users sitting on the floor. Pieces taller than five *ch'ok*s (150 cm) were too tall to be convenient. Therefore, bi-level wardrobes gained popularity. Cabinet makers generally built drawers into the top section of

wardrobes; but in pieces taller than 160 cm, they put drawers in the lower section. The "head" chests, *mungap*s (writing supply boxes), or *pandaji*s (clothes/ blanket chests) all conveniently fell between one to three *ch'ok*s (30-90 cm).

The list contained in the domestic section of *Sallimkyongje* sheds some light on the types of *anbang* furniture used during Chosun Period. Out of 230 types of furniture, 10 were found in the *anbang*. They included *nong*s (stackable chests), bamboo wicker trunks, wicker boxes, wooden chests, boxes, tables, shelves,

145. Photo: The furniture and accessories of the ancient Ch'usa estate. A *poryo* (large cushion) occupied the central spot in the *araenmok* (warmest section of the room). In front of it rested the *soan* (low desk) and *yonsang* (inkstone box). A low *mungap* (writing supply box) was set under the window sill. A large cabinet to store clothing and bedding occupied the opposite side of the *araenmok*.

wardrobes, measuring sticks, and vanities.

A sorcerer's song dedicated to a household guardian god listed the *anbang* furniture.

Included in the list were small utensils, folding screens, and furniture pieces such as *chang*s (wardrobes), *nong*s (stackable chests), and *pandaji*s (clothes/blanket chests). Furniture used for storage of clothes and other household items listed here included nine objects: a *hongchang* (wardrobe painted in red), *pongchang* (wardrobe decorated with the inlay of the birds of paradise), *kumch'imchang*, (bedding cabinet), tri- and bi-level wardrobes, *moritchang* (cabinet placed at the head of a bed), *tulmichang* (ash wood wardrobe), and *hamnong* (stacked chests) with mother-of-pearl decoration. Among these, the tri-and bi-level wardrobes, *moritchang*s, and *pandaji*s became popular and were commonly available among common classes; but painted pieces like red *hongchang*s, birds-of-paradise-inlaid *pongchang*s, or mother-of-pearl chests, all

being extremely ornate, appeared only in upper class households.

Compared to the list contained in the domestic section of the *Sallimkyongje*, the inventory described by the sorcerer's song to Songju god seems to dwell on the extravagance that characterized the furniture used by women. In general, however, this was not the case.

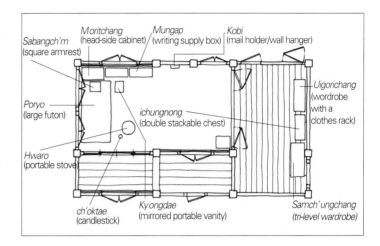

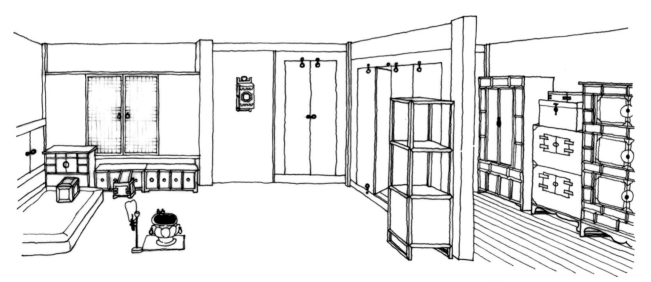

146. Illustrations: The furniture arrangement (reconstructed for historical accuracy) in the *anbang* and *wuitpang* (upper room adjacent to *anbang*) of the ancient Ch'usa estate. A silk covered *poryo* and *sabangch'im* (square armrest) rested upon the *araenmok*. A *hwaro* (portable stove or room warmer), *kyongdae* (portable mirrored vanity) and *ch'ottae* (candlestick) were set near the *poryo*. A *mungap* (writing supply box) occupied a spot under the windowsill while a tri-level shelf (with cabinet space in the lower part) stood at the *wuinmok* (coldest section of the room). In the back room larger pieces of furniture designed for storage of clothes and bedding such as a tri-level wardrobe, double *nong* (stackable chests) and tall wardrobe with a coat rack lined up along the back wall.

Because the primary function of *anbang* furniture was the storage of the entire family's clothing and bedding, the *anbang* furniture usually took modest forms, with only occasional exceptions. Historic artifacts remaining today seem to support this view. Whether such extravagant types of furniture as *yongchang*s (wardrobes highlighted with a dragon design), *hongchang*s, and *pongchang*s described in classic novels or sorcerers' songs truly existed and how common they were, even among the upper class, remains uncertain. Since historic artifacts came from royal palaces, it remained unproven whether or not non-royalties also had access to similarly ornate furnishings.

Having said this, and with the remaining samples of Chosun artifacts in mind, one can conclude that the *anbang* furniture was limited mostly to storage pieces. They included *moritchang*s, (cabinet places at the head of a bed), tri- and bi-level wardrobes, clothes cabinets with racks, stackable chests, and blanket chests, and decorative pieces such as *mungap*s and shelves. In addition to these, there were small objects, including silk-covered futons, square armrests, chests, boxes, vanities, comb boxes, sewing boxes, and portable stoves. (illustration 146). All these household items were arranged with an eye toward the design principle of leading the visual line of movement from small objects to larger pieces.

The *anbang*s of the upper class households came in rather modest sizes, considering the large amounts of clothing and bedding prepared and stored in that space for the extreme Korean weather conditions.

They were especially small when one considers that these rooms were expected to fulfill many functions—as a bedroom, dining room, living room, and special events room.

This spacial constraint necessitated the manufacturing of small sized furniture and the placement of only a few essential pieces of furniture in the *anbang*. To accommodate socializing and other activities that occurred in this space, meals and snacks were brought in on portable tables. Because Koreans sat on cushions placed on the floor, the floor space was not occupied by superfluous furniture like chairs; and, once the tables were cleared, the center of the *anbang* remained free of furniture, with only a portable stove and a pair of candlesticks remaining. During meals or social activities, the hostess or the eldest occupied the *aranmok* (the spot closest to the fireplace) and the younger people sat at the *wuinmok* (the upper part further from the fireplace).

The size of the floor space left free of furniture during the day was related to the volume of beddings stored in cabinets and spread on the floor at night. In other words, people left free of furniture an area of floor space equalling the length of an adult's mattress plus the space reserved for a *moritchang* (cabinet places at the head of a bed) - about seven to eight *ch'ok*s (210 - 240 cm). This space equalled to one *kan*, which Koreans considered an ideal size for a room. Surplus furnishings not fitting into this area went into an adjacent room, or the attic, reached by way of a door set into the *aranmok*-side wall of the *anbang*.

Generally, a *poryo* (mattress-sized cushion) occupied a central spot of the *aranmok*. Usually, only a square armrest accompanied the *poryo*, but occasionally an *ansok* (back rest), and a *changch'im* (long armrest) came into use. When the floor became a bit too warm, the *poryo* served to reduce the heat coming in contact with a person sitting on the cushion. When the floor was not heated, the cushion helped to maintain some body heat. Folding screens generally stood behind the *poryo* to reduce drafts and brighten the room with cheerful decorative designs and colors. If the screens hindered taking and replacing bedding or utensils out of the attic, people did away with them.

Furniture pieces such as a *moritchang* cabinet and *mungap* were placed alongside each other, which created a long horizontal visual line under a window. The narrow and long writing supply box was placed under a window facing the courtyard. Craftsmen built the box to fit under the window's wainscot, so that the box would not impede the line of vision of a person looking out. Women often placed small items like a mirrored vanity on top of the writing supply box; but if this impeded traffic in and out of the room, they arranged the vanity and other small objects on the *aranmok* side. The wall above the writing supply box was generally left empty to help create a sense of openness, but sometimes small decorative items like a *kobi* (mail holder doubling as a wall hanging) accented the area.

If the *anbang* did not come with an adjacent upper room, large-size item, such as a wardrobe, stackable chests, and furniture pieces not used often, occupied the upper part of the *anbang*. If the *anbang* came with an adjacent upper room, shelves displaying decorative items went in the upper area of the *anbang*, and large storage pieces such as a tri- or bi-level wardrobe, a wardrobe with clothes racks, and blanket chests, found their place in the adjacent (upper) room. Boxes and chests topped the wardrobes, and objects such as a basin and chamber pot were tucked under them. A set of sliding doors finished with rice paper on both sides divided the two rooms, but by opening the door women could expand the area into one large room, as needed.

People placed a second wardrobe against the wall facing the back courtyard, and storage containers like a chest or a comb box on top of the wardrobe. A fabric screen placed inside the door served to cut draft and

brighten the atmosphere of the room.

For obvious financial reasons, fewer types of furniture and accessories appeared in lower class homes than in upper class residences. People of the lower classes spread a thinly padded comforter in the *aranmok* of the *anbang*. A coat rack hung on one of the walls. Furniture, including a headside chest, blanket chest, storage boxes, and bi-level chest lined the upper portion of the room or stood against a side wall. Women stacked folded bedding on top of the headside chest, blanket chest, or storage box. (photo 147)

As seen so far, furniture occupied space along walls, leaving the middle of the room free for various activities.

147. Photo: The *anbang* of a lower class house. Furniture was arranged along walls, clothes were hung on a *hwaettae* (rack) and a lamp stand and other domestic necessities were placed.

2 The *sarangbang* (room of the gentleman of the house located in the men's quarters)

The central space in *sarangch'ae* (men's quarters), the *sarangbang* faced south. As the room was occupied by the male head of household, it doubled as a reception area for visitors (illustration 148).

A microcosm for a world steeped in Confucian social and cultural principles and traditions of the Chosun Period, a *sarangbang* reflected the spirit, intellect and education of the man of the house and the heritage of his family. In the Confucian view classic literature provided the basis of all learning and principles of life; therefore, the *sarangbang* — the site of such scholarly pursuits — was carefully constructed and decorated to create an atmosphere of order and grace.

In upper class houses, *sarangbang* was not only a man's bedroom and dining room, but also a reading room, a place for meditation, an area for reception of guests, and a place for relaxation and artistic endeavors. People equipped the room with simple yet elegant furniture, designed for writing and the storing of related supplies and accessories. Chosun people took great care to strip men's furniture of decorative elements in order to convey the idea that men, as Confucian scholars, dedicated themselves to the elimination of greed, sensuality, and interest in such triviality as decorations.

Therefore, men limited furniture placed in their *sarangbang* to the barest minimum essential for the study of classics. The furniture in the households of the literati during the Chosun Period indicates that rather than serving as a symbol of status and authority, it fulfilled simple functions, while displaying modest, graceful and underdecorated appearance. (photo 149)

The domestic section of *Sallimkyongje* contains a

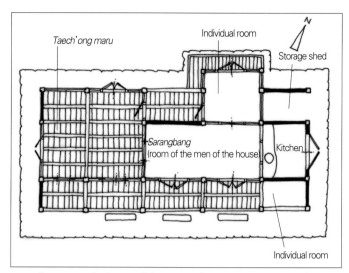

148. Illustration: The layout of the *sarangch'ae* (men's quarters) of a traditional house. The *sarangbang* (the room of the master of the house) generally faced south and towards the front gate.

description of furniture types — which was five times more than those used in *anbang*s — 26 were made of wood or bamboo. The wood or bamboo objects included hobby items and various practical accessories. These included six-stringed Korean harps; bamboo flutes; desks; wooden beds; pillows; chests used as safes; lanterns; reading lamps; ink stone boxes; water containers for ink; pencil boxes; wall hanger/mail holders; enclosed bookcases; cherry wood wardrobes; bamboo blinds; chess boards; reed mats; fans; magnets; wooden shoes; canes; umbrellas; and cone-shaped hats.

The dramatic musical "*Hungbuga*" ("The Song of Hungbu") also described the interior decorations of *sarang*. According to this, the furniture housed in the *sarangbang* included those items used for writing, various writing supplies, *poryo* and bedding, books, and accessories. The furniture and equipment described here seem to be of extremely high quality material; however, because the literati during the Chosun Period practiced Confucian principles of self-restraint and avoided luxury, the majority of furniture was crafted

149. Photo: The furniture and accessories of the *sarangbang* in Wunhyon Palace. A folding screen, *poryo* (large cushion), *ansok* (backrest), *sabangch'im* (square armrest) and *changch'im* (long pillow) occupied the *araenmok* (warmest section of the floor). To the front of these items like a *soan* (low desk) and candlestick were arranged. The central space of the room was reserved for smoking paraphernalia and cushions. A *mungap* (writing supply box) also served as a stand for small writing supplies.

on the simple and modest side. Therefore, one must assume that the description of Hungbu's household was exaggerated.

From these accounts and Chosun Period artifacts, one can classify the *sarangbang* furnishings into several types: pieces used for storage, things designed for writing, small writing supplies, and hobby items. Wardrobes with clothes racks and bookcases with doors were for storage. Furniture pieces needed for writing included supply boxes, shelves, and desks. Small supply items included pencil cases and brush holders. On the wall hung the *kobi*, into which scrolls or stationary were tucked. The remaining artifacts and supplies included cast-iron candlesticks, wood lamps, incense holders, fragrant tobacco, and smoking para-

phernalia. Depending on the interests of the head of the household, items such as a collection of beautiful stones and planted oriental orchids accented his room. Hobby items like a Korean harp, flute, or chess board might complete the furnishings.

In an upper class *sarangbang*, in order to present a scholarly and somber atmosphere, people finished walls with white paper, the ceiling with muted blue paper, and the floor with oiled flooring paper.

To reiterate, in general, the members of the upper class avoided cluttering the *sarangbang* with unnecessary furniture. Therefore, certain paraphernalia remained in an adjacent room while furnishings such as stackable and other storage chests took up space in the attic. In the absence of an adjacent room or bedroom, a wardrobe with clothes racks stayed in the *sarangbang*.

In arranging *sarangbang* furniture, an atmosphere of subtlety prevailed. On one wall — the one behind the *aranmok* — only an attic door broke the stark plane. A folding screen, generally of six or eight panels, stood along this wall, and featured quiet, graceful landscape paintings, brush paintings of the four most favored motifs (oriental orchids, plum blossoms,

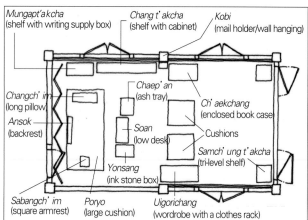

Mungapt'akcha (shelf with writing supply box)

Chang t'akcha (shelf with cabinet)

Kobi (mail holder/wall hanging)

Changch'im (long pillow)

Ansok (backrest)

Chaep'an (ash tray)

Ch'aekchang (enclosed book case)

Soan (low desk)

Cushions

Yonsang (ink stone box)

Samch'ung t'akcha (tri-level shelf)

Sabangch'im (square armrest)

Poryo (large cushion)

Uigorichang (wordrobe with a clothes rack)

bamboos, and chrysanthemums), or calligraphed poems. If the owner did not care for screens, only one was placed at the headside in his bedroom for the practical purpose of cutting off drafts. A *poryo* (a large cushion), similar to that used in the *anbang*, occupied the center spot at the *aranmok*. While women used only a *poryo* and a square armrest in the *anbang*, in the *sarangbang* men generally had the backrest, the long armrest, and several individual cushions in addition to the *poryo* and square armrest. The backrest cushion stayed in the center of the back edge of the *poryo*. The long armrest lay within reach of the master's left arm. The square armrest remained on the right side.

Because the books of the Chosun Period were bulky, a low desk was always kept handy. For reading convenience, a stand with a slanted top was on hand. A desk worked as a functional item, but also served as furniture item signifying the position of the master of the house when he interacted with his visitors. Next to

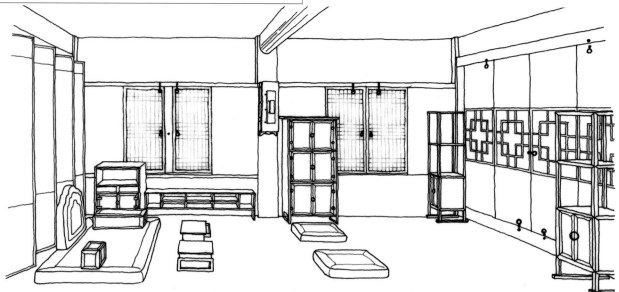

150. Illustration: The furniture arrangement (reconstructed for historical accuracy) of the *sarangbang* of the ancient estate of Ch'usa. A *p'yongp'ung* (folding screen), *poryo* (large cushion), *ansok* (backrest), *sabangch'im* (square armrest), and *changch'im* (long pillow) occupied the *araenmok* (warmest spot on the floor). A *soan* (low desk) and *yonsang* (ink stone box) were set to the front of the *poryo*. Cushions occupied the center of the room while a *mungap* (writing supply box), *t'akcha* (open-sided shelf), *changt'akcha* (shelf with cabinet) and *ch'aekchang* (book cabinet) lined up against the wall facing the front courtyard. A tri-level open-sided shelf was set in the corner by the door leading to the *sarang taech'ong*.

the desk lay a writing supply chest which held small items such as paper, brushes, and small water pitcher for making ink. A tray holding smoking paraphernalia, like a tobacco box, lighting stones, a spittoon, and an ashtray lay next to the desk or in the center near the portable stove and cushions.

Along the wall and window opening out to the *apt'oi* (small front side veranda), one placed a pair of *mungaps* (writing supply boxes) or an extra long *mungap* below the window. One lay sundry writing supplies or a brush holder on top of the boxes; however, for neatness, one sometimes stored all these items in one box. A bit higher on the wall, or on an exposed post, hung a *kobi* (decorative wall hanging doubling as a letter or document holder), used for the storage of documents in scroll forms. A simple shelf or enclosed bookcase of understated design flanked the *mungap*s. One added another set of *mungap*, shelves, and enclosed bookcase along the opposite wall. Against the wall with a window opening to *twit'oi* (small back side veranda), either a wardrobe with clothes racks or an enclosed bookcase took their places. Depending on the size of these pieces, a painting was added as an accent. People avoided displaying several paintings or calligraphy plaques in a row or creating a symmetry with two paintings as such a practice was considered poor taste. They preferred to leave a certain amount of empty surface in order to generate an open feeling.

Men chose scroll paintings or calligraphy for their *sarangbang* for more than their decorative quality. They shied away from paintings of bright colors in favor of neutral-toned landscapes or calligraphy with passages of significance to them. A pair of open-sided shelves or tri-level bookcases claimed the space in the upper section of the room, generating a sense of balance for the whole area (illustration 150).

3. The arrangement of furniture in the kitchen

Upper class homes generally came with two or more kitchens. Most food preparation occurred in the main kitchen while the others were small and constructed mainly for the hypocaust fireplace that heated the floors of rooms. Each of these fireplaces came with cooking slots where pots of water boiled or some simple food preparation was done. In upper class homes, the *anbang* (room of the lady of the house) and *konnobang* (room of the wife of the eldest son) each had an attached kitchen, and in some cases each of these kitchens featured two fireplaces with identical cooking slots and counters. For the convenience of the lady of the house, who presided over food preparation, the heaviest cooking was done in the kitchen attached to her room.

The kitchen was divided into several areas: the fireplace built with fine clay and brick, a storage space, and a meal preparation area. Utensils hung from pegs driven into the upper cross beam above the fireplace. The remaining utensils were stored in the built-in cabinet behind the *aranmok* of the *anbang* or in the attic. The entryway to these storage spaces was through the *anbang*.

Of the 69 kitchen utensils listed in the *Sallimkyongje*, 22 came in wood and bamboo. These included rice scoops, wooden tubs, treadmills, pounders, rice-washing bowls grooved on the inside, wooden mills for hulling rice, grain leveler, grain measuring containers, china cabinets, grain bins, vats, tables, rice-wine strainers, winnows, bamboo trays, wicker trunks, small traveling boxes, rice colanders, trays, baskets, and mortars.

One sorcerer's song described kitchen items as

151. Photo: The kitchen furniture and equipments of the Norank-dang Building at Wunhyon Palace. At a corner against a wall stood a *ch'ant'ak* (cupboard shelves) and small tables.

pots, bins, cabinets, various items of chinaware, and implements for hulling powdering, and measuring grains. Pots for cooking rice, boiling water, and heating soups were placed on the slots made in the cook-top counter of the fireplace. Strainers, brushes, and grilling racks hung on the cross beam above the fireplace.

Water-carrying yokes, water jugs, and water jars lined the floor of the kitchen. Water-jug-carrying head pads and gourds hung on the wall above them. In upper class homes, a well was placed to the back of the kitchen; however, because of the beliefs of the Yin-and-Yang-and-Five Elements School, people rarely drilled wells too close to the kitchen.

Following the Confucian teaching of the "separateness of functions" of men and women, the two sexes did not share meals. Separate tables were set according to the gender, age, and position. This custom naturally necessitated a large number of tables. These were stored on shelves and cabinets; however, when storage space was not sufficient, women stacked them in one corner. When even such a corner space was not available, people had shelves or cabinets constructed in the back of the wood-floored veranda and there stored various tables, chinaware and brass bowls, wine bottles, and stackable portable food containers (photo 151).

When a family had a food storage room, here they kept kitchen cabinets, shelves, grain bins, and hulling tools and extra foods. In upper class homes, people had separate storage structures built, including *tojangbang*s for the storage of various jars, other storage rooms, and attics.

The furniture arrangements in the upper homes differed from those of the lower classes. In the homes of the common people, china cabinets and grain bins occupied a corner in the *taech'ong*. Small portable tables were stored on shelves installed on a wall while a table reserved for ancestor worship ceremonies was set on the rack constructed between cross beams in the ceiling. Toward the back of the tops of the grain bins, jars were stacked three deep. Some jars featured dragon designs; others were small, plain, white jars. These were used for the storage of seasoned radish strips, pickled oysters and other seafood, and highly spiced side - dish items.

Unlike in upper class houses where the kitchen and its secondary structures were scattered throughout the building compound, the kitchen in the common class home was contained in one structure located either at the very end of the row of rooms or at the elbow, if the building was of L or similar shape. As all food preparation activities had to be performed in this one area and because the lady of the house or her daughter-in-law often took her meals there, the kitchen was built in a larger size than other rooms in the house.

The kitchen could be divided into three large areas: the hypocaust fireplace with a cook-top counter, a large wood floored food preparation area, and firewood storage space. As in the case of upper class kitchens, the fireplace was constructed against the wall of the *anbang* (room of the lady of the house).

Three cooking slots accommodated pots of various sizes. Across from this area was a waist-high wood-floored food preparation space. Food, utensil and chinaware storage areas occupied the back side of this ledge.

Below this ledge, large clay water jars were set into the ground. When people could not afford such a ledge, a counter was built with clay on the dirt floor of the kitchen. In one corner, across from the fireplace, firewood and kindling, such as pine branches, were stacked against the wall. Sometimes, people built low clay walls around this area.

The storage facilities of common people were similar to those of the upper class; however, the lower class folks lacked the furniture specifically designed for storage. They used simply constructed, built-in cabinets for all around storage. Large jars of *kimch'i*, supplemental utensils, tools, and plates all went into a single storage shed.

As reviewed in this chapter, the furniture used in the *anbang* consisted mostly of the pieces needed for the storage of household items while those placed in the *sarang* were related to scholarly activities and the reception of guests.

The arrangement of furniture in the two areas differed as well. The dissimilarity also occurred between the upper and lower classes in terms of the volume and types of furniture and their arrangement. The upper class, for example, used a larger volume of furniture that were decorative as well as functional, while the lower classes limited their furnishings to minimum necessities. Such disparity showed especially in kitchen furnishings. However, there were some exceptions because of the differences in taste and life styles.

olors and color schemes used in traditional Korean houses owe much to the ideas of the Yin-and-Yang-and-Five-Elements Theory. Through the adoption of these ideas, colors gradually accrued symbolic significance in addition to their aesthetic properties. The same occurred with patterns, which served as mediums that conveyed symbolism as well as human emotions they evoked. A close look at the colors and patterns is offered here.

1. Colors

Korean language involving colors seems to indicate that Koreans understood scientific concepts about how colors were perceived. The fact that words meaning "color" and "reflected shades"were used interchangeably leads one to the conclusion that Koreans were aware of the relationships between colors and light rays. As other peoples have formed and expressed their own unique color concepts, developed in response to the nature of light rays received in their parts of the world, Koreans exhibited their own preconceived, archetypal notions of colors.

Koreans also held color concepts that were characteristic of their region and preconceptions. For example, in the Korean vocabulary, blue and green are used interchangeably. This demonstrates that Koreans did not perceive colors as part of the innate properties of objects, but as rays they absorbed or rejected.

1 Traditional colors

Koreans, like other peoples, have used colors as a means of expressing emotions as well as their learned aesthetic sensibility. Traditionally Koreans placed emphasis on colors as a way of expressing their philosophy of life and universe--namely, to convey symbolisms based on the world view embraced by the concepts of the yin and yang, and five elements. In other words, Koreans sought to bring about order and harmony to the world through their use of *obangsaek* (five basic colors), chosen for their philosophical significance. A discussion follows on the significance held by these colors and how Koreans used them in their daily lives.

(1) The significance of *obangsaek*

The five elements described in the Yin-and-Yang-and-Five-Elements Theory refer to wood, fire, earth, metal, and water. According to this philosophy, all objects in the universe can be explained in terms of how they relate to directions, colors, seasons, yin and yang, and feng shui (water/wind). In short, the mysteries of heaven can be understood by examining the five ways of heaven, the earth through its five materials, and humans through their five natures (chart 1).

The *obangsaek* (five basic colors) of blue, red, yellow, white, and black corresponded with the five directions of east, west, south, north, and center. Mixed colors fell between these basic colors. Namely, dark blue fell between east and west; green between east and center; bright red between south and west; purple between south and north; and rust color between north and center. These ten colors formed the basis of traditionally selected colors.

[Chart 1] The *obangsaek* and their meaning

Elements	Wood	Fire	Earth	Metal	Water
Direction	East	South	Center	West	North
Color	Blue	Red	Yellow	White	Black
Season	Spring	Summer	·	Autumn	Winter
Yin Yang	Yang	Yang	Yang	Yin	Yin
Feng Shui	Dragon	*Ponghwang*	·	Tiger	Tortoise

The Korean word *p'arang* (blue) came from the root word *p'al*, which derived from *p'ul* (grass). Blue signified the color of trees, sky, and water. It symbolized the east, birth, youth, *pyoksa* (repelling of evil spirits), and lower or humble positions. As blue and green were used interchangeably, the adjective *p'uruda* (blue), which derived from *p'ul* (grass), applied to trees, oceans, mountains, and the sky alike.

The traditional meaning of the color red was the south, brightness, greatness, and *pyoksa*. The "red cloth wrap that flowed down from the sky" described in the creation fable of the Karakkuk Kingdom was an attempt to narrate the birth of the nation through a symbolic use of the color red (greatness) and the brightness of the sky. The story of "a black frog dying after fighting with a red frog," as told in the History of Three Kingdoms, could be interpreted as the Puyo in the north (the black frog) being defeated by Koguryo in the south (the red frog).

The *norang* (yellow), deriving from the word *nul* (the ground or soil), symbolized the center, the earth, the emperor, and authority. The "center" signified a moist, level, and fertile plain. The word P'yongyang (the capital of North Korea) carries this same meaning. When worship ceremonies were held to honor and appease the heaven, a yellow offering was placed in the center among blue, white, red and black objects because yellow corresponded with the center.

The *hinsaek* (white) related to the west, the sun, purity, and a good omen. The white color, perceived as the color of the rays of the sun, was a particularly significant color to Koreans. Many names of mountains in Korea contain the suffix *paksan* (a white mountain), because Koreans saw them as sacred, having absorbed the spirit of the sun's rays. Koreans called themselves *paedal minjok*. By this self-description, Koreans showed their belief and pride in themselves as the descendants of the bright and pure heaven.

The *komunsaek* (black) referred to the north, deity, water, and the color of bears. Names of animals like *kom* (bear), *kobuk* (turtle), or *komi* (spider) all have roots in *kom* or *kam* because these animals were believed to possess the status of deities.

(2) Colors in relation to daily lives

Because colors were used for symbolic purposes based on the Yin-and-Yang-and-Five-Elements concepts, rather than men's aesthetic need for expression, a host of rules and restrictions were applied. Confucianism also provided influences. Teaching self-cultivation of man through the development of higher moral consciousness, the observance of propriety, and transcendence of emotions and sensuality, Confucianism viewed using colors a sign of underdeveloped character. In this context, the government regulated the use of colors and restricted the color choices people could make, even among government titled classes. The end result was that the common class people were left with only white. The gold-bordered, red costumes belonged to royalties, and bright reds, dark blues, and greens went to titled officials, depending on their ranking. Yellow was taboo, as it was the official color of the emperor of China. Violets and certain shades of greens were also forbidden, except at ceremonies, on the grounds that they were colors of luxury.

People exhibited their displeasure with such restrictions, but only in minor ways. Women wore colorful underwear and brilliantly colored trinkets, and satirical folk paintings emerged, which made light of color restrictions. But such rebellion remained feeble gestures, and the repressive culture led to a tradition lacking in the aesthetic use of colors. Only at special ceremonies, such as weddings, were colors permitted, allowing Koreans to display their taste for color; however, even then established rules and patterns, derived from symbolic and superstitious concepts, operated.

For example, blue, being a yang color, and being associated with the force that repels yin (evil), was used for situations dealing with the conquering of

152. Photo: A *saktong durumagi* (girl's coat with multi-colored, striped sleeves). To make this coat, women pieced together strips of fabric in blue, red, yellow, pink, and green colors, all of which represented luck, health, and long life.

destructive ghosts or illnesses.

Another example of the superstitious use of colors can be seen on *saktong chogori*s or *saktong durumagi*s (women and girls' coat with sleeves that are striped with five colors) still in use today. The three yang colors of blue, red, and yellow appear, but instead of white and black, the yin colors, pink and green are added to form the five-color scheme (photo 152). Also, in traditional weddings, a bride still wears a green *chogori* (blouse) and red *chima* (long skirt) both being yang colors.

The word *ch'ong* (blue) is still contained in many expressions for youthfulness, as in the examples of *ch'ongwun*s (youthful dreams) and *ch'onggwa*s (fresh fruits). During the Chosun Dynasty, this color also signified a lowly ranking. Red was associated with the south. An example showing such a relationship can be found on wall paintings on Koguryo tombs, where a red phoenix shows on the south wall. The color also signified the power to overcome evil. An example of the red being used for this purpose can be seen in the custom of dashing red azuka bean stew against the gate of a house that required special protection. Also, at the

153. Photo: A *kumjul* (straw rope announcing the birth of a boy) strung across a doorway. At the birth of a boy baby, Koreans decorated a piece of rope with red peppers and draped it across their doorway to announce the good news and to forbid entry of outsiders.

onset of spring or on *tano* (the fifth day of the fifth month), people hung red talismans on walls or doors. For a similar reason, Koreans strung a piece of rope with red peppers and charcoal chunks and draped it around earthenware jars. For the same reason, when a boy was born, people adorned the front gate with a string of red peppers (photo 153). The custom of little girls dying their finger nails red with the coloring from balsam flowers traces its origin to a similar symbolism.

Red also signified a high status. In Koguryo tomb paintings, the pillars of buildings were depicted in red. The extra high and ornate gates of the Chosun Dynasty palaces and mansions were painted red, while lesser gates received a coat of blue. Except for the furniture belonging to the queen, furnishings and accessories were not permitted to be lacquered or otherwise coated in red. According to historical records from Chosun Dynasty, those passing exams for higher

government office were awarded red certificates, while those passing lower ranks were given white ones. The official costume for the upper officials were red, while the lower rank came in dark blue.

Because yellow, the color reserved for the Chinese royalties, was seldom used in Korea; and when used on the costumes of Korean royalties, it showed only as gold borders. In China, yellow tiles often graced palace roofs, but never in Korea.

As for the white clothes favored by Koreans, it is difficult to conclude that such a practice came into existence only because of government restrictions on the use of colors. Even aside from such external pressures, Koreans on the whole seemed to have possessed an inclination toward the color. Also, because of their philosophical reservations toward colors and decorations, they practiced restraint from ornamentation and sought more spiritual expressions, thereby favoring white as the color of cleanliness and purity. Expressions such as *sunbak* (pure white), Korean's near fanatical reverence for symbolic creatures such as white cranes, and the custom of making white rice cake on the hundredth day after the birth of a child and distributing them to one hundred households, and the eating of white noodles at weddings all seem to indicate Koreas' preoccupation with the white as a symbol of many good things in life, including the rays of the sun, the sanctity of births, and their hope for a bright future. Koreans, on the other hand, viewed black as a color of bad omens and death. The decorations at ancestor worship ceremonies or the alters were in that color. Black was also associated with one of the five elements: water. Koreans predicted floods if black clouds appeared at the vernal and autumnal equinoxes and summer and winter solstices; and they prepared black talismans to avert suchdisasters. Furthermore, if people saw extra dark dirt in the ground, even if the spot was divinated as an auspicious grave site, they believed that water would spring forth, causing poverty to the descendants and stripping them of good positions. Thus, the plot was abandoned.

2 | Colors in the house

Colors used in the house can be divided into three types: the natural colors of the materials, colors added to them during processing, and finish coats. Generally, Koreans preferred to make use of the natural colors in such materials as lumber, stone, tile, and brick.

However, the wall paintings on Koguryo tombs depicting scenes of hunting, fourteen girls dancing, and the four symbolic animals show various colors with red on the pillars of buildings and reddish brown or gray on roof tiles. According to *Samgukyusa* (A History of Three Kingdoms), five different colors and even a gilded coating appeared on roof tiles. From the red roof-end tiles unearthed at Anapchi pond, one can conclude that colors were used on residences.

According to the section on the use of colors in residences contained in *Samguksagi* (Annals of Three Kingdoms), the government imposed many restrictions. Even officials ranked *chingol* (persons of partly royal lineage) were forbidden to use gold, silver, or brass ornaments as well as the five basic colors. Neither were they permitted to use white plaster for their walls, nor embroidery on their folding screens. The painting of their homes was permitted to only those of a *songgol* (persons of royal lineage) rank and higher. Therefore, it appears that colors were used on residences during the Three Kingdom Period, but only occasionally.

According to historical records, the Koryo Kingdom imposed restriction on the use of colors on non-royalties. But numerous powerful people broke the rules and caused scandals. Records show that temples and mansions of the noble class in particular were brilliantly painted. For example, the Anhwa-sa temple became famous for its extremely beautiful *tanch'ong* (multi-colored decorative painting). One nobleman's residence was known for its pavilion, which boasted gilded decorations, eaves painted in red, *tanch'ong*-painted pillars, and silk-covered walls.

During the Chosun Dynasty, restrictions on the use of colors became even more rigid. According to *Kyongguktaejon* (Administration Code), those painting their buildings, except for temples, those using silk, flower-designed, or embroidered cushions, and those using red lacquered utensils were to be given 80 lashes. During King Sejong's reign, the government forbade the painting of all structures, even public build-

154. Photos: Examples of the conservative use of colors practiced in houses during the Confucian Chosun Dynasty. Only the use of the natural colors found in wood, stone, and roof tile was encouraged by the government. The result was a serene, tidy, and natural-looking atmosphere.

ings and temples. However, by the reign of King Munjong, despite objections by some cabinet members, the government relaxed the restrictions and legalized the painting of public structures and temples. This practice stood for the rest of the Chosun Dynasty.

The fact that eventually color use was legalized seems to indicate that the number of powerful and rich people breaking the government rules and flaunting their wealth and position became significant. A few good examples of such cases can be found in official records. The color red in particular gained its symbolic significance as the color of status. Therefore, while the history books of the Three Kingdoms refer to status colors as "five colors," the Chosun Dynasty records use the word "red."

Korean kings generally did not engage in excesses in building and decorating palaces, but after the introduction of Confucianism, this self-restraint became more evident. If they seemed to lean toward grandiosity, their cabinet members apparently offered frequent advice to the kings to heed Confucian ideals of modesty and propriety. Thus, some structures within palace compounds do not show a *tanch'ong* decoration. Even those so adorned displayed less bright colors. Overall, partly because of Koreans' attraction toward the white color and the restrictions imposed on colors in the context of the Yin-and-Yang-and-Five-Elements ideas as well as Confucianism, traditional Korean houses generally did not display much color. Rather, natural colors of such materials as lumber, stone, tile, and brick blended with the subtle colors used in the interior, creating an understated residential atmosphere (photo 154).

3 Colors of the interior

The colors visible in the interior consisted of three types: the colors of building materials, finishing treatments, and furniture.

(1) Colors of building materials

Traditional Korean houses were generally built with wood; and the wooden pillars, cross beams, and rafters were often left exposed. As a result, wood played an important role as a design element. The most commonly chosen lumber was pine, and in common class houses, bark was peeled off and the *paeggol* (exposed white pine wood) was used without any special coating or finishing. With the passage of time, the pale color of pine turned dark brown, losing its luster. In time when the wood grain became pronounced, the wood tended to twist and show cracks.

To prevent such deterioration, among the upper class houses the pine was first wrapped in ramie, which was sometimes substituted with high quality silk; then, a litharge glaze made of oxidized lead was applied as insect repellant. Finally, the surface was lacquered.

Before using the pine to build houses, men smoke-stained the wood over a fire made with freshly cut pine branches or pine cones. If people had sufficient time for the completion of the house, or if they could afford this special processing, they had all the lumber prepared in such manner. Otherwise, only the timber to be used for the pillars and rafters got the treatment. The process involved holding the lumber over fire until resin flowed out and coated the surface.

Just before resin dried, people rubbed the wood with ash to get rid of the smoke stains and soot. This polishing process left the surface smooth and shiny, exposing the wood grain and providing, from the resinous coating, resistance to humidity, insect damage, and other deterioration. This also prevented warping. A pine cone method worked in a similar fashion. People smoke-stained the logs by holding them over pine-cone fire and rubbed the wood with luffa to scrub off the soot and reveal wood grain.

Builders treated the lumber used for framing the wood floor of the *tae-ch'ong* and that used for the railings of verandas differently. They boiled animal skin to a brown colored glue. To this substance, they added red clay. The resulting glue-like paint covered the wood. An alternative method was waxing the lumber with bean oil. If the oiling process left the coloring of the wood too inconsistent, people added dye from gardenia seeds to the oil to achieve a little more uniformity. Sometimes, workers treated the wood with water mixed with ash before applying coloring. Wood products treated in the various ways mentioned above lacked color consistency, but overall they acquired natural, neutral colors.

(2) Colors of finishing materials

The floor

The dugout huts and clay shelters of ancient times had well-patted dirt floors. At first the inhabitants spread leaves or dried grass on them. Eventually, they discovered woven reed or straw mats. Then people began to spread stones on the floor; these stones later evolved to *chon*s (square bricks) of brown or reddish color. Records indicate that during the Three Kingdom and Unified Silla Periods, lamb's wool or animal fur was spread over the layer of square bricks;

however, no examples of this remain today. Square bricks were used for the flooring of palaces or temples; however, in private residences, only a few were laid occasionally on the platform leading up to the *taech'ong*.

During the Chosun Dynasty, as the *ondol* (hypocaust heated floor system) was popularized and the general living standards improved, people equipped individuals rooms with *ondol* floors. Such floors were covered with oiled-paper, dirt floors remaining only in areas such as kitchens, storage rooms, or animal pens. The flooring paper received a coat of bean oil mixed with yellow coloring from gardenia seeds. Thus finished, the waxed *ondol* floor shone in warm yellowish hue, giving otherwise stark appearance of the white-walled rooms warm and inviting look (photo 155).

In some upper class households, soft silk displaying subtle patterns substituted paper. Such fabric was then oiled for a smooth and water-resistant surface. Occasionally, people used cotton, applying same oiling process. The end result was a textured floor of woven fabrics shining through the waxed surface. For an extra fancy finish, people used a melted-resin coating. This left the floor a beautiful yellowish pumpkin color. With use, the floor became smoother, and the color deepened to a rich reddish pumpkin hue. Sometimes, people mashed ginkgo leaves in a mortar and spread them on the floor to create a greenish.

The *maru* of traditional Korean homes was wood floored. A glue-like substance mixed with red clay coated the wood. If more even coloring was desired, people added gardenia dye to the bean oil mixture. With use, however, the wood floors of the generally turned very dark brown.

155. Photo: A floor finished with an oiled paper covering. The paper coating produced a warm yellow tint, which contributed to the creation of a comfortable and cozy atmosphere in individual rooms for the Korean people, who enjoyed sitting on floors rather than on chairs.

Walls

In general, windows were installed into the walls facing the courtyard while the side and back walls remained uninterrupted and were finished with white paper or plaster. Koreans had used plaster since the Three Kingdom Period, and the fresco paintings on Koguryo tombs indicate this practice. In a Koguryo fresco, as with those in the West, the plaster was painted before it dried.

Plaster was the most widely utilized finishing method applied to the walls of the *taech'ong* among the upper class during the Chosun Dynasty. Once finished, the white surface contrasted sharply with the dark wood floor and the exposed beams and rafters. This

156. Photo: A typical *taech'ong* where the color of exposed wood beams and rafters contrasted sharply with the color of the plaster filling the space between beams and rafters, providing a pleasing and lively appearance.

contrast, along with the textual difference between the plaster and wood, generated a stunning design that imbued a sense of liveliness (photo 156). The interior walls of the kitchen were also often completed with plaster, too. However, common class households generally featured brown or white clay walls. During the time when reed mats served as the floor covering, wallpapering was yet to be discovered and popularized.

Even among the upper class, because of the scarcity of paper, people draped curtains or nets on walls. According to ancient documents, even down to the early years of the Chosun Dynasty, drapes were always used in upper class homes throughout the winter.

About the time oiled paper came into use as a floor covering, clay interior walls also began receiving paper finishes. The walls of the *taech'ong* were generally left as plaster surfaces, but occasionally they were wallpapered for additional insulation and to cover up cracks. The upper class population used a thick, smooth, and durable ivory colored paper made from mulberry pulp. The most commonly used wallpaper was white; however, gradually subdued colors of light blue, jade, or green appeared. The lower classes used paper painted gray with India ink or a rough-textured yellow paper.

157. Photo: A beautifully constructed and decorated upper class house. Elevated on a high foundation, this typical upper class house with its decoratively designed latticework provided a satisfying appearance.

Mass production of Korean rice paper called *hanji* began around the 16th century. Before this, windows were mere openings left without any finishing touch. After the popularization of paper, people fitted various lattices across the window frames and glued paper on the interior sides. Because the dark wood latticework remained exposed on the exterior side, the design provided stunning visual element (photo 157). Looking out from inside, these lattice windows presented a different aesthetic experience: that of light filtering softly through the rice paper and the dark, muted lattice strips. In the northern regions, to prevent the paper from disintegrating when snow blew on the windows, people applied a layer of paper to the exterior of windows as well.

In private residences, the lattice was generally a

natural wood darkened with time. However, beginning in the 19th century, people began to paint the wood strips on windows with green or yellow. The brown latticework on the Myongjongjon of Ch'anggyong Palace and the Injongjon of the Ch'angdok Palace exemplify this. In the latter part of the 19th century, green became more popular.

The total effect of the white walls, the soft light filtering through white rice paper and latticework, and the corn-colored waxed paper floors was a warm and rich natural atmosphere that characterized traditional Korean houses.

Ceilings

As discussed in Chapter 3, the ceiling of the *taech'ong* generally featured the exposed-rafter finish, while that of individual rooms received drop ceiling treatments. The white plaster surfaces between beams and rafters, and the dark natural wood color of the beams provided the beauty in this style ceiling.

A drop ceiling method was used for rooms with *ondol* floors. At first, plain white rice paper was applied to such ceilings; however, gradually, blue, green, and yellow tints were added. In the second half of the Chosun Dynasty, various ceiling papers became popular. Some came with a pale pink background, accented with light green patterns. Some had a subdued blue background sprinkled with gold or silver dust, while others came in various shades of pinks and greens alternating and forming patterns. To give a neat, finished look, people covered moldings with blue paper or yellowish oiled paper. If the wood board of the drop ceiling was to be left exposed, people applied yellow clay to it for color. However, the wood was generally covered with paper.

(3) Colors on furniture

Over 1,000 types of trees flourished on the Korean peninsula, as it bridged a wide span latitudinally and 70 percent of the land was covered with dense forests. From this variety of timber, dozens of beautifully grained, hard woods were easily available for furniture construction.

A majority of traditional Korean furniture was wood; however, a piece of furniture was rarely made of only one type of wood. Rather, taking advantage of the diverse properties of various types of wood, different lumber was selected for certain parts of furniture. Certain wood pieces were sliced thin before use, but applying thin veneers to give an impression of an improved appearances was not practiced. So, traditional furniture was solid wood and acquired luster and richness with use. Generally, people preferred natural wood, but occasionally they had the surface painted, and for an extra fancy touch, a thin layer of sliced, painted ox horn applied. Lacquer, mother-of-pearl, or red paints were also chosen for a more luxurious appearance.

From the time of the Koryo Kingdom, Koreans diligently planted pines. As a result, pine proliferated and emerged as the most plentiful timber. Showing a reddish brown tint, the central part of a pine log looked distinctly different from the outer section. Because of its availability and its drying properties, pine became particularly popular among the common class.

Persimmon trees grow well amid the sunlight and oceanic breezes. The timber of these trees is known for its soft, yet dense texture; but it does not dry well. Because of the beautiful, very dark wood grain patterns at its center, black-persimmon wood was considered a valuable wood (photo 158) and went into making *chang*s (wardrobes), *nong*s (stackable chests),

158. Photo: A detail of a *chang* (wardrobe). Crafted of highly prized persimmon tree wood, with its distinctively beautiful symmetrically-arranged wood grains, this furniture piece added dramatic visual element to a room.

*mungap*s (writing supply boxes), open-sided shelves, and *yonsang*s (ink stone boxes). How the dark swirl grains were formed is not certain; however, Chosun Period scholars believed that they were caused by rain water that seeped into the wood.

Koreans also enjoyed the big-cone pine or Korean white pine, well known for its beautiful wood grains, pleasing scent, and the ease with which it could be worked. Cabinetmakers made *pandaji*s (clothes/book chests) and other storage boxes with this timber.

The ginkgo tree wood has straight, linear grains and is of a dense texture, exuding a wonderful scent. The pale-yellowish-brown wood also has elasticity, so that when pressed or nicked, the damage does not easily show. For this reason, craftsmen used this wood for objects like portable meal tables or checker boards.

Walnut is a dense, hardwood, and, because of its oily nature, the wood contains a luster, and does not warp or crack. Therefore, this material was considered valuable and went into forming structural pieces or the backing boards for furniture.

Lightweight, paulownia wood has reddish and white tints with straight linear grains. Its growth rate is rapid. It does not warp, and because of its worm-resistance, it was widely used for furniture making. However, because it is not strong wood, it generally went into backing boards of wardrobes or stackable chests that did not need to bear a lot of weight.

Because of its beautiful, yellowish brown wood grains in the center, its luster, and durability, zelkova wood was considered high quality timber. However, if not properly dried, it tended to warp or crack. Because of its durability, people liked to use this wood to make grain bins, china cabinets, and good quality storage chests for clothes.

The lime tree wood is of a very pale yellowish tint. It splits easily because of its soft yet dense texture and is easy to work with. Because of these characteristics, people made portable meal tables and checker boards out of this material. Sometimes this wood was used to produce decoratively carved goods. A *sungsungi*-style chest from Pakch'on of the P'yongan Province serves as an example of furniture made with this wood.

Bamboo grows best in gravelly and sandy soil, and was the main product of Chonju, Tamyang, and Namwon in South Cholla Province. It is easy to grow, and its growth rate is rapid. It does not give under pressure and shrinkage from dryness is low. Because dyeing bamboo is easy and has many benefits, the practice is used widely in furniture making and crafts. In making bamboo furniture pieces, people wove bamboo strips into a mat-like form and attached it to the surface of furniture pieces made of ginkgo or paulownia. Or, craftsmen split the bamboo branches and attached these directly to the furniture. Because it symbolized of unflinching loyalty, a virtue deemed the most important by scholarly men, bamboo was used in making *sarangbang* (the room of the master) rather than *anbang* (the room of the lady of the house) furniture.

The techniques for applying extra luxurious finishes included the attaching of *hwagak* (ox-horn decoration), coating with lacquer, and painting with red. For the ox-horn ornamentation, the root section of an ox horn was sliced paper thin and designs were painted on the reddish or yellowish surface. Craftsmen attached such a decorated layer to furniture to create a splendidly colorful masterpiece (photo 159).

Originating from Chinese techniques of decorating with amber or crystal painted on the back side, so that the design would show through to the front, the painted ox-horn-veneer method imbued zest into women's modest, rather drab, Confucian-style furniture of the Chosun Dynasty. However, because just the most luxurious quality furniture items were treated with such ornamentation, only women of the upper class or of royal lineage had access to them. Generally, such small furniture pieces as sewing thread boxes, or wedding chests received such a fine finish.

The technique of mother-of-pearl lacquerware work traces its origin to the Unified Silla and Koryo Periods. However, popularization among the common classes did not occur until the mid Chosun Dynasty. The patterns of mother-of-pearl works displayed a great variety. Koryo style, for example, offers extremely detailed, densely textured designs formed of tiny bits of sea shells covering the entire surfaces. The objects crafted in this style made brilliantly fancy accent pieces, while those of the Chosun used larger bits of sea shells; and, instead of covering whole surfaces, designs appeared only in small well-placed clusters (photo 160). This style generated an appearance of order and modesty.

159. Photo : A very colorful *hwagakham* (box adorned with thin veneer of painted ox horn). Decorated with thin slices of ox horn painted on the underside and applied to the surface of the box, this served as a highly treasured personal possession for the upper class population.

160. Photo : A mother-of-pearl *pitchop* (comb box). Chips of sea shells were arranged carefully to create various patterns on these boxes, producing a visual treat quite different from that of ox horn boxes.

2. Patterns

The term "pattern" refers to distinguishing marks made onto surfaces. In prehistoric eras, before the emergence of languages, symbols served as a means of communication. Gradually, they gave way to more advanced forms of expressions--letters and drawings, from which paintings and design motifs derived. The interior and exterior spaces of traditional Korean houses and their furnishings showcased a rich variety of such design patterns. A study of these design elements yields glimpses into the lifestyles of the Korean people of the past, their social mores, and their personal hopes and faiths.

1 Traditional patterns

As with the use of colors, patterns exhibited symbolic, sometimes mythical properties beyond the merely decorative. Patterns likewise relayed messages about the Koreans' complex philosophies of life and their views of the universe as well as their affective aspect of life.

The wall paintings on the Koguryo tombs depict human figures, folk landscapes, the four symbolic animals, and various decorative patterns. The paintings Muyongch'ong tomb and Ssangyongch'ong tomb are resplendent with magnificent scenes of the heaven, accented with a great number of Taoistic and Buddhist patterns. Patterns derived from Taoism included the *ponghwang* (bird of good omen with a chicken's head, a snake's neck, a sparrow's chin, a turtle's back, and a fish's tail), giraffe, and the faces of ghosts and mythical animals. The patterns of lotus blossoms, honeysuckles, and flame-shapes were all Buddhist symbols.

The symbolic and stylized figures of fantasy animals shown on Koguryo paintings reflect the Koguryo people's religious view of the next life. Pakche Kingdom patterns remain on such artifacts as earthenware, tile, and brick. In their patterns Buddhist characteristics depict honeysuckles, plants, lotus blossoms, auspicious birds, and scenes of the heavens. These patterns are marked by a gentle and warm atmosphere created by soft curves.

The patterns of the Unified Silla exhibited a particularly rich variety; nevertheless, the technique of repeating patterns characterized arts and crafts of the Silla period. Influenced by Buddhism, the highly developed imprinting technique of this period featured realistically rendered Buddhist motifs of clouds, linden trees, *posanghwamun*, and honeysuckles. During the Koryo Period, the inlaying method gave way to plain surfaces for a while, but the Silla-style patterns returned around the 12th century. The Koryo inlaid pottery showed design motifs including landscapes, animals and plants, and human figures.

Overall, traditional Korean patterns fell into the categories of objects found in nature--such as clouds, stones, and the sun; animals and plants; geometric forms; and the letters signifying propitiousness.

(1) Patterns of natural objects

Mountains, streams, stones, clouds, and the sun and moon represented timelessness and man's desire to emulate their qualities. The patterns of the Big Dipper, the moon, and the sun depicted on the ceiling section of the wall paintings on the Koguryo tombs reflect the early custom of worshipping the "sky" or heaven--a deity that was closely related to the agricultural life of Koreans. Incorporated into Buddhist art, the moon-and-sun motifs--along with the ten objects symbolizing immortality (the sun, streams, mountains, stones, clouds, pines, the *pulloch'o* or the herb of eternal youth, turtles, cranes, and deer)–became the most commonly used patterns. The picture painted on the back of a throne depicted the sun, moon, mountains, oceans, pines, and waterfalls, all symbolizing the source of life, long life, and benevolent government (photo 161). Also, the sun represented the masculine while the moon signified the feminine.

The cloud designs, symbolizing plentiful blessings, long life, and numerous descendants, often appeared on the metal fixtures of furniture and on *tanch'ong* (bright, multi-colored painting done on pillars, eaves, roof lines, and ceilings). Also, the cloud patterns accented ceremonial bowls and platters used at

rituals ancestral worship. In this case, the design carried the descendants' wish for the immortality of the ancestors' spirits to reach the heavens. The wall paints and lacquerware of the Three Kingdom Period display either realistic renderings of clouds or those stylized with S-shape curves. On the Silla Period pottery as well as painted or otherwise finished craft items, cloud patterns appear in very fancy, transformed, flowery shapes, reflecting the influence of Buddhist symbolisms. The queen's wood footstool, excavated from the tomb of King Munyong, features feather-like cloud patterns symmetrically painted on either side on the red painted surface. The painting on the back of a throne depicts the sun, moon and five famous-mountains as emblems of the source of life, long life, and benevolent government.

(2) Animal and plant patterns

Animal patterns

Called *sosusogummun*, predominant animal patterns included dragons, cranes, tigers, bats, *ponghwangs* (mythical birds), deer, turtles, wild geese, fish, and butterflies. The dragon, serving as a guardian of benevolent power, was an imaginary animal vested with the head of a camel, antlers of a deer, eyes of a rabbit, ears of a cow, body of a snake, belly of a frog, claws of an eagle, and the sole of a tiger. Koreans equated the dragon with the force that energizes nature, with the spring and with powerful phenomena like the rain and storms that refresh nature.

Along with clouds and pines, a single crane or a pair of cranes served as powerful propitious symbols. They appear on pots of the Unified Silla Period. Koryo blue inlaid celadon pottery called *sangamch'ongja*

161. Photo: An *Ilwol-o-ak-do* (painting of symbolic motifs—the sun, moon, mountains, ocean, pine trees and waterfalls) behind a throne. The various patterns shown in this art work told the story of the origins of life and expressed good will for a long and auspicious life for both the king and nation.

162. Photo: Bat patterns found on a metal fixture. A metal fixture on a woman's furniture piece displaying a bat design symbolized a desire for many sons.

163. Photo: Tortoise patterns found on a wooden fixture. The tortoise patterns on a front gate of a house belonging to the common class population symbolized long life and perfect health.

shows cranes "soaring and dancing" among clouds. The Chosun Dynasty crafts display even a wider range of the cloud/crane patterns.

Tigers represented power, authority, and the guardian of the west. The Koguryo wall paintings of the four symbolic animals on Koguryo tombs exemplify such symbolic use. Tigers enjoyed a long-standing status in folk belief as the animal of faithfulness, always remembering to "repay" kind deeds done on their behalf by humans.

Among animals with a long life span, bats were the most prolific; therefore, they fit perfectly as a symbol of *tanam* (producing many sons), and their shapes graced women's trinkets and metal fixtures on women's furniture (photo 162).

Bats were also called *p'yonpok, pok* being a pun meaning blessings. So, bats' symbolic significance extended to good fortune and appeared as design elements on various objects, including clothing, pots, rice cake presses. Craftsmen often paired bat designs in a symmetrical fashion, to convey "double blessings." Five bat designs used together referred to the five blessings: long life, wealth and fame, good health, integrity of character, and an easy and natural death.

The *ponghwang* (imaginary bird), symbolizing virtuousness, benevolence, faithfulness, righteousness, and propriety. It was believed to make its appearance during peace time, and was used widely as an especially auspicious design pattern. While a dragon represented the masculine, the *ponghwang* served as an emblem of the feminine.

Beginning with the Old Stone Age Period, Koreans worshipped tortoises as an animal with a 10,000-year life span, symbolizing long life, perfect health, or princely positions (photo 163).

Called *yangjo* (birds that migrate in winter to the south, "following the sun"), wild geese enjoyed popularity as an animal of faithfulness between male and female, as they always flew in pairs and mated for life. Naturally, at weddings, wood geese played a symbolic role.

Implying a bountiful oceanic harvest, fish images also functioned as important design patterns, appearing on rock wall paintings from the New Stone Age, the accessories, earthenware, and silver- and gold-coated receptacles of the Three Kingdom Period, and the belts of official costumes of Koryo. These patterns also served as symbols of wealth and fame, good omens, and the fortune of having plenty of descendants. Thus, they graced tools and equipment as well as nuptial outfits.

Emblems of joy, summer, and affection between husband and wife, butterflies decorated folding screens, furniture (photo 164), and pottery used in the *anbang* (the room of the lady of the house) and garments worn in nuptial ceremonies.

164. Photo : A *samch'ungchang* (tri-level wardrobe) decorated with metal fixtures of butterfly patterns. The butterfly patterns emblemed joy and affection between husband and wife was favored by women for their use in *anbang*.

Plant patterns

Plant patterns especially of honeysuckles, lotus, peonies, grapes, pines, bamboos, plum blossoms, and oriental orchids played prominent roles, as these symbolized the good things in life, including harmonious relationships, the happiness of having many sons, and long life.

The *tangch'o-mun* (arabesque pattern) showed intertwining stems and leaves, with a scattering of a few flowers; it served as an emblem of long life or eternal spring (youth). This popular design pattern's graceful lines, carrying forth the rhythm of the interweaving of stems and leaves, were simple yet elegant. The motifs included patterns of honeysuckle, grapes, peonies, and chrysanthemums.

The *posanghwamun* consisted of halved leaf shapes arranged in circles of 4, 6, 8, or 10 symmetrical shapes. At first, this design motif did not hold any special religious overtones; however, during Unified Silla Period it assumed Buddhist symbolism and appeared on such artifacts as bricks, roof tiles, and earthenware.

Representing wealth and fame, lotus blossoms became the scholars' favorite flowers. Men of learning appreciated the purity shown by this flora--because of its ability to remain clean (white) when its roots are buried in mud. They saw a parallel between such quality and the scholarly ideal of maintaining purity and integrity of character which they tried to develop in themselves.

Peonies, known for their beauty, served as the symbol of harmonious relationships and appeared on clothes, furniture, pottery, and chimney (photo 165). The arabesque patterns were often interwove with those of peonies.

165. Photos: A chimney decorated with plant motifs and a Chinese character. The peony blossom design symbolized harmonious relationships (left). The grape and grape vine motifs on a wall between a railing and a gate represented a desire for a long life along with many sons and blessings (right).

Because of its luscious-looking clusters of fruit, the grape plant also represented blessings in life, including long life, having many sons, and good fortunes. Women's accessories generally featured this pattern, rendered in a very realistic manner (photo 165).

Along with bamboo and plum blossoms, pine trees graced craft items and implied eternal friendships and faithfulness between a male and female. Pines generally did not appear alone as design patterns; they appeared in the backgrounds of figure or landscape paintings.

Typifying the most revered ideals of loyalty and open-mindedness, bamboo decorated writing supply paraphernalia used in the *sarangbang* (room of the master) and symbolized man's scholarship and character. Also, because bamboo lasted a long time and remained green throughout the winter, it embodied long life.

Representing the Confucian ideals of maintaining pure-heartedness and modesty, oriental orchids figured prominently in art beginning the latter part of the 17th century. They reemerged during the 19th century in a more refined and modest form, adorning writing supply furnishings.

(3) Geometric patterns and those formed from Chinese characters implying auspicious omens

Geometric patterns

Geometric patterns are probably the oldest forms of design elements in Korea. From the beginning, they seemed to have carried a superstitious significance. Typical examples of geometric patterns included the shapes of lightening, tortoise shells, and the characters of *wan* (卍), *hoe* (回), and *chi* (之).

The lightening design, sometimes called *noemun*, appeared after the Bronze Age. A pattern that predates the lightening design is a comb design found on earthenware of the New Stone Age.

The tortoise-shell or hexagonal pattern symbolized long life, happy augury, and animals deemed to possess supernatural power (photo 166). In the wall painting of four mythical animals on the Koguryo

166. Photo: A fence decorated in a tortoise shell pattern. Adopted mostly by upper class families, this pattern represented long life and auspicious omens.

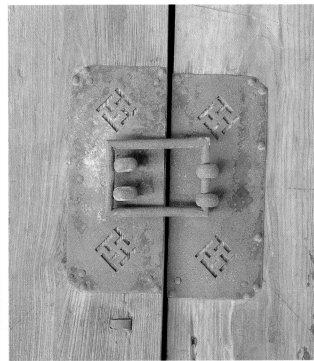

167. Photos: The *wan* (卍) character patterns seen on front gates of traditional houses. The *wan* character conveyed philosophical ideas about the principles by which the universe operates and expressed a man's wish for good luck in all his ventures.

tombs, a tortoise appears as the guardian of the north. Because of its longevity, people included the tortoise among the ten animals symbolizing long life and used its pattern in crafts. The hexagonal design on the chests that stored official government uniforms signified wishes for good health and a long life.

The character *wan* (卍) used as a design is believed to be associated with Buddhist symbolism; however, it is more closely related to the basic shape of a cross that gained tails as it spun around in circles--symbolic of the movement of the universe and the course of the sun. So, this very commonly used design can be understood as a geometric pattern or a character used as a design element (photo 167). The character *wan* (卍) also has a meaning "smooth sailing in ten thousand matters," or "smooth sailing for ten thousand years".

168. Photo: *Ansang-mun* (elephant eye design) on a *kyungsang* (a desk for books). The pattern was symbolic of good fortune.

Designs formed of characters meaning good omens

This category included the patterns of ten longevity symbols, the Eight Trigrams for divination, *t'aeguk* (the central circle design on the Korean national flag), the *yo-uidu-mun* (swirly cloud-like shapes representing fulfilled hopes), the *ansang-mun* (elephant eye design) (photo 168), and Chinese characters signifying happy augury.

The pattern formed of the ten shapes symbolizing longevity included the sun, mountains, clouds, streams, stones, pines, cranes, deer, tortoises, and *pul-loch'o* (the herb of eternal youth). These appeared on furniture, other household possessions, and chimneys (photo 169).

The Eight Trigram pattern represented the wish for happiness and blessings. Originating from Chinese philosophy, the trigrams were associated with the various phenomena occurring in the heavens and on earth.

Representing the three primal elements responsible for the existence of all things, the *t'aeguk* pattern appeared in metal fixtures on furniture.

169. Photo : A chimney decorated with the ten motifs representing longevity. These patterns related directly to the family's wishes for prosperity and the perpetuation of their proud family heritage.

The *youidumun*, a type of swirls which derived from the shapes of things symbolizing fulfilled dreams, such as clouds and mushrooms, was a popular design that decorated items used to induce good luck.

Patterns using characters signifying happiness became popular, especially during the Japanese invasion of Korea in 1592. At that time the aversion of traumatic experience occupied people's minds and these symbolic patterns appeared widely on metal fixtures of furniture pieces, chimneys (photo 170), and walls (photo 171).

The characters *subok* (long life and blessings) decorated women's clothing as well as furniture. Other characters, including *kangnyong* (health), *mansumugang* (long life), and *pugwidanam* (wealth, fame, and many sons) were widely used as well .

170. Photo : A chimney of a traditional house. Even chimneys were decorated with a Chinese letter representing joy.

171. Photo: An example decorated with various motifs of plants and Chinese letters symbolizing good omens contributed to the creation of these visually pleasing walls. In addition, this design expressed Koreans' desire for a wide range of good things in life.

2 Patterns and interior space

(1) Patterns created by finishing touches

Paper floor coverings did not feature any special patterns printed or painted. However, during the process of finishing the floor with oiled paper, the seams created by the overlapping of the pieces of paper formed square patterns. In addition, the glue that was brushed onto the paper left gentle, curvy strokes showing through the paper. Though unintended, such patterns contributed to the creation of visually pleasing and uniquely Korean flooring.

On the *maru* (wood-floored hall), too, Koreans placed no particular effort into producing patterns; however, laying down pieces of boards to fill the floor frame resulted in naturally formed patterns. Two typical examples were the *wumulmaru* and *changmaru* design.

The *wumulmaru* showing the character *chong* (井) pattern graced the *taech'ong* of lower as well as upper class homes.

The *changmaru* pattern appeared as the result of arranging short boards across the space left by two parallel framing boards.

At first wallpapers did not feature any patterns. However, during the Kings Yongjo and Jungjo periods, paper with flower patterns was produced by placing the paper on a wood press and rubbing the surface. Later, the characters *paksubakpok* (living one hundred years with one hundred blessings) replaced the flower pattern. Many different variations of the characters *supok* provided an interesting array. Wallpaper of subtle colors printed or stamped with designs came into fashion for the walls of the *anbang* (room of the lady of the house) while plain white paper graced the *sarangbang* (master's room).

At first, the paper used to coat the drop ceilings was plain. Gradually light blue, green or yellow tint was added to the paper. During the latter part of the Chosun Period, paper of pink background printed with green designs or paper of light blue color dusted with gold or silver specks appeared among certain classes of households. Another type of paper featured patterns formed by varying the different shades of pinks and greens.

(2) Patterns on windows, doors, and railings

Contrasting with the understated ornamentation shown on the finishing touches of floors, ceilings, and walls, the intricate lattice-work patterns formed by dark, natural wood strips on windows, doors, and railings provided welcome sense of change and movement to the interior and exterior spaces of traditional Korean homes.

Patterns on windows and doors

During pre-Koryo periods, latticework consisted of wood rods simply arranged in a vertical manner across the frame of a window or door. It was not until the Koryo Period that fancier patterns, such as *chong* (井) and *a* (亞) shapes emerged, symbolizing a noble status. With the advancement of Confucianism during the Chosun Dynasty, simpler and more graceful designs found favor. However, patterns deriving from the characters *a* (亞), *wan* (卍), and the *pissal* (a hatch design) of the Koryo Period continued to enjoy popularity.

Private residencies generally adopted simple yet charming designs of *ttisall* (vertical lattice combined with grouped horizontal lines), *yong* (用), *a* (亞), or *wan* (卍) characters. Meanwhile the heavier designs of *chong* (井) character, or a hatch pattern highlighted

172. Photos: Various patterns in latticework. A pattern resembling crisscrossed kaoliang branches, the *suttaesal*-pattern was used widely among the common class population as a substitute for the more elaborate and aristocratic *a* (亞) character latticework (top left). The *ttisal* pattern was formed by vertical lattices accented with horizontal lattices grouped into three sections (bottom left). Sometimes, the middle section was omitted. The use of the *chong*- (井) pattern was favored for palaces and temples, as well as private houses. The latticework combined the dense *chong* (井) character patterns with more coarsely constructed patterns (right).

the windows and doors of palaces. A variety of flowery patterns were chosen for temples.

The *sesal* design referred to very dense lattice-work, while *pomsal* designated a more coarsely constructed work that left wide spaces between wood strips. The latter appeared on sliding doors between rooms or in men's quarters. An example of this type was the *yong* (用) character pattern, which generated a sense of simplicity; however, when moonlight cast shadows of leaves against this latticework, the view could look exquisitely poetic. For the *suttaesal* pattern, one repeated the arrangement of two horizontal lattice strips across two vertical pieces. At first glance, the design looked like a mat woven with Indian millet stalks (photo 172). Lower class people used this design as a substitute for the *a* (亞) character pattern.

Among the densely constructed latticework were patterns of *ttisal, chong* (井) character, *kyosal,* and *sosulsal.* In the *ttisal* pattern, vertical lattice pieces were at equal distances from one another, but horizontal ones were closely grouped in the top, middle, and bottom sections (photo 172). If the height of the window was low, people skipped the middle group. The *chong* (井) character pattern resembled the shape of the Chinese character *chong* meaning a well (photo 172). This pattern gained popularity during the Chosun Dynasty, appearing in residences as well as in palaces on *pulbalgichang* (papered section with the middle part decorated with lattice windows), *kwangchang* (horizontally wide windows used strictly for allowing in light), and *putpagich'ang* (immovable, blind windows).

The *a* (亞) and *wan* (卍) character patterns did not develop until tools for fine craftsmanship became available.

The stone pagodas of the Silla and Koryo Periods featured *salch'ang*s (windows with evenly spaced vertical wood strips). During the Chosun Dynasty, out of Confucian emphasis on modesty, fancy latticework of the *a* (亞) and *wan* (卍) character patterns found expression only among the rich and vain, particularly on windows and doors in women's quarters.

Double doors, windows of plain lattice design, or of plain planks were installed on the exterior of the fancier windows and doors (photo 173). The *a* (亞) character pattern looked neat and orderly, generating a sense of security, while the *wan* (卍) character pattern, with some of the lattice pieces bending outward, gave a fancier, more eye-catching appearance. What was unique about these two patterns was that the latticework looked different, depending on the position of the observer or the way the sunlight hit.

173. Photo : An example of space with double windows and doors. The exterior of the windows were usually decorated with fancier patterns like as *wan* (卍) or *a* (亞) latticework than interior patterns.

Patterns on railings

Because traditional houses were very rarely two stories or higher, railings appeared on first story verandas or enclosures facing the outside and functioned as important decorative elements. From the examples of the railings around the Changgunch'ong tomb of the Koguryo Kingdom and the latticework excavated from Anapji pond site from the Unified Silla Period, it appears that railings might have been in use in the Three Kingdom era. Also, the railings on the Pakwun (White Cloud) Bridges and Ch'ongwun (Blue Cloud) Bridges of Pulguk-sa Temple and those found around the Tabotop Pagoda indicate the variety of railing patterns used. The railing on the ten-story stone pagoda of the Koryo Kingdom featured carved lotus decorations on the upper portion of the support posts. Such railing designs realized further development throughout the Chosun Dynasty.

During the Chosun Dynasty, there were some men's quarter *taech'ong*s constructed in a *numaru* form, but such cases were rare. Unlike the *taech'ong*, *numaru*s were open on three sides. People enjoyed *numaru*s with fancy railings that provided better views of surrounding vistas as extended living space. Railing were generally wood. While some installed between pillars were purely functional, most displayed elegant designs and served a highly decorative purpose. Depending on the shapes of the support posts, railings can be divided into two types: the *kyoran* and *keja*.

The *kyoran* type featured latticework between the top and bottom rungs, some showing the *a* (亞) or *wan* (卍) character patterns. Also popular were those accented with cloud-like swirl designs carved out of the backing board between the top and bottom rungs. In

the *keja* type, the tops of the support posts jutted out in sculpted chicken-leg-like forms. Therefore, the top board set across these sculpted posts extended farther outward than the edge of the floor upon which the railings were erected. The railings of the Wunju-ru Pavilion in Kurae of South Cholla Province and the Ch'unghyo-dang at Hahoe in Andong are good examples.

(3) Patterns on furniture

Patterns in finishing touches

Human figures and geometric designs appeared on bamboo boxes of Nangnang Period, whereas the lacquerware of the Three Kingdom Period displayed arabesque patterns. By Koryo Period, traditional, distinctive Korean designs were firmly established and showed greater variety of patterns than during the Three Kingdom Period. The designs found on Chosun furniture were similar to those used on white celadon pottery of the 15th and 16th centuries. The honeysuckle and peony patterns popular during those periods continued to serve as dominant design elements in the 17th century, accenting many mother-of-pearled furniture pieces. These patterns underwent transformation during the 18th century, but dominated until the end of the Chosun Dynasty. Plum blossom and bamboo patterns emerged during the 16th century. Plant motifs dominated during the 15th and 16th centuries, but during the 17th and 18th, after the two invasions by Japan in the year of Imjin and by China in the year of Pyongja, other patterns including trees, insects, fish, birds, and the ten longevity symbols began to be incorporated to decorate furniture. By this time, the Confucian doctrine of modesty was in full swing.

174. Photo: A round mother-of-pearl box. The intricately patterned, mother-of-pearl chrysanthemum designs provided one of the most important motifs seen in Korean furniture and accessories.

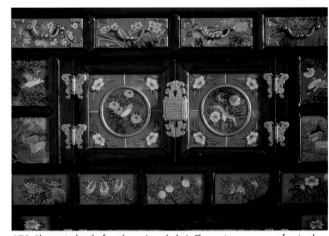

175. Photo: A detail of a *chang* (wardrobe). The various patterns of animals and plants graced women's furniture in *anbang*.

176. Photo: An *uigorijang* (wardrobe with a coat rack) used in a *sarangbang* displayed various Chinese-character patterns.

With the mass production and popularization of crafts, the quality of craftsmanship and design suffered. Meeting the diverse demands of the general public as well as the more discerning population, countless patterns joined the already popular, traditional motifs of plum blossoms, oriental orchids, chrysanthemums, and bamboo. The new designs, to mention only a few, included peonies, honeysuckles, lotus, ten longevity symbols, dragons, *ponghwang*s (imaginary birds), bats, fish, flowers with birds, landscapes, human figures, and various character designs. The most popular were the ten longevity symbols and letter patterns symbolizing wealth, fame, long life, blessing, and good health, and landscapes. One of the genre landscape paintings, dealing with mountain hideaway or cliff motifs admired during the 17th and 18th centuries in China, gave way to stylized landscape designs popular among the general population of Korea in the 19th century.

Mother-of-pearl works (photo 174), along with furniture and accessories featuring *hwagak* method (painting designs on thin veneer of ox-horn) also exhibited the new motifs including pairs of cranes and clouds; the ten longevity symbols; birds and flowers; wild geese; butterflies and bats; peaches and pomegranates; and letter patterns.

Following the Confucian *teaching*s of "attention to the separate functions" of men and women, design motifs used on male and female furnishings differed. The *ponghwang*s (imaginary bird), cranes, clouds, butterflies, fish, bats, peonies, and chrysanthemums graced women's furniture (photo 175), whereas patterns deemed to represent masculine character and ideals decorated men's furnishings. The latter included the four basic motifs (plum blossoms, oriental orchids, chrysanthemums, and bamboo), carp, and various letter patterns (photo 176).

Patterns on metal fixtures

Metal (mostly cast iron, nickel, and tin) fixtures on furniture served utilitarian as well as decorative purposes.

Traditional Korean furniture items were wood, and its natural color, texture, and grain harmonized well with the metal fixtures that came in a variety of shapes and designs, depending on the type and size of furniture to which they were attached. Metal fixtures served to strength the joints and often compensated for the weather-related shrinkage or expansion of furniture. The patterns used on metal fixtures were character-based designs, symbolizing the desire of people for a propitious future. An aesthetic sense was employed in designing these fixtures, so that their proportions and understated decorative elements would enhance the natural beauty of wood.

The Silla period metal fixtures of buildings excavated at the Anapchi pond and the metal fixtures on the wooden coffins and other wooden craft items from Koryo period tombs suggest that metal fixtures came

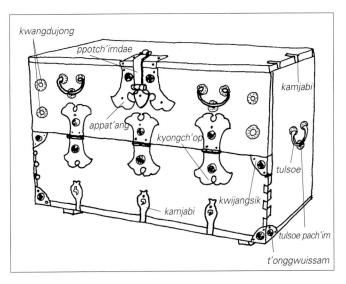

177. illustration and photo: The metal fixtures used on a typical *pandaji* (clothes chest). Metal fixtures served functional as well as decorative purposes on *pandaji*s and included an *appat'ang* (lock plate), *ppotch'imdae* (lock rod), *kyongch'op* (hinges), *tulsoe* (handles), *tulsoe pach'im* (handle plates), *kamjabi*s (corner pieces) and *kwangdujong*s (round, purely decorative pieces) (top). The metal fixtures used on a small wardrobe included *appat'ang, kyongch'op, tulsoe, kwijangsik* and *kamjabi* (bottom).

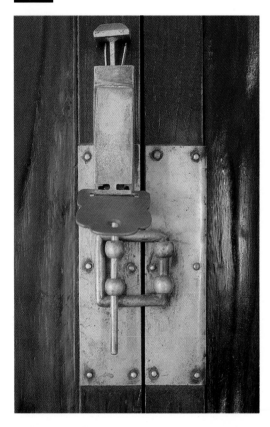

178. Photos: Two different examples of lock plate pattern, Korean square cookie shape (left) and butterfly shape (right). Lock plates came in a variety of patterns because of their highly visible location on the front.

into use after the Iron Age. These artifacts also indicate that the shapes, patterns, and functions used during Koryo period were similar to those of Silla. With the mass production of furniture and household accessories during Chosun, the use of metal fixtures underwent rapid development. During the early Chosun, the patterns for metal fixtures remained rather simple, modest, and utilitarian. Later, more ornate types with regional flavors emerged. Also, as the manufacturing of these goods transferred from government-operated shops to private enterprises, mass production moved into a higher gear, producing countless varieties of metal fixtures to suit the taste of all classes and to furnish entire households.

Metal fixtures fell into two types: functional, including hinges, hooks, loops, and locks; and structural, including splice plates, lock plates, corner and three-corner cover pieces (photo 177).

A great variety of hinges used on doors fulfilled functional as well as decorative roles. Craftsmen paid more attention to decorating exposed hinges, fashioning them into a great number of sizes and shapes. Most popular patterns included circles, squares, and the shapes of calabashes, spools, swallow tails, and butterflies. Enhancing already decorative metal fixtures, engraved designs displayed the *wan* (卍) character pattern (photo 177 top), yin and yang, clouds, swirls, and characters meaning long life and many blessings enhanced already decorative metal fixtures.

Metal handles or hooks were devices by which doors or windows were held open and drawers were pulled out. They were functional, but were often added merely for decoration. The most common shapes used for these handles included *pulloch'o* (the herb of eternal youth), bats, fish, butterflies, bows, a Korean character *tigut* (ㄷ) and *wan* (卍) characters. On top of these, the designs of bats, *wan* (卍) and *a* (亞) characters, and the Eight Trigrams were engraved or filigreed. Sometimes the handles featured handle plates.

Lock plates fastened to the body of a piece of furni-

180. Photo: Metal fixtures used on doors to fulfill the structural enforcement. The bird-claw cover is a kind of *kamjabi* wrapped corners where two pieces of wood met.

179. Photo: Various types of metal fixtures. The lacquered comb box featured in its upper section a cookie-patterned lock plate, an L-shaped *ppotch'imdae* (lock rod) that fit into a turtle-shaped lock, several *t'ongwuissam*s (three-corner cover) and *kamjabi*s (corner cover). The lower section featured a *posanghwamun* patterned lock plate, *kwangdujong*s (purely decorative pieces), *kori* (ring), and swallow-shaped hinges.

ture supported handles and locking devices. Because of their highly visible location on the front and center of a furniture item or accessory piece, lock plates came in a variety of patterns (photo 178). Most popular were the shapes of Korean square cookie shapes, carp, bats, deer, grapes, and *pulloch'o* (the herb of eternal youth), all of which symbolized wealth, fame, longevity, and blessings. The surface of plates often displayed engravings.

A *ppotch'imdae* was a thin, long piece fastened onto the top lid of a chest. The hasp of a padlock passed through a ring held down by the cover plate. These long fixtures generally featured simple line or geometric patterns. Depending on the length of the fixtures, the ends displayed flower and other designs which gave them an additional dimension. A *kwangdujong* (metal cover) covered the front of a chest for decorative as well as functional purposes. Depending on the size

of this metal covering, two-dimensional designs of the moon, squares, cherry blossoms, and oriental orchids accented it. A *kamjabi* (corner cover) wrapped corners where two pieces of wood met (photo 179). Because its appearance was similar to that of a leech, it was called a leech fixture. The size of the cover facing the front often featured shapes of squares, swallow tails, and the herb of eternal youth. The "bird-claw" covers appeared where joints formed (⊥), (ㅓ), (ㅜ) Korean character shapes (photo 180).

A *t'onggwuissam* (three-corner cover piece) served to strength joints where three pieces of wood formed corners (photo 179). In summary, this chapter discusses the characteristics of the traditional Korean use of colors and patterns. Colors served symbolic rather than aesthetic functions. Meanwhile, the natural colors of building and craft materials gave the interior and exterior spaces of traditional Korean houses an appearance of order and peace. Finally, traditional Korean patterns exhibited simplicity, modesty, and order rather than superfluous, ornamental characteristics.

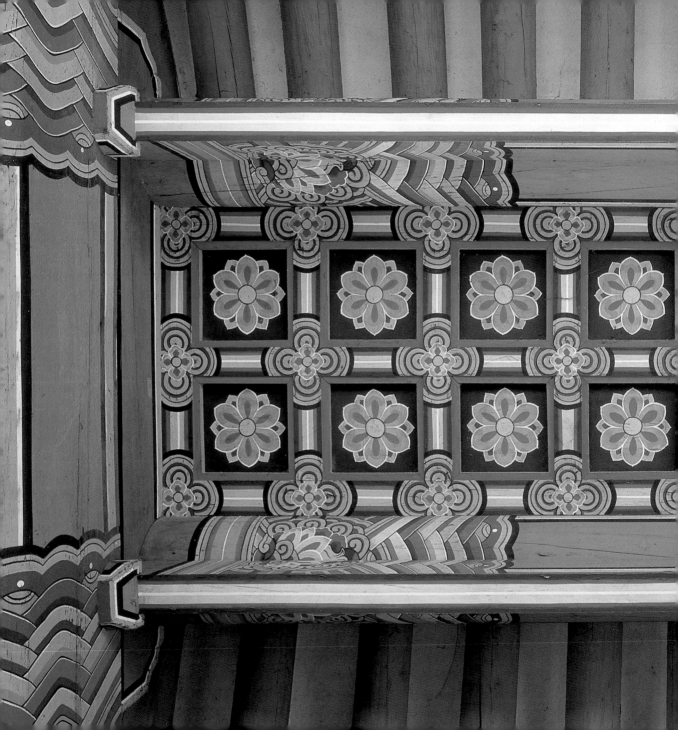

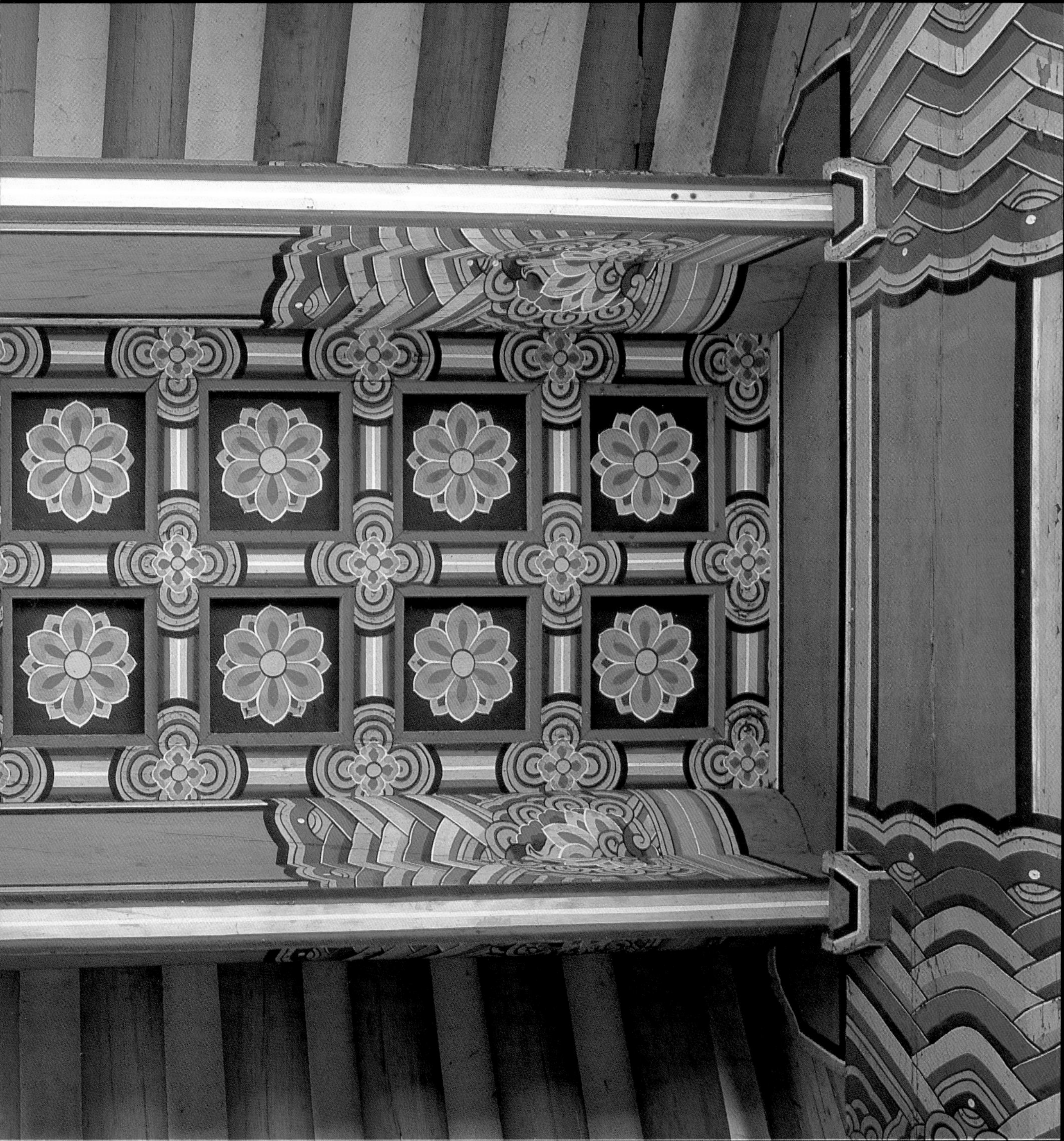

P revious chapters dealt with the natural and cultural forces that influenced the structural development of traditional Korean houses. These chapters examined the long history of the evolution of housing through the study of numerous examples. This chapter presents an overview of the Korean concepts of and interactions with interior spaces and examines the aesthetic characteristics Koreans imbued in them.

1. The concept of space in traditional houses

One often hears the comment that Korean sense of aesthetics is synonymous with the pursuit of the beauty in nature. This fundamental attitude remained constant throughout the periods of changes brought about by waves of ideological influences that swept through Korea at various points of her history.

Some of the shifts in aesthetic sensibilities that occurred can be seen in the general characteristics exhibited by the societies of the Three Kingdoms Period, the United Silla, Koryo, and Chosun. For example, the arts and crafts of the Three Kingdoms Period, are distinctive in their emphasis on the overall completeness over excessive details, warmth of subjectivity over the coolness of objectivity, and the striving for the natural and realistic over the surreal and abstract.

The artifacts of the Unified Silla Period display spirited rhythms and a mature sense of the aesthetic striving for the type of refinement that was embedded

with dignity and restraint. Koryo Period likewise exhibited highly creative spirit of warmth. However, influenced by Confucianism during the Chosun Period, the Korean focus shifted to a more severely restrictive stress on simplicity and modesty.

Despite these fluctuations, the basic concept of pursuing harmony with nature persisted. Koreans shied away from creating objects of superfluous brilliance, embraced the simplicity and grace reflected in nature, discovered order among the commonplace, and reached for the quiet and the soft, all of which sometimes looked almost stark and childish. The overall emotion evoked was a feeling of comfortable familiarity.

Therefore, scholars of Korea and her art often conclude that Korean aesthetics spring from understatements that capture non-artificial beauty and the order that reflects nature before being altered by man. Subdued colors and color schemes, the organic integration of simple and clean lines, resistance to artificiality, the elegance that is characteristic of nature untouched by man, and the quiet humor seen in Korean art all support such a view. To reiterate, Korean art exhibits artistry achieved through harnessed creativity, schemes that appear to lack schemes, and attentiveness that seems to lack attention. This distinctively Korean aesthetic applies to all areas of art: paintings, crafts, architecture, and interior designs.

Thus, in the design, arrangement, and decoration of interior spaces in traditional Korean houses, one can observe such predominant artistic principles at work. A discussion of these principles follows. For the sake of discussion they have been categorized simply here into modesty, inclusivity, non-artificiality, and contemplativeness.

1 Modesty

This characteristic signifies the act of moving away from creating art that draws excessive attention to itself and pulling beauty out of the depths to move observers. Naturally, the overly expressive has no place in this art form. Rather, what appears to be common place but speaks from a depth and truth receives attention. This concept originated from the Buddhist philosophy of nothingness; and, more closely, from Confucian ethic of viewing human desires and instincts as unworthy while observing the practice of the happy golden mean. Striving for the flawlessly finished or outstandingly refined appearance, let alone going for the over-sized or loudly decorative, went against this principle.

Reflecting these characteristics, the interior spaces of traditional Korean houses showed manageable rather than overpowering scales. Such modest sizes, even of larger structures, generated a feeling of security and comfort. As for the exterior appearances of residences, they rarely exhibited structural lines and shapes that conflicted with those found in the surround-

ing landscape. Such design principle clearly speaks of the Koreans' choice: submissiveness to nature.

This tendency toward modesty materialized more prominently in the houses of common class people. Compared to the residences of the literati class, the living spaces in the houses of the general public were smaller and fewer. Thatch-roof houses in particular were of modest size, structure, and materials. Even the residences of the nobility, which were grander and more elaborately structured, still retained a degree of orderliness and reasonableness, resulting from maintaining restraint in the choice of structural style and furnishings.

Take, for example, the Yongyong-dang at Ch'angdok Palace, which was the residence of a prominent member of the literati. It consisted of an *anbang*, *andaech'ong*, *konnobang*, and *numaru*; and its *anbang* and *konnobang* were each 245cm × 489cm with the ceiling height of 214cm. Compared to the estates of nobility of comparable status in the Western world, the Korean counterparts were of a modest scale (photo 181).

181. Photo: An individual room in a traditional house. The height and size of a room were in a comfortable proportion to the stature of the average Korean. Rooms were generally decorated in simple and graceful taste.

2 Inclusiveness

This characteristic refers to the act of embracing what is found in nature, even imperfections, as acceptable or even valuable. Building houses with such an attitude meant that materials obtained from nature found acceptance for what they were—without much alteration from man. Even changes made to the materials that occurred during the process of crafting were considered a part of nature. This aesthetic tolerance made it possible for nature's natural state and its spontane-ity to continue to exist in crafted objects. Thus, in Korean arts and crafts, characteristics such as accurately measured repetitions, perfectly symmetrical formations, or technically immaculate geometrical schemes were rarely found. Koreans went further and even incorporated a certain amount of imperfections or asymmetry in the creative process in order to retain the type of spontaneity found in nature. This spirit of inclusiveness concerning imperfections and flaws carried over into the area of the designing and decorating of interior spaces.

183. Photo: The harmony between nature and the man-made world. Utilizing materials found in nature, Koreans strove for a complementary relationship between the lines created by nature and those produced by man.

3 Non-artificiality

182. Photo: Exposed wood rafters of a ceiling. The curved lines of rafters were left uncorrected, showing the Koreans' respect for the natural.

For example, when selecting timber for rafters or support pillars, slightly curved pieces of wood were not discarded. Korean pine was particularly curvy and knotty, but Koreans welcomed such peculiarities as natural and included them in their building schemes. The end result was that such natural shapes and lines contributed to the creation of an overall warmth and a spontaneous appearance (photo 182). The *maru* area particularly exemplified this aesthetic sense; here its various naturally-shaped lines found on exposed beams, posts and pillars remained unaltered. Curved lines were allowed to stay not because Koreans lacked the tools with which to trim them into straight shapes, but because they desired to live in harmony with and submission to nature. As discussed earlier, such spirit of acceptance germinated from the religious influences of Confucianism, Buddhism, and Taoism. Through such submissiveness and despite the appearance of being dominated by nature, Korean art gained mastery, perfection, and richness (photo 183).

Traditionally, Korean art resisted excessive processing of natural objects by man. Recognizing the innate characteristics of materials as natural--therefore, good and acceptable-and viewing detailed or precise renderings as artificial, Koreans applied only minimal shaping or decorating. Rather than attention to details, Koreans placed emphasis on the overall effect and balance. This emphasis sometimes led to art works that appeared simplistic or rough, but they evoked a sense of familiarity and ease.

This concept, as discussed earlier, also had its origin in nature worship. Based on such a belief, external ornamentation received minimal attention, so that the observer's focus would be directed to the essence of the art work and not its superficial exterior or details. Thus, Korean art work can be better appreciated when studied from a distance, as such a perspective affords a look at the piece as a whole rather than as a sum of brilliantly decorated and detailed parts. Also, as with the modesty and inclusiveness already discussed, this non-artificiality carried over into the area of the design of interior spaces in traditional Korean houses and molded its characteristic elegance.

Nowhere on the walls, floors, ceilings, or other surfaces in Korean houses would one find ornateness and artificiality, either in structure, arrangement, or decorations. Only natural beauty shining from under-altered materials formed an atmosphere that, while not instantly captured the fancy of an observer, offered a feeling of ease and warmth.

For example, the walls of *pang*s (individual rooms) were generally finished with plain white rice paper. So were the floors — with plain, oiled paper covering. White plaster covered the walls of the *maru* while its floor was of unpainted wood showing natural grains. The decorations consisted of metal fixtures on furniture and accessories, paintings, folding screens, and embroidered cushions.

Even these objects could not be deemed overly decorative or artificial, as they made modest uses of colors and patterns only enough to enliven an otherwise subdued environment, maintaining the characteristic elegance which stemmed from taking inspiration from nature (photo 184).

4 Contemplativeness

This characteristic refers to the act of striving for the expression of the innate beauty in objects rather than reaching for a superficial aesthetic. Korean traditional art explored the deeper, more mature level of beauty as compared to beautifying the exterior of art objects.

Buddhism, more than any other influence, gave rise to this aesthetic philosophy. In Buddhist thinking, the present does not exist.

Meaning can be found only to the extent that the present life helps advance a person's life goal—attaining perfection—to be reached in the afterlife. This premise causes individuals to accept life as it is and to meditate on it. An aesthetic principle based on such a view of life, therefore, leads the artist to look beyond the glitter of colors and ornamentation and strive for the beauty that may appear to be bland, but attracts the observer in a quiet way and can be discovered only by those with a searching heart.

Carrying these four distinct attitudes into interior design, Koreans chose to leave large portions of their interior spaces unadorned. The spaces unoccu-

184. Photo: The spatial arrangement of a *taech'ong*. Because Koreans strove for understated aesthetics, more spaces were left empty, or only minimally adorned, than filled or decorated in traditional Korean houses. The floors, walls, posts, and doors all received minimal amount of decoration, producing a modest and contemplative atmosphere.

pied by furniture or paintings caused the interiors to look a bit stark; at the same time, however, they generated a sense of spaciousness, solitude, and peacefulness. One may say that much of the floor space had to remain empty because Koreans sat on the floor and their furniture pieces were small in size, compared to those used by Westerners.

However, the fact that even those rich enough to afford more massively scaled furniture pieces contented themselves with standard furnishings indicated that the Confucian ethic of maintaining modesty and the golden mean influenced such a choice.

Also at work was the meditative and humble character Koreans were taught to develop by Buddhist teachings on mercy and wisdom and Taoist philosophy on achieving a long life, all of which emphasized the importance of transcending the traps of the present world. On the basis of these philosophical views, Koreans generally obtained only very essential pieces of furnishings.

Thus, the modest appearance of the interior spaces of traditional Korean houses provides a contrast to those of the Western culture, those of China—which exhibit a very active use of colors, and those of Japan--which show a highly developed sense of decoration (photo 184).

2. Aesthetic characteristics of interior spaces

This section discusses the overall design characteristics found on surfaces such as floors, walls, ceilings, windows and doors, presenting correlations between their spaces, forms, textures, colors, and the aesthetic principles discussed above.

1 Spaces

(1) The balance between the closed and open spaces

Except for the one-room shelters that existed in ancient times, most residences of later periods consisted of several divided living spaces. The layout of these rooms varied from one period to another and from region to region. Comparing Western-style housing structurally with that of Korea, the former generally exhibits an unmistakable division between the interior and outside world. Even within the interior space, the Western-style homes feature more solid divisions between rooms that provide higher levels of privacy than do traditional Korean homes. The Korean counterparts erected walls to separate the outside from inside, but distinctions between rooms were not always clear.

When building a house, builders first constructed walls around the perimeter of the site. As part of the wall structure, rows of rooms to serve as servants' quarters were built — generally, one wing on each side of the front gate. Within this walled compound, another set of low walls, which included the middle servants' quarters, divided the *anch'ae* from the *sarangch'ae*, the *sarangch'ae* from an annex, and so forth.

To an onlooker, the imposing front gate and the high walls around a residence could give an impression that the traditional Korean house was a solidly closed space. However, within the walled area, divisions between rooms were flimsy as most walls featured rice-papered windows and doors and much of the time these windows and doors remained open. Particularly in the summer, doors were raised upward and fastened to hooks, allowing free traffic between rooms and affording hardly any level of privacy (photo 185). In other words, the living spaces of Korean homes were extremely open.

The *taech'ong* was an especially wide open area. It even came with a back door, which stayed open in warm weather to allow cross breezes. Therefore, a person sitting in the *taech'ong* could command a view of the outside beyond the courtyard and front gate, as well as that of the back courtyard and perhaps even a

hill beyond. The doors on either side of the *taech'ong* leading to the *anbang* and *konnobang* were pulled upward and anchored with loops, allowing the three areas to serve as one very large space.

To create more private areas, double doors or windows were installed inside another set of windows or doors. Over these, a *pangjang*, a kind of a fabric shade, was draped. After this, if needed, folding screens were arranged for additional privacy.

185. Photo: The courtyard seen from a *taech'ong*. Once doors and windows were lifted up for the summer, the *taech'ong* became a wide open area looking out at a spacious courtyard.

(2) Lineally interrelated spaces

Korean houses featured a layout of rooms that allowed a high degree of movement from one room to another. Even though such structurally fixed divisions as walls, ceilings, floors, and windows remained constant, the use of removable room dividers and doors allowed various areas to be accessible to different members of the family, as well as visitors at numerous times throughout the day. The *anbang, taech'ong,* and other rooms could remain as individual areas or combine in a variety of ways to accommodate every household activity. No room served only one purpose, such as sleeping or eating. The same area used as a living room also served as the dining room at meal times and turned into a bedroom at night. Such a multi-purpose arrangement made it possible for residents to move about — from a less bright place to a sunnier spot, from a closed space to an open one, from a small to a larger area, from a higher to a lower place — and thereby experience variety and achieve productivity.

Stepped into the imposing, tall front gate, one entered a small, rather dark entryway flanked by servants' quarters on either side. The next step led the visitor into the wide, open, bright courtyard of the servants' quarters. One then faced another door—the middle gate-which featured another set of servants' quarters similar to those built on either side of the front gate. The middle gate opened to another small and dark entryway connected to the large, sunny courtyard of the women's or men's quarters. One walked across the courtyard to alight a few steps and reached the central space, *andaech'ong,* or *sarang-daech'ong.* When the back door of the *taech'ong* was open, one could enjoy the view of a large and sun-drenched back courtyard while the *taech'ong* was

186. A series of connected spaces. Rooms opened up, particularly during summer months, leaving viewers with a sense of openness and interrelatedness.

an open space with a high ceiling, the individual rooms on either side of the *taech'ong* were enclosed, cozy space with low ceilings (photo 186).

(3) Spaces with a strong visual axis

A space formed by four walls creates in the center an axis. The axis can be vertical or horizontal. In the case of a rectangular-shaped space, the axis appears along the long horizontal line. Windows or doors placed on either side of this axis will visually connect the interior with the exterior and heighten the observer's consciousness of the exterior world. When posts, beams, or a type of an opening form a repetitive pattern along a visual axis, the pivotal focus becomes even stronger and provides the room with a strong sense of direction.

The *taech'ong* was a connective space located between two enclosed rooms, and it served as a central space where important ceremonies, such as *chesa*

187. Photo: The view of a back yard seen from a *taech'ong*. When the small back door of a *taech'ong* was opened, a strong visual axis or continuum formed, with the front door as the starting point, moving through the front courtyard and *taech'ong*, and finally leading all the way out to the back courtyard.

(memorial services) and other major events, occurred. Also, as a space where the axis intersected, it also held a symbolic significance as the command post of the household and as a reception area.

The entire front side of the *taech'ong* opened to the courtyard, commanding a sweeping view of the outside. A small door located to the back and about the size and shape of a picture frame formed a powerful antithetical visual line in relation to the open front side (photos 185, 186 and 187).

2 Forms

Aesthetically, form refers to the shape created by dots, lines, surfaces, or three dimensions. The dot form signifies a point of visual strength that relates to the surrounding area in a relationship of contrast or antithesis. Because traditional Korean interior spaces were designed to reflect inclusiveness and natural beauty, dot forms that monopolized the observer's visual attention rarely appeared. Therefore, the following discussion will focus on the forms of lines and planes.

(1) Lines

In design terminology, line refers to linear or contoured form defined by thin borders. Window frames, for example, constitute lines. Posts or pillars also are treated as lines, even though they may be of significant volume. Typical of linear elements found in interior spaces are vertical, horizontal, oblique, or curved lines, and those that attract the strongest focus determine the character of each sphere.

A space dominated by a vertical linear elements produces an atmosphere of dignity and solemnity, while one accented by horizontal lines evokes a sense of calm and peace. An area characterized by oblique lines tends to suggest instability and imbalance; on the other hand, change and movement in such a space can provide a stimulating sense of liveliness and anticipation. Curved lines imbue the sensation of comfort, softness, mystery, and elusive beauty.

The *pang*s (individual rooms) consist mainly of plane elements—floors, walls, and ceilings—while the *taech'ong* contains both plane and linear elements. However, because of the strong visual components formed by the exposed dark wood pillars and beams contrasting sharply with white plastered walls, students of traditional Korean houses generally view the *taech'ong* as a line-dominant space.

To take a closer look at this linearly stimulating sphere, one must sit in the middle of the *taech'ong* facing the front courtyard. The pillars on either side of the structure come into view first. They stand in a wide open area, unobstructed by such devices as windows or doors.

Then come the horizontal and oblique lines of beams, cross beams, and rafters, all of dark wood protruding from a white plaster background (photo 188). The eye then moves to the doors on either side of the *taech'ong*. Their artfully crafted, delicate lattice work—honeycombs of linear elements—loom as a sur-

prise, providing a visually stunning and satisfying experience (photo 71).

Thus, the *taech'ong* serves as a splendid display case for a plethora of lines ranging from massive pillars to pencil-thin lattices, all displaying an atmosphere of dignity and solemnity created by the vertical lines. The sense of stability emanates from the horizontal beams, while a lively atmosphere of change and movement springs from the oblique lines of the rafters (photo 72).

In addition, the well-shaped, square, smooth forms of the posts, beams, and cross beams contrasting with the rafters—left natural with knobs and curved lines—and the finely crafted thin lattices of the doors and windows provide an additional dimension to the

188. Photo: The linear elements seen on the ceiling of a *taech'ong*. The horizontal lines of *toris* and *pos*, the vertical lines of the posts, and the diagonal lines of the rafters provided a lively interplay of contrasting linear elements.

aesthetically stimulating whole.

The reason that the *taech'ong* does not evoke the impression of a cluttered, complex area (despite the various directions taken by a number of lines) but rather generates a sense of simplicity and order lies in the fact that the lines retain a naturalness instead of appearing artificial because of excessive "correcting" or shaping. For example, for the rafters builders used logs with hardly any finishing treatment and never sawed them into straighter shapes. The beams and cross beams received more attention, but still these retained certain curves, although the corners were shaved slightly for a rounder appearance. Window and door frames were treated with more refining, their corners generally being rounded for a natural look. In short, all this detail work, or the lack of it, contributed to the creation of the simple, gentle, dignified, and natural appearing whole.

As seen so far, simple lines of varying thicknesses and lengths worked together in traditional houses to harmonize spaces that combined lively rhythms with subtlety and a vigorous, near-empty appearance, revealing an elusive beauty appreciated by seekers of such an aesthetic.

(2) Planes

Planes refer to exterior surfaces, including walls, floors, ceilings, doors and windows. The planes found in the interior spaces of traditional Korean houses are generally rectangles.

The areas where planes dominate as design elements are individual rooms like the *anbang, sarangbang,* and *konnobang.* This occurs because in those spaces the linear elements like posts, beams, and cross beams were covered with wallpaper. Even the windows and their lattice work were covered on the interi-

or side with rice paper. Thus, even though the sunlight filtered through, from the inside the lattice work was seen only dimly, with the effect that the window surface looked like a plane.

A drop ceiling also formed a plane as it was generally finished with a layer of paper. Also, the floor represented a plane since it was finished with a thick layer of oiled paper; although, because of the overlapping of the paper strips, certain subtle patterns formed of linear repetitions emerged.

While the ceiling and floor provided planes lacking in decorations, the walls that featured windows or the doors of a *pyokchang* (cabinet recessed into a wall) produced linear design elements. This was particularly the case if the natural wood of the window frame remained exposed. However, often the doors of the *pyokjang* or the attic doors were covered with paper in order that their planes might blend better with the surrounding wall surfaces. In this case, the windows or doors did not provide any significant linear divisions to the walls (photo 76).

In short, the surfaces of the interior spaces of rooms were rather plain. However, there were several elements that imbued vitality into such scenes--furniture, lattice work on windows and doors, and asymmetrically arranged linear elements. A look at each element follows.

Furniture pieces of varying heights and sizes were arranged to maximize visual interest and their variety provided otherwise drab wall surfaces with welcome change. The lattice work on windows and doors also offered interesting diversion. Even though the lattices remained exposed only on the exterior and their linear patterns remained subtle when seen from the inside, once strong sunlight hit the rice-papered windows and doors, lattices emerged as visually stir-

189. Photo: Walls showing various linear dimensions. The vertical posts and horizontal lintels divided the wall surfaces into rectangles of different sizes, creating an aesthetically satisfying harmony born out of variety.

ring and stimulating elements. The asymmetrical juxtaposition of the vertical attic door next to the horizontal door frame of the *pyokchang* also played an important role in adding vibrancy.

Although the *taech'ong* serves as more of a line-dominated space, it contained plane-rich elements as well. Its floors and walls exhibited various planes with walls especially divided into many white plastered planes framed by vertical posts and horizontal

cross beams. The arrangement of the planes in the *taech'ong* was typically asymmetrical, which added aesthetic vigor to the entire scene. Not much study has been done on the exact proportions of the various planes; however, the outcome generated by the diverse geometrical shapes of the planes resulted in the creation of an extremely appealing, elegant atmosphere (photo 189).

3 Texture and color

Texture and color are closely related as they are both innate properties of material objects. Texture refers to the sensation one gets when touching a surface, or how the surface appears in relation to the amount of light reflecting off it. Also, depending on the amount of smoothing and polishing applied, the texture can be shiny or dull, or smooth or rough. Such variations add much to the creation of ambiance in a space. Color is just as important in determining atmosphere.

As discussed in earlier chapters, materials used to furnish the traditional Korean interiors came from nature and were used without much artificial processing. Woods and color pigments serve as examples. Occasionally, some processing was applied to natural material, as in the case of paper. But overall, in their creative endeavors Koreans took care to preserve and utilize the natural textures of materials.

As for the colors used in individual rooms, wood and wood products were used without applying colors. However, if any color was applied, very subtle and neutral tones were chosen, creating an overall appearance of elegance (photo 155).

The use of textures and colors in the *taech'ong*, on the other hand, contrasted somewhat with those used on individual rooms. The *taech'ong* featured stark contrasts between the textures and colors of the natural wood of the posts, beams, and rafters—with their grain, knobs, and cracks all exposed—and the smooth, white plaster walls or ceilings.

The plaster walls also contrasted with the well-patterned dark wood floor. In other words, unlike individual rooms, the *taech'ong* served as a piece of art work that demonstrated bold visual contrasts which imbued a sense of vitality.

What has been discussed in this work deals with the two cultures of the Chosun period: the lower classes — the culture of simplicity; and that of the upper class (the literati) — the tradition of elegance. At first glance, they might appear to be distinctly different, but a closer examination reveals similarities. Because of the influence of Confucianism, even the members of the economically well-off literati class, who could afford more luxurious residences and furnishings, on the whole exercised self-restraint and strove to minimize conspicuous consumption. They limited, for example, the *sarangbang* furnishings to only those required for scholarly pursuits and a few items used for leisure activities, such as musical instruments, tea sets, and incense burners.

As for the commonalities between the classes, the desire to live in harmony with nature and the intention to live modestly according to Buddhist and Confucian teachings could be found in both the upper and lower classes.

This is exemplified in Korean architectural designs, furnishings and decorations. The Korean aesthetic and philosophical views practiced with so much zeal by the Chosun people and their more remote ancestors offer a challenge to modern day Koreans. Perhaps some of these ideals should be emulated and passed on to posterity.

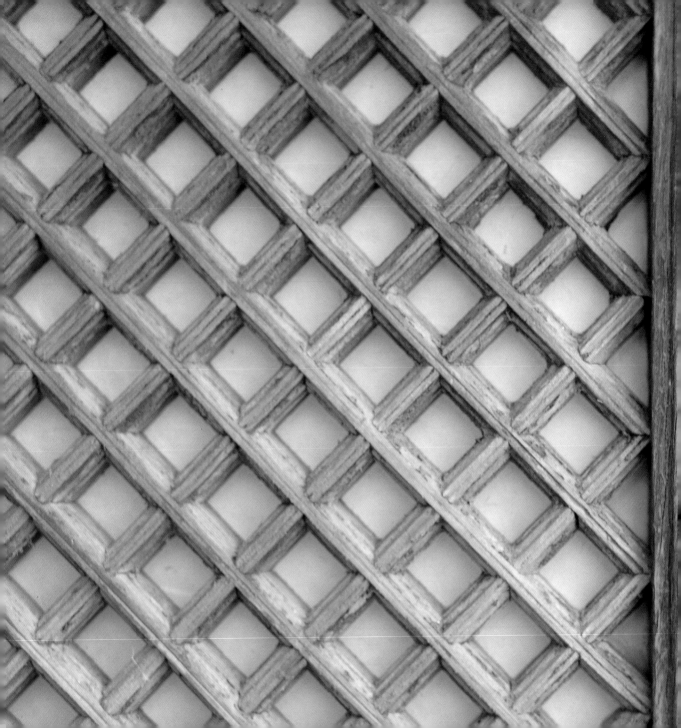

G·l·o·s·s·a·r·y

ank'ori, pakk'ori, mok'ori (안커리, 밖커리, 모커리)
Words used on Cheju Island for inner, outer, and corner quarters. These areas were self-contained compounds complete with separate kitchens. This arrangement developed as the result of the unique "independence" type inheritance system practiced on this island.

ansarangch'ae (안사랑채)
An annex near the *anch'ae*, used by retired grandparents or, on their visits home, married daughters.

aranmok (아랫목)
The warmest spot of a room, closest to the fireplace.

ch'aekchang (책장)
An enclosed double- or tri-level bookcase. Because the storing of books was the primary function of this piece, cabinetmakers kept compartmentalized spaces to a minimum and placed a window separate door on each level.

ch'ang (창)
A window. As its structure was similar to that of a door, and the Korean words for a window and door were often interchangeable. Generally, however, if an opening sits on above a window sill, it was considered a window.

ch'angbang (창방)
Wood eave pieces that supported decorative blocks like *p'yongbang*s, *hwaban*s, and *soro*s.

ch'anggan (찬간)
A waist-high wood- or *ondol*-floored food preparation area set up next to a kitchen, where chinaware and prepared foods were stored.

changgwitul (장귀틀)
Long floor framing beams. These were joined with shorter framing beams, and filler boards to create a wood floor.

ch'anghoji (창호지)
A rice paper covering for windows and doors.

changjimun (장지문)
A sliding door installed between two rooms.

changmaru (장마루)
A *maru*, built with long and narrow wooden strip boards. This floor was laid on second story *maru*s or verandas.

changyo (장여)
Long, narrow beams fitted on top of another set of beams called *ch'angbang* and under the *tori* cross beams. The *changyo*s increased the durability of the beams and strengthened joints.

ch'anhap (찬합)
Picnic boxes.

ch'anjang (찬장)
Double- or triple-level cupboard, built with sturdy lumber to accommodate the storage of a large number of heavy items, such as brass, chinaware, and prepared foods.

ch'ant'ak (찬탁)
Shelves structured like book shelves, used in kitchens to store food and dishes.

Glossary

chich'on (지천)   A modest finishing material covered with a layer of paper over a sheeting of woven arrow-root vine.

ch'imbang (침방)   Bedrooms.

ch'obaeji (초배지)   The first coarsely-textured layer of wallpaper applied with a very thick glue.

ch'ok (척)   A *cha*, or a unit of measurement equalling 30 cm.

chokcha (족자)   Scroll paintings.

chongbo (종보)   High cross beams set on top of two short support posts called *tongjagidung*s.

chongch'im (정침)   A space reserved for ancestor worship ceremonies in the main quarters. Later, the name changed to *chongbang*s, and during the latter part of the Chosun period, this space moved into the *anch'ae*.

chongdori (종도리)   The highest beam (running the length of the house from side to side) mounted on top of *chongbo*s (highest cross beams running the length of the house from front to back) via support posts called *marudaegong*s. The *chongdori*s were also called *marudori* or *marudae*.

chong'ibanja (종이반자)   A drop ceiling finished with three layers of rice paper.

ch'ongp'an (청판)   Various wood boards used in building and cabinet making.

chudori (주도리)   Cross beams that fitted across two pillars.

chukpuin (죽부인)   A piece of *sarangbang* furnishing, this "bamboo wife" was made with twelve long bamboo strips woven loosely in the shape of a woman. The inside was hollow, allowing ventilation. Bamboo wives kept men cool in summer time as they slept hugging them.

chungdori (중도리)   Mid-level ceiling cross beams.

churyon (주련)   A wooden plaque with poems or flower designs carved into it.

chwadung (좌등)   A square or hexagonal interior lighting device in which a candle or a lamp was set.

chwagyong and pitchop (좌경, 빗접)   A *chwagyong* (mirrored vanity) which evolved from a *pitchop* (comb box) after mirrors were developed.

chwibyokkan (쥐벽간)   The spaces created by horizonal posts of architecture or furniture.

Haejuban (해주반)   A portable table produced in Haeju of Hwanghae Province. Its top was made of thick solid woods featuring a *p'angak* (wood engraving) on each side.

ham (함)   A wood chest which is not equipped with hinges in the top lid. Its entire top opened.

hamasok (하마석)   A stone step that aided a man when dismounting a horse.

hamnong (함농)   Two chests stacked together.

hamsil (함실)   A flue built without a cook-top counter.

hanoak (한옥)   Traditional Korean house.

hapgak (합각)	Triangular side sections of a roof. The interior ceiling sides of these sections were finished in the same manner as the walls.
hojokpan (호족반)	A tiger-legged portable table.
honham (헌함)	The railing installed around a small side *maru* and extending outside the main *maru* pillars.
hotchip (홑집)	A single-row house (rooms laid out in a single row).
hot'ungorae (허튼고래)	A bottom flue stone without grooves and supported by stones on four corners.
hwach'ang (화창)	A window installed high up on a kitchen wall for light and ventilation.
hwagongch'ogong (화공초공)	A way of decorating pillars by topping them with ornately carved head pieces.
ichungjang (이층장)	A double-level wardrobe typically found in the *anbang*.
ichungnong (이층농)	A simply structured wardrobe-like double chest with no corner posts, cover board, or decoratively-pieced front.
ilgakmun (일각문)	A one-*kan*-wide gate built between two posts.
kabujangje (가부장제)	An extended family system with the eldest male as the nucleus.
kaejari (개자리)	Under an *ondol* floor, a dip located toward the back end of the flue and at the bottom of the chimney. Ashes collected in this dip, and smoke rested here briefly before flowing out the chimney.
kakkesuri (각계수리)	A safe equipped with many drawers and a set of sliding doors.
kam, kamsil (감, 감실)	A display case for ancestral tablets.
kamyoje (가묘제)	The institution of ancestor worship, whereby each household was required by the government to maintain a space to perform ceremonies.
k'an (kan, gan, 칸)	A unit of measurement, referring to the size of a square space created by four pillars set roughly at a distance of one-*kan* (about seven to eight feet).
keja nangan (계자난간)	A railing featuring hens.
kilsangmun (길상문)	Designs patterned after Chinese characters signifying long life, many blessings, and health.
kobi (고비)	A word referring to deceased parents and used in written communication. Or a wooden mail holder on the wall or post.
koe (궤)	Wooden chests. The *wuittaji* style opened to the top; the *apttaji* style opened to the front.
koesang (궤상)	An armrest or pillow for the arm.
koju (고주)	An extra-tall pillar.
koju oryang (고주오량)	A house with an additional, extra-tall pillar and an extra-high exposed-rafter style ceiling. The extra pillar enabled an addition of a small, wood-floored side *manu*.

kolp'anmun (골판문) A wooden board door, used as a double door or as the door of a storage room.

komagidol Maru (고막이돌 마루) crawl space over stones.

k'ongdam (콩댐) An oily substance made by mixing ground beams and wild sesame seed oil, applied to flooring paper to give it water resistance and a smooth, shiny, and corn-colored appearance.

konggosang (공고상) A portable table with a twelve-sided table top and eight- or twelve-sided legs.

kongnangan (곡난간) A railing with posts whose top parts were curved and extended outward, or a railing with an end section that curved from the top end post down to the bottom board.

korae (고래) The pathway through which heat and smoke traveled from the ondol fireplace toward the chimney.

kosat (고살) A narrow alley way leading up to the front gate of a traditional Korean house.

kujokpan (구족반) A table with legs shaped like those of dogs.

kuldori (굴도리) Round pillars used on upper class residences or palaces.

kupt'ong (굽통) The vertical, weight-bearing portion of the leg of a furniture piece.

kwit'ul (귀틀) Beams used to build the frame for the *maru* (a wood floor). The shorter beams were called *tonggwit'uls* and the longer ones *changgwit'uls*.

kyoch'ang (교창) A wide, horizontal window placed high on the wall of a kitchen or a storage room, or above paneled, latticed doors or windows.

kyopchip (겹집) A double-row house (rooms lined up in double rows).

kyoran (교란) A railing featuring latticework between posts. Typical lattice designs included patterns of the Chinese characters *a* (亞) and *wan* (卍), and a *pissal* (hatch) design.

kyunbun sangsokche (균분상속제) An inheritance system which left an equal share to all children.

mangjangji (맹장지) A window or door covered with several layers of rice paper, both on the interior and exterior sides. This treatment was used to reduce the amount of sunlight penetrating an interior space.

mangnabinulmaru (막나비널마루) A wood floor laid with boards of irregular widths.

maru (마루) A wood-floor laid with thin flooring boards.

maruch'ong (마루청) A room with a wood floor, sometimes called *marubang*.

marudaegong (마룻대공) King posts supporting the highest cross beam.

marutul (마루틀) The framework into which boards were fitted, sometimes called a *marugwitul*.

midaji (미닫이) A sliding window or door.

minga (민가) The houses of the general populace, as compared to official structures, such as temples and palaces. A narrower definition referred to the houses of non-literati class.

Glossary

misegi (미세기)   A single-paneled sliding window or door.

momch'e (몸체)   The main portion of furniture.

moritpang (머릿방)   The upper (or back) room of a two-room *anbang*.

morumch'ongp'an (머름청판)   Boards that filled the space between the middle and bottom beams.

morumdongja (머름동자)   Short posts fitted between the middle *morum* beam and *morumdae*s.

morumgan (머름간)   The spaces between short wainscot posts *morumdae*. The bottom lintel installed below a sill.

mulhwak (물확)   A stone water fountain.

mun (문)   A door.

mungap (문갑)   A writing supply box, sometimes used in pairs.

mun'olgul (문얼굴)   An opening between the posts and beams where a window or door was fitted.

munp'ungji (문풍지)   Strips of rice paper glued along cracks of a window or door; served to reduce drafts as well as facilitate air circulation.

nangan (난간)   Safety railings, often with decorative lattices, installed around verandas, ledges, staircases, and galleries.

naptori (납도리)   Square pillars used mainly on the houses of those classes who did not hold government titles.

nudarak (누다락)   An attic constructed above a room with a fireplace.

numaru (누마루)   A wood-floored veranda with a railing, built off the *konnobang* (the room occupied by the wife of the eldest son, across the *taech'ong* from the *anbang*) or *sarangbang*.

nunghwaji (능화지)   Paper patterned with diamond shapes, made by laying paper on a wooden board carved with the diamond shapes and rubbing the paper.

nun'gopchaegi ch'ang (눈곱재기창)   A tiny window installed next to a door for the purpose of peeping out.

nunsop ch'onjang (눈썹천장)   A small area of the ceiling specially constructed to cover the triangular shaped area at either end of a roof, where the central roof line and eaves met.

nuran (누란)   A railing installed around a veranda or an attic above a room with a fireplace.

ondol (온돌)   A hypocaust heating system. Heat from the fireplace flows through a flue and heats a room by warming the stones that form a sub-floor.

oryangjip (오량집)   A house with a ceiling built with five *tori* cross beams.

pach'imjangyo (받침장여)   A strip of wood supporting a *tori* (a cross beam running the length of a house from side to side).

Pakch'on pandaji (박천 반닫이) — A chest named after the Pakch'on area of the P'yongan Province where it was produced. Sometimes called *sungsung'i pandaji* for its cast-iron decorations featuring very roughly filigreed (punched hole) patterns.

p'alchakchibung (팔작지붕) — A roof with triangular shaped sides.

p'alkoe (팔괘) — Eight Trigrams devised by a man named Pok Hi of ancient China. These trigrams symbolized various elemental phenomena occurring in the universe. For example, in the trigram, heaven is represented by the sign "–" and the earth by "– –."

panbikkan (반빗간) — A detached storage and food preparation space, constructed separately from the kitchen. Kitchen utensils were stored here.

panch'inyong (반친영) — A marriage arrangement whereby the couple held their wedding ceremony at the bride's home and lived there until the end of the month or year before moving to live permanently with the groom's family.

pandaji (반닫이) — A chest whose front panel was divided into two sections. The upper part opened. Sometimes called *aptaji* (a front-opening chest).

panghwajang (방화장) — A method of erecting stone or brick facades half way up the exterior side of a wall for fire prevention.

pangjang (방장) — A fabric screen set up against the interior side of a door for heat preservation.

panja (반자) — A drop ceiling.

panjach'onjang (반자천장) — The finishing treatment for drop ceilings. Among various styles, including the plain board, "well-shaped" board, and paper, the last one was the most commonly used.

p'anjangmun (판장문) — Wooden board doors used on kitchens and storage rooms or as double doors.

panjikkurut (반짇그릇) — A sewing box containing needles, threads, thimbles, scissors, and fabric pieces.

pitpanja (빗반자) — A ceiling, or portion of it, finished at a slant.

po (보) — Cross ceiling beams running the length of a house from front to back.

pongch'ang (봉창) — A permanently open window with no lattices.

pulbalgi (불발기) — A square or octagonal window set into the middle section of a thickly rice-papered door. This window featured latticework of various designs, including a checkered pattern or *chong* (井), *wan* (卍), or other designs based on Chinese characters.

pulbalgimun (불발기문) — The door between the *anbang* and *anbang taech'ong*, or between *sarangbang* and *sarang taech'ong*. This door featured octagonal *pulbalgi* windows in its middle section. The *pulbalgi* area was covered with only one layer of rice paper; the remainder received several layers. At night, when the room was lit, light brightly shone through the latticework of the *pulbalgi*.

pulch'onjiwi (불천지위) — An ancestral tablet presented by the king to the descendants of an exceptionally loyal subject. The descendants were required to hold ancestor worship ceremonies on such a tablet for all generations to come.

Glossary

punhammun (분합문)   Four-paneled doors installed between an enclosed room and an open space. In the summer, they were kept propped up, allowing the two spaces to serve as one large, open area.

punomgi (부넘기)   A dip made behind the initial sharp uphill incline in the sub-floor flue. This depressed area facilitated the forward movement of the fire toward the chimney and kept the fire from moving backwards into the fireplace.

puttumak (부뚜막)   A cook-top counter constructed over a fireplace in order to utilize the heat to both warm the floor of a room and cook food.

puyon (부연)   "Flying" rafters (short rafters installed toward the bottom edges of eaves).

pyokchang (벽장)   A built-in cabinet recessed into the wall on the *aranmok* (the spot closest to the fireplace) side. For the convenience of a person sitting on the floor to turn and reach the door of the cabinet, this storage space was built about 1.5 *ch'ok*s (45 cm) high from the floor.

p'yonaek (편액)   Wooden plaques, with paintings or calligraphy on paper or silk, mounted above door frames.

p'yongbanja (평반자)   Finishing a drop ceiling with boards. Sometimes, this wood ceiling was covered with a coat of clay or paper. In cold regions, this ceiling finish served as extra insulation.

sabangch'im (사방침)   A square cushion serving as an armrest, used for reclining.

sabangt'akcha (사방탁자)   A shelf style furniture with four levels with a drawer and cabinet in the lower compartment; used to store writing supplies as well as to display knickknacks.

sabunhammun (사분합문)   A four-paneled door installed to the front of a *taech'ong*.

Sach'ang (사창)   A window screen made with coarsely textured silk or ramie, used for ventilation and to keep insects out.

sagaetchaim (사개짜임)   A finger joint technique.

salch'ang (살창)   A window with lattice pieces fitted vertically at even intervals across the frame. Such a window was installed in a kitchen for increased ventilation.

Sallimgyongje (산림경제)   A well-known book on home economics authored by the realist philosopher Hong Man-son during the reign of King Sukchong of the Chosun period. A section on domestic implements contained in this twelve-volume work gives escriptions of the household possessions of the upper class as well as those of lower class homes.

salp'yongsang (살평상)   A wooden bed with a latticed bottom section. Two or three such sections were put together to be used as a bed.

samryangjip (삼량집)   A house with a ceiling having only three *tori* cross beams.

sanjongsarang (산정사랑)   An additional *sarang* located at a spot with a great view for the enjoyment of nature by the man of the house.

sarang (사랑)   A room addition during early Chosun period, it later evolved into separate quarters for the heir and his son. The *sarang* began to take on symbolic significance as the place of authority and status for the man of the house and the heritage of the entire household.

sasinsu (사신수)   The four symbolic animals believed to guard the four directions.

satkatch'onjang (삿갓천장)   A cone-shaped ceiling built to the contour created by rafters. This ceiling style was chosen if the ceiling clearance was not high enough to allow a drop ceiling.

simbyok (심벽)   A wall constructed by placing framing beams at the bottom, middle, and top portions, applying clay mixed with chopped straw, and plastering the surface.

sinwi (신위)   An ancestral tablet.

soan (서안)   Low desks *yangban* men used in a sitting position; they came in two types, *kyongsang* and *pomsang*.

soemok (쇠목)   A wooden beam horizontally fitted between posts.

soesiri (쇠시리)   A building technique applied to the corners of wood pieces making up eaves.

sokham (석함)   A decorative stone chest set in a garden. People placed a stone box on top of a *sokham* for decoration.

sokkarae (서까래)   Rafters.

soloe (설외)   A sheeting formed of vertically hung thin strips of bamboo or kaoliang. Used on walls or ceilings under a plaster covering.

sonjasokkarae (선자서까래)   The rafters placed in a fan shape, starting from the point where middle cross beams intersected and stretching outward toward the edge of a side eave.

so'ol (서얼)   Children of mistresses. These offsprings faced serious difficulties such as ineligibility for high positions and restriction from marriage to members of the *yangban* (upper class). These people were considered *chungin* (middle class), even if their fathers were *yangban*s.

soro (소로)   Square pieces of wood that supported other pieces of wood, such as *changyo*s or *kongp'o*s, all of which formed the eaves of fancy houses.

sosuldaemun (소슬대문)   An extra high front gate constructed to accommodate the passage of carriages carrying government officials of *chongip'um* (*Chong* Class Two) rank or higher.

sujangjae (수장재)   Various wood pieces fitted horizontally from posts.

suksok (숙석)   Sculptured stones used for corner stones.

taech'ong (대청)   A large, wood-floored *maru*.

taedulbo (대들보)   The main ceiling beam.

taettol (댓돌)   The stones lining the edges of a foundation.

t'akchajang (탁자장)   Shelves enclosed on three sides. This relatively short, highly decorated piece came with many shelves and enclosed compartments for the storage or display of knickknacks and writing and other supplies.

tanch'ong (단청)   An extremely ornate way of painting buildings in five different, very bright colors. This treatment was reserved for the ceilings and eaves of temples, palaces, and official buildings.

tanch'ungjang (단층장)   A single-level wardrobe, sometimes called *moritchang* because it was placed at the head of a bed.

tanggolbyok (당골벽)   The wall that filled the spaces between rafters resting on beams.

tanggolmagi (단골막이)   The ceiling sheeting between the rafters above cross beams.

tasikp'an (다식판)   Cookie presses. They came in wide variety of designs.

tchokmaru (쪽마루)   A ledge made with only a couple of boards.

tchongmae (쪽매)   A teachnique of piecing together boards to make a large wooden plane.

todummun (도듬문)   A paper sliding door with a frame of natural wood rather than one covered with rice paper completely.

t'oech'im (퇴침)   A small napping pillow.

t'oegan (퇴간)   A room addition of about one half *kan* size.

t'oenmaru (툇마루)   A small side *maru* or ledge.

tojangbang (도장방)   A storage room widely used throughout the Yongnam, Honam, and Ch'ungch'ong regions. Large and small size jars containing *kimch'i* or rice were stored in this space.

tonggwit'ul (동귀틀)   Short boards that fitted between long boards to form a wood floor.

tongja (동자)   Short posts that held pieces of boards together.

tongjagidung (동자기둥)   A short pillar or post.

tori (도리)   Cross beams that supported raftes.

ttoksal (떡살)   A rice-cake press that imprinted designs on the *cholp'yon* type of rice cakes.

tukkoptae (두겁대)   An upper lintel on a wall, or the cover board of a railing.

tukkoptajimun (두껍닫이문)   A sliding door with wall pockets into which the door panel slid when opened. The entire surface, including the frame, was covered with rice paper and a scroll painting or calligraphy was hung on this surface.

tulmijang (들미장)   An ash wood wardrobe, a product of the Kangwon Province, known for its beautiful wood grain.

tulsoe (들쇠)　Metal handles attached to the front of furniture pieces, or the metal handles attached to the sides for easier handling.

turigidung (두리기둥)　Round pillars which, according to oral history, were not to grace private residences. In actuality, many upper class homes in the country side featured such pillars.

twiju (뒤주)　A rice or other grain bin.

uigorichang (의걸이장)　A tall wardrobe with a bottom section in the form of a front-opening chest, and the top compartment came with a rack for hanging clothes. This piece of furniture was developed during the latter part of Chosun period.

wonangsamch'ungchang (원앙삼층장)　A tri-level wardrobe equipped with a pair of doors in one of the three sections. Symbolizing conjugal happiness, this wardrobe was commonly presented to newlyweds.

wumulbanja (우물반자)　A drop ceiling finished in a well-shape. A framework was filled with boards to complete this ceiling, sometimes called *soranbanja*.

wumulch'onjang (우물천장)　A *chong* (井) or well-shaped ceiling section put into an area of the ceiling where rafters spread out in a fan shape. Into a wooden framework boards were laid to fill the space.

wumulmaru (우물마루)　A "well-shaped" *maru*. Floor boards were fitted together to fill a framework built with two long cross beams and two shorter cross beams. This type of flooring was used most commonly on the floor of the *taech'ong* and storage rooms.

wunmok (웃목)　The spot in a room farthest from the fireplace.

yodaji (여닫이)　A window or door that came with hinges that opened in or out by pushing or pulling the door.

yondungch'onjang (연등천장)　A ceiling that left the rafters and beams exposed and the spaces between them plastered in a white finish.

yongwitchaim (연귀짜임)　The miter joint technique. The surfaces to be joined were cut at 45 degree angles and fitted together.

yonsang (연상)　A box in which an ink stone was stored. Writing supplies such as paper, ink sticks, a small ink water pitcher, and brushes were held in a compartment above the legs supporting the box.

yuji (유지)　Oiled corn-colored paper.

R·e·f·e·r·e·n·c·e·s

Arnheim, Rudolf, *Art and Visual Perception*, University of California Press, 1970.

Arnheim, Rudolf, *Visual Thinking*, University of California Press, 1969.

Chang, Sun-Joo, *The Kan and Spatial Composition in Upper Class Houses of Chosun Era*, Unpublished master' s thesis, Chungbook National University, 1994.

Cho, Yeo-Han, *Philosophy of Art*, Kyung Moon Publishing, 1994.

Choi, Byong-Wu, *A study on the residential space of Korean traditional Architecture*, Unpublished master' s thesis, Yongnam University, 1983.

Choi, Chang-Jo, *Feng-shui idea of Korea*, Mineumsa, 1984.

Choi, Dgei-Heui, *The Perceptual factors and the Planning principle in a Dwelling Space*, Journal of the Korean Home Economics Association, vol 37(3), 1986.

Choi, Hyung-Sun, *Changes and Norms of Hygienic Lifespaces in Korean Family Houses*, Unpublished master' s thesis, Yonsei University, 1991.

Choi, Jung-Sin · Kim, Dae-Nyun, *Interior Design*, Munundang, 1994.

Choi, Sang-Hun, *A Study on the Relationships between Human Dimensions and Interior Space of the Upper Class Residence of Late Chosun Dynasty*, Unpublished doctoral dissertation, Seoul National University, 1992.

Choi, Sun-U · Park, Young-Kyu, *Korean Furniture*, Kyungmi Publishing, 1993.

Chosunilbosa, *Tomb Paintings of Koguryo*, Chosunilbosa, 1993.

Chu, Nam-Chul, *Korean Architectural Design*, Ilji Publishing House, 1990.

Chun, Byung-Ok, *Decorative Designs in the houses of Chosun Dynasty Period*, Po-Chin Chai Publishing Co.,1995.

Chun, Jin-Hee, *A Study on the Space Planning in Korean Traditional Houses*, Journal of Sangmyung Women's University No.4, 1996.

Chun, Jin-Hee, *An Evaluation of the Composition and Elements in Korean Traditional Interior Spaces*, Journal of Korean Society of Design Studies No.16, 1996.

Chung, Si-Choon, *A Study on the Visual Qualities of Traditional Korean Architecture*, Journal of the Architectural Institute of Korea, vol 5(4), 1989.

Editorial Committee of Dictionary of Korean Myths and Symbols, *Dictionary of Korean Myths and Symbols*, Dong-A Publishing Company, 1992.

Ha, Jong-Han, *A study on the storage space in the Traditional Houses*, Unpublished master's thesis, Yongnam University, 1986.

References

Hong, Hyung-Ock, *A Study on the Korean Traditional Family Living and Housing Arrangement (I), -with Special Reference to the Family Living in the Chosun Dynasty-*, Kyunghee University, Vol.11, 1982.

Hong, Hyung-Ock, *A Study on the Korean Traditional Family Living and Housing Arrangement (II), -with Special Reference to the Structure of Family Relationship in the Chosun Dynasty-*, Kyunghee University, Vol.14, 1985.

Hong, Hyung-Ock, *Korean Housing History*, Mineumsa, 1992.

Hong, Hyung-Ock, *The Housing Adjustment and Adaptation in Korea-from Chosun Dynasty to Korea-*, unpublished Doctoral Dissertation, Korea University, 1987.

Hong, Jin-Kyoung, *A Study on the Korean Significance of the Architectural Details & Finishing of Traditional Housing*, Unpublished master's thesis, Ewha Womans University, 1985.

Hong, Soon-In, *A study on the formation of traditional village and private house form*, Unpublished master's thesis, Seoul National University, 1982.

Huh, Mi-Young, *Study on the Storage Chest, Bandaji, in Junla Province Furniture.* Unpublished master's thesis, Junbuk University. 1987.

Jang, Soon-Yong, *A Methodological Study of the Korean Traditional Residence Planning*, The Journal of Korea Institute of Registered Architects No.283, Cheong Moon Printing Co, 1992.

References

Jang, Soon-Yong, *A Methodological Study of the Korean Traditional Residence Planning*, The Journal of Korea Institute of Registered Architects No.286, Cheong Moon Printing Co, 1993.

Jang, Suk-Ha · Kim, Il-Jin, *A Study on the proportion method of plan on Traditional Architecture*, Journal of the Architectural Institute of Korea, vol 8(5), 1992.

Jeong, Yoo-Na, *A Study on the Characteristics of Architectural Coloring in the Palaces of Chosun Dynasty, Korea*, unpublished Doctoral Dissertation, Seoul National University, 1995.

Jungangilbo, *Korean Furniture:Art of Korea*, 1997.

Kang Hee-Soo, *An Analysis of Design Elements of the Stacking Chest (Nong) in Chosun Dynasty Furniture*, Unpublished master's thesis, Yonsei University, 1991.

Kang Kyung-Sook, *History of Korean Pottery*, Ilji Publishing House. 1985.

Kang, Young-Hwan, *Social History of Korean House*, Woonjin Publication, 1993.

Kim, Bong-Ryol, *Architecture of Korea*, Gonggansa, 1985.

Kim, Hae-Eun, *A study about the actual situation for Traditional Furniture on Modern Interior Space*, Unpublished master's thesis, Ewha Womans University, 1987.

References

Kim, Jong-Sung, *A study on Architecture and by Hermeneutic philosophy*, Unpublished master's thesis, Seoul National University, 1985.

Kim, Ki-Seok, *The story of house*, Daewonsa, 1995.

Kim, Kwang-Sook, *A study on the Decorations of Wood Furniture during Chosun Dynasty*, Unpublished master's thesis, Seongsin Womans University, 1980.

Kim Kyung-Ok, *Study on the Furnitures in men's Living-room during the Yi-Dynasty*, Unpublished master's thesis, Ewha Womans University, 1972.

Kim, Kyung-Won, *A Study on the Composition of Interior Space in Korean Traditional Houses*, Unpublished master's thesis, Korea University, 1987.

Kim, Ran-Ky, *A Comprehensive Analysis of the Dwelling Spaces in the Korean's Manor House*, Kumim No.62, Total Design Co., Ltd, 1986.

Kim, Sam-Dae-Ja, *Traditional Korean Wood Furniture*, Daewonsa. 1994.

Kim, Sun-Woo, *A Historical Study on Dwelling Heating System in Korea*, Journal of the Architectural Institute of Korea No.90, 1979.

Kim, Yeon-Ok, *Climate and Culture of Korea*, Ewha womans University Publication, 1985.

Kim, Yong-Jin, *History of Korean Folk Art*, Hakmunsa, 1978.

References

Kim, Young-Hee, *A Study on the Phenomenon of Visual Perception in Korean Traditional Houses*, Unpublished master's thesis, Ewha Womans University, 1989.

Kim, Young-Ki, *Korean Formative Consciousness*, Chang-Ji Co., Publisher, 1995.

Klein, D.Ballin, *The Concept of consciousness*, University of Nebraska Press, 1984.

Koo, Bang-Hee, *A study on the Lighting Devices of the Yi-Dynasty*, Unpublished master's thesis, Hongik University, 1980.

Kum, Jang-Tae, *Confucian Ideas and Religious culture*, Seoul National University Press, 1994.

Lee, Cha-Sook, *Korean Living History*, Kyomunsa, 1989.

Lee, Jin-Young, *A study on the modernization of Korean Traditional Furniture*, Unpublished master's thesis, Ewha Womans University, 1980.

Lee, Jong-Seok, *Wood and Lacquer Art of Korea*, Youlhwa-Dang Publisher, 1993.

Lee, Sang-Hae, *Enviromental recognition of feng-shui in Korean traditional culture*, Space, 1988.

Lee, Yi-Sun, *A Morphological Analysis of Design Elements of the Storage Chest, Bandaji, in Chosun Dynasty Furniture*, Unpublished master's thesis, Yonsei University, 1993.

Lim, Young-Ju, *Collection of Traditional Pattern*, Mijinsa, 1986.

Lim, Young-Ju, *History of Korean Pattern*, Mijinsa, 1983.

Moon, Chang-Man · Sakata, Izumi, *A Study on characteristics of symbolic proportion in openings of the Korean Traditional wooden Architecture*, Journal of the Architectural Institute of Korea, vol 12(6), 1996.

Pai, Man-sil, *Korean Furniture*, Kodansha, 1984.

Pai, Man-Sil, *The Traditional Style of Korean Wood Furniture*, Ewha Womans University Publishing, 1995.

Park, Eon-Kon, *A Border and Territory of Space in Korean Traditional Architecture*, Plus 8908, Plus, 1989.

Park, Sun-Hee, *A study on the Housing life style and space use of Yang-ban during the Chosun Dynasty*, Unpublished doctoral dissertation, Yonsei University, 1991.

Park, Young-Kyu, *Korean Wood Furniture*, Sam Seong Publishing Co., Ltd., 1982.

References

Shin, Yung-Hoon, *The Traditional Residence of Korea*, Youlhwa-Dang Publisher, 1993.

Son, Seung-Kwang, *A Study on Human Scale of Traditional Houses,* "*Han-Ok*" *in Chosun Dynasty*, Unpublished master's thesis, Seoul National University, 1985.

Yi, Yu-Mi, *A Study on the Development of* "*An-Chae (Inner Quarter)*" *of the Upper-Class Houses during the First of the Chosun Dynasty*, Unpublished master's thesis, Yonsei University, 1988.

Yoon, Bok-Ja · Chi, Soon · Park, Young-Soon, *Korean Furniture and Culture*, Shinkwang, 1988.

Yoon, Jeong-Ok, *A Study on the Korean Traditional Cookery Space*, Unpublished master's thesis, Korea University, 1981.

Yoon, Sa-Soon · Ko, Ik-Jin, *Korean Thought*, Yul Eum publishing, 1990.

A·u·t·h·o·r·s

Choi, Jae-Soon, Prof. at Human Ecology, Inchon Univ., Inchon, Korea.

Chun, Jin-Hee, Prof. at Dept. of Interior Design, Sangmyung Univ., Cheonan, Korea.

Hong, Hyung-Ock, Prof. at Housing & Interior Design, Kyunghee Univ., Seoul, Korea.

Kang, Soon-Joo, Prof. at School of Architecture, Konkuk Univ., Seoul, Korea.

Kim, Dae-Nyun, Prof. at Dept. of Architecture, Sewon Univ., Cheongju, Korea.

Min, Chan-Hong, Prof. at School of Design, Dongduk Women's Univ., Seoul, Korea.

Oh, Hye-Kyung, Prof. at Housing & Interior Design, Kyunghee Univ., Seoul, Korea.

Park, Young-Soon, Prof. at Dept. of Housing & Interior Design, Yonsei Univ., Seoul, Korea.

Translator

Maija Rhee Devine, Professional writer

Photographer

Suh, Jai-sik, Professional photographer
Author and photographer of *Beauty of Korea*, Hollym Corporation; Publishers.
To contact him, call 011-891-8088 or 442-8084.

Cover photos for 7 chapters

Selected photos